OXFORD THEOLOGY AND RELIGION MONOGRAPHS

OXFORD THEOLOGY AND RELIGION MONOGRAPHS

COMEDY AND FEMINIST INTERPRETATION OF THE HEBREW BIBLE
A Subversive Collaboration
Melissa A. Jackson (2012)

THE STORY OF ISRAEL IN THE BOOK OF QOHELET
Ecclesiastes as Cultural Memory
Jennie Barbour (2012)

THE ANTI-PELAGIAN CHRISTOLOGY OF AUGUSTINE OF HIPPO, 396–430
Dominic Keech (2012)

VISIONARY RELIGION AND RADICALISM IN EARLY INDUSTRIAL ENGLAND
From Southcott to Socialism
Philip Lockley (2012)

REPENTANCE IN LATE ANTIQUITY
Eastern Asceticism and the Framing of the Christian Life *c.*400–650 CE
Alexis C. Torrance (2012)

SCHELLING'S THEORY OF SYMBOLIC LANGUAGE
Forming the System of Identity
Daniel Whistler (2013)

PATMOS IN THE RECEPTION HISTORY OF THE APOCALYPSE
Ian Boxall (2013)

THE THEOLOGICAL VISION OF REINHOLD NIEBUHR'S
THE IRONY OF AMERICAN HISTORY
"In the Battle and Above It"
Scott R. Erwin (2013)

HEIDEGGER'S ESCHATOLOGY
Theological Horizons in Martin Heidegger's Early Work
Judith Wolfe (2013)

ETHICS AND BIBLICAL NARRATIVE
A Literary and Discourse-Analytical Approach to the Story of Josiah
S. Min Chun (2014)

Theology and Economic Ethics

Martin Luther and Arthur Rich in Dialogue

SEAN DOHERTY

OXFORD
UNIVERSITY PRESS

OXFORD
UNIVERSITY PRESS

Great Clarendon Street, Oxford, OX2 6DP,
United Kingdom

Oxford University Press is a department of the University of Oxford.
It furthers the University's objective of excellence in research, scholarship,
and education by publishing worldwide. Oxford is a registered trade mark of
Oxford University Press in the UK and in certain other countries

First Edition published in 2014

Impression: 1

Published in the United States of America by Oxford University Press
198 Madison Avenue, New York, NY 10016, United States of America

British Library Cataloguing in Publication Data
Data available

Library of Congress Control Number: 2013945565

ISBN 978-0-19-870333-4

As printed and bound by
CPI Group (UK) Ltd, Croydon, CR0 4YY

Acknowledgements

I began work on my doctoral thesis, of which this monograph is a revision, in the summer of 2005, just before getting married to Gaby. To her, and to my parents, go my deepest love and gratitude. I was hugely fortunate to have Dr (now Professor) Bernd Wannenwetsch as my supervisor, who was unstintingly generous with his time, guidance, and friendship, as was Professor Oliver O'Donovan, whose graduate seminars it was a privilege and joy to attend. I am so grateful to them, and to my fellow graduate students, for all that I learned from them.

To Bishop Pete Broadbent and Revd Jane Morris go my heartfelt thanks for allowing me to serve my curacy in a creative and flexible way, in order to give me time to work on the thesis. Similarly, Revd Dr Graham Tomlin and Revd Dr Andy Emerton not only gave me a job at St Mellitus, but Andy made sure I completed the thesis once I arrived! There, Dr Chris and Anja Tilling and Revd Christoph Lindner were kind enough to check (and correct) my German.

Several bodies gave my family and me generous financial support, including the Ministry Division of the Church of England, the Squire Marriott Bursary Fund, and the Kirby Laing Institute for Christian Ethics (KLICE). A happy side effect of receiving assistance from the last was the opportunity to attend KLICE's graduate seminar, and there to get to know its Director, Dr Jonathan Chaplin, who has been a wise and supportive advisor.

I drew on various parts of the thesis in my essay, 'Money', in *Living Witness: Explorations in Missional Ethics*, eds. Andy Draycott and Jonathan Rowe (Leicester: Apollos, 2012). In turn, I draw on that essay in the conclusion of this monograph, and I acknowledge that here.

Contents

Abbreviations

BEE Rich, Arthur, *Business and Economic Ethics: The Ethics of Economic Systems*, ed. Georges Enderle, trans. David W. Lutz and Albert Wimmer (Leuven: Peeters, 2006).

LW Luther, Martin, *Luther's Works*, 55 vols. (Philadelphia: Fortress and St Louis: Concordia, 1955–1986).

ST Aquinas, St Thomas, *Summa Theologica*, 2nd rev. edn. 22 vols., trans. Fathers of the English Dominican Province (London: Burns, Oates & Washbourne, 1912–36), <http://www.newadvent.org/summa/> accessed January 2006–May 2011.

WA Luther, Martin, *Luthers Werke: Kritische Gesamtausgabe*, 65 + vols. (Weimar: H Böhlau, 1883–), <http://luther.chadwyck.co.uk> accessed August 2005–May 2011.

Introduction

WHAT THIS MONOGRAPH TRIES TO DO, AND WHY

This monograph seeks to expand the self-critical resources of contemporary theological approaches to economic ethics. It does so by bringing a detailed engagement with the method of a particular pre-modern theologian and social commentator, Martin Luther (1483–1546), into interaction with an analysis of the method of a modern contribution to economic ethics, that of Swiss theologian Arthur Rich (1910–92). It is thus not the study of the economic *ethics* of these two thinkers (although an element of this is required), but of their *method* as they approach the particular field of economic ethics. The book thus seeks to open up fresh horizons for economic ethics today and to pose self-critical questions, which might remain unasked if its methods were studied only on their own terms. This is not to suggest that modern theological economic ethics has nothing to add to its older variants, still less that Martin Luther is superior to Arthur Rich per se. Indeed, at times I point out ways in which Rich's method improves on Luther's. But it does not set out to be an even-handed comparison of the two thinkers, since its emphasis is not on historical study but on the ways in which contemporary economic ethics may benefit from breaching some of its accustomed habits of mind. Rich's method *does* have some significant gains over Luther's, some of which we will point out in passing, but a detailed consideration of them lies outside the scope of this work.

The book seeks to break new ground in the following three ways. First, there is extensive scholarly literature exploring the question of the relationship between economics and theology and/or ethics.[1] And, due to his hegemonic

[1] We will not attempt a full-scale literature review in this introduction, but for a sample of recent forays into ethics by economists, see the collection of essays edited by Peter Groenewegen, *Economics and Ethics?* (London: Routledge, 1996) and Amartya Sen, *On Ethics and Economics* (Oxford: Blackwell, 1987). As for theological explorations in economic ethics, see, for example: Max L. Stackhouse with others (eds.), *On Moral Business: Classical and Contemporary Resources for Ethics in Economic Life* (Grand Rapids: Eerdmans, 1995) and J. Philip Wogaman, *Economic Ethics: A Christian Inquiry* (Philadelphia: Fortress, 1986). Several valuable discussions of the

influence in some theological quarters, there is no shortage of literature on Martin Luther, including full-length studies of his economic ethics.[2] Yet, while it is true that contemporary theological ethics generally seeks to root itself in the Christian tradition of thought and is therefore otherwise well equipped to critique modern trends, there is very little which takes Reformation theology seriously as a resource for reflection on *economic* matters.[3] However, groundwork for such a step *has* been laid in recent historical scholarship on Luther, which has helped to correct some of the misperceptions of his ideas, and we will draw on the findings of this research in order to establish our claims.

Second, the significant contribution of Arthur Rich to economic ethics has received little attention in English-speaking circles, although it has enjoyed influence on the continent. There has yet to be a substantial treatment in English of *Wirtschaftsethik*, Rich's magnum opus.[4] So there is clearly a need for elucidation and analysis of Rich's thought to be more readily available. Furthermore, while there has been a reasonable amount of secondary literature on Rich published in German, there is less that exposes his work to more critical scrutiny. As we have indicated, this monograph will draw on the method of the pre-modern Luther as a resource for interrogating the possible strengths and weaknesses of Rich's own method. Insofar as Rich is like other recent practitioners of theological economic and social ethics, such discoveries will clearly have a wider significance. Therefore, in several places I will draw attention to ways in which Rich is similar to other thinkers in this field.

Third, there is need for theological work on the question of method in Christian social ethics, especially economic ethics. As Anna Robbins has shown, twentieth-century Protestant contributions to social thought have been marked by a bewildering confusion as regards the proper method for such work, but the way in which she confines her discussion to the contemporary period means that she is unable to bring fresh resources to bear

issue have been penned by Christians who also happen to be economists, such as D. L. Munby, *Christianity and Economic Problems* (London: Macmillan, 1956), and Donald Hay, *Economics Today: A Christian Critique* (Leicester: Apollos 1989).

[2] For example, Hans-Jürgen Prien, *Luthers Wirtschaftsethik* (Göttingen: Vandenhoeck & Ruprecht, 1992), and Ricardo Rieth, *'Habsucht' bei Martin Luther* (Weimar: Hermann Böhlaus Nachfolger, 1996).

[3] One attempt to appropriate Luther's thought for today is the relatively brief and relatively popular work by Ulrich Duchrow, *Global Economy: A Confessional Issue for the Churches?*, trans. David Lewis (Geneva: WCC Publications, 1987). The book is no less useful for its brevity and popularity, but clearly there is scope for more sustained work.

[4] Arthur Rich, *Business and Economic Ethics: The Ethics of Economic Systems*, ed. Georges Enderle, trans. David W. Lutz and Albert Wimmer (Leuven: Peeters, 2006). This single-volume edition is a translation of two original volumes: Arthur Rich, *Wirtschaftsethik I: Grundlagen in theologischer Perspektive* (Gütersloh: Gerd Mohn, 1984), and *Wirtschaftsethik II: Marktwirtschaft, Planwirtschaft, Weltwirtschaft aus sozialethischer Sicht* (Gütersloh: Gerd Mohn, 1990).

on the matter.[5] Forced to choose only between recent options, she adopts what she designates a dialogic, Niebuhrian approach while trying to synthesize it with what she regards as the valid features of other twentieth-century methods. This yields real insights, but restricting oneself to a single period means that the assumptions of that period may remain unquestioned. By contrast, it will be assumed that contemporary theology cannot be sufficiently self-critical if the conversation remains within its own chronological horizon.[6] This monograph therefore sets out to discover resources in an earlier theological generation, which may help to liberate us from potential tunnel vision with respect to economics. Thus it sets out to address the still somewhat uncharted methodological question of economic ethics in a way that, where necessary, has the capacity to reshape the assumptions of contemporary discourse.

THE METHOD

The demonstration of our claims will be undertaken by means of a close engagement with a selected publication of Luther (his 1519/20 *Großer Sermon von dem Wucher*) and of Rich (his masterwork *Wirtschaftsethik*, published in two volumes in 1984 and 1990 respectively).[7] Our assumption is that, given our aim is to understand the *method* of these particular thinkers, it will be more illuminating to grapple in a concentrated manner with one particular work than to survey insights collected from across their corpus, although as the discussion proceeds, parallels with their other works will be adduced in order to illuminate and clarify the work under discussion, or to note points of development or discrepancy. It therefore favours a limited but meticulous approach above a compendious but less detailed one. Studying primary material thoroughly will enable us to see the steps each writer takes in approaching his chosen matter, the issues he considers pertinent, and the theological moves he makes in order to respond.

The monograph will therefore describe Luther's and Rich's methodologies in a way that they do not themselves render explicit, and will use what we have learned from each in order to understand better and critique the other. For example, to anticipate a later observation, Rich is quite self-conscious about his method, and often describes and defends it overtly, in contrast to the

[5] Anna M. Robbins, *Methods in the Madness: Diversity in Twentieth-Century Christian Social Ethics*, (Carlisle: Paternoster, 2004).

[6] For discussion of this notion, see Bernd Wannenwetsch, 'Conversing with the Saints as they Converse with Scripture: In Conversation with Brian Brock's *Singing the Ethos of God*', *European Journal of Theology* xviii (2009), pp. 125–35.

[7] The full German text of Luther's sermon can be found in WA v. 6, pp. 36–60. The standard English translation is in LW v. 45, pp. 273–308.

more intuitive Luther. At other times, he is less self-aware, and his manoeuvres are more concealed. At such times, our prior study of Luther will better enable us to notice and describe what Rich does. Luther, however, tends not to reflect explicitly on what he is doing, although his execution is masterful. This alerts us to the possible discrepancy between how good one is at doing something, and how good one is at describing it. Our proposal is therefore that it is worth delving into these methodological steps and exploring the reasons for them, and it will establish this by enumerating what we can learn from such a process. At times the critique will be mutual, but more often the evaluation will be of Rich's method from the perspective of Luther's, for the reasons that we have already set out.

In summary, the key words in what follows will be 'why' and 'how' rather than 'what'. I will not simply describe Luther's and Rich's economic ethics, and situate them in the context of their times, nor the theological conceptuality which gives rise to them. Rather, I will study the interplay of these two things, to demonstrate *the way in which* their theological insights inform their moral vision and shape their methodology.

THE STRUCTURE

The ordering of the material is reasonably self-explanatory, first setting out the analysis of the method of the pre-modern Luther, then of the modern Rich, followed by a further exposition of Rich in which questions and insights from Luther are brought to bear on Rich's thought in order to discover ways in which Luther's theology can expand the self-critical resources of Rich's approach to economic ethics, and by implication others which resemble his. Let us pause briefly to map out the terrain that we will be exploring.

Chapter 1 briefly introduces Luther's sermon on usury, and situates it in the context of his day. It then gives a commentary on Luther's method in the sermon, discussing inter alia such matters as its genre, Luther's moral understanding of 'the gospel' and its relation to financial and commercial matters, and the way in which Luther reads and deploys Scripture in social ethics. Also analysed are the ways in which Luther exploits particular doctrines (such as creation and justification by faith alone) with respect to a moral question, and his core theopolitical concept of the twofold government of God, and how he brings these theological motifs to bear on a pressing economic question which confronted him: the rise of the *Zinskauf*, a method of lending money at interest which circumvented canonical prohibitions on usury. I then summarize my findings from my close engagement with this particular text of Luther's, in readiness for the subsequent discussion of Rich in the light of Luther.

Since this material represents commentary on Luther's particular work, the structure of the chapter follows that of the primary work being discussed.

Chapter 2 briefly sketches Arthur Rich's life and work, and situates his thought contextually in certain key ways. It indicates some of the lines of the development of Rich's thought, up to the publication of the two volumes of *Wirtschaftsethik*. It then presents lineaments of Rich's theological method as set out in *Wirtschaftsethik*, such as Rich's understanding of what he calls 'the basic ethical question', the general human moral experience, his approach to Scripture, and his adoption of aspects of the thought of Max Weber and John Rawls. Here, Rich's thought is expounded on its own terms, certain critical notes sounded only occasionally. I also note ways in which Rich's method is similar to other contributions to theological economic ethics, in order to provide evidence for our later suggestions of ways in which our reading of Rich might have implications for other approaches to theological economic ethics. The analysis of Rich's *Wirtschaftsethik* is slightly more thematically organized than that of Luther's sermon, but it broadly follows the structure of his own work. The chapter concludes with a brief survey of Rich's conclusions.

The evidence has now been assembled for the task of Chapter 3, which is the heart of the monograph. As stated above, our undertaking is to augment the resources available to contemporary economic ethics by comparing the method of an eminent modern practitioner with that of a skilful pre-modern one. We therefore bring our study of Luther to bear on what we have found in Rich's approach, in order to note potential strengths and weaknesses of Rich's method, which might have been less evident had we confined our comparison to Rich's contemporaries and ours. Matters are examined such as Rich's concept of ethics, his treatment of social ethics as the primary matrix for ethics, his anthropology and its implications for his ethical method, his use of the doctrine of eschatology, and of Weber and Rawls, and his characterization of the relationship of ethics to the discipline of economics.

As one might expect, as contemporaries of Rich, we frequently find ourselves in sympathy with him. Yet in the light of our reading of Luther, we will question some of Rich's assumptions, and note ways in which a more self-critical approach could have made his project more successful. For example, we will suggest that Rich is far too ready to take economics for granted as a morally neutral science, and that Luther's ostensibly more individual approach to ethics (which has sometimes led to him being regarded as socially conservative) enables him to adopt far more socially radical conclusions than Rich's, despite Rich's attempt to address economic questions in a radical way.

A short conclusion then summarizes the argument and, noting parallels between Rich's method and those of other Christian contributions to economic ethics, makes tentative suggestions as to the wider applicability of the critical questions posed to Rich's method by the analysis of Luther. It therefore shows how the study of the pre-modern Luther in relation to the modern Rich has provided resources for more self-critical reflection on the practice of economic ethics.

Having explained our own method, and the evidence that we will be seeking to gather, we proceed now to our first chapter, and our discussion of Luther's *Sermon von dem Wucher*.

1

Luther's Moral Theological Method in His *Sermon von dem Wucher*

This chapter will situate Luther's *Sermon von dem Wucher* in its theological, political, and social context, and give a commentary on Luther's theological method in the sermon, touching on matters such as the genre of the sermon, Luther's approach to Scripture and tradition, his method in engaging with particular Christian doctrines, and the way he brings all this to bear on the particular economic questions which prompted him to write. It will primarily follow the flow of the sermon itself, although we will also pause to analyse and take stock of our findings at relevant junctures.

THE CONTEXT OF THE *SERMON VON DEM WUCHER*

Luther had already tackled the matter of usury late in 1519, in a shorter *Sermon von dem Wucher* (WA v. 6, pp. 3–8), of which this work is an expansion. The sermon apparently did not have the desired effect, and Luther became increasingly frustrated with the growth in what he regarded as usurious practices. The socio-economic backdrop to this growth was as follows.[1]

[1] The various interconnected contexts of the treatise have been analysed in recent scholarship and therefore rather than attempt an exhaustive enquiry, what follows is a condensed summary of relevant aspects of such treatments. Clearly the reality was far more variegated than this synopsis indicates. For further information on the socio-economic context, see Friedrich Lütge, 'Agriculture', in *The New Cambridge Modern History: II. The Reformation, 1520–59*, ed. G. R. Elton (Cambridge: Cambridge University Press, 1962), pp. 23–36 and Prien, *Luthers Wirtschaftsethik*, pp. 31–68. On the ecclesiastical-theological context, see Carter Lindberg, *Beyond Charity: Reformation Initiatives for the Poor* (Minneapolis: Fortress, 1993), pp. 18–67, which draws on the seminal but dated work by Gerhard Uhlhorn, *Christian Charity in the Ancient Church*. No translator given. (New York: Scribners, 1883). On the 'left wing' of the Reformation, see Martin Brecht, *Martin Luther: Shaping and Defining the Reformation, 1521–1532*, trans. James F. Schaaf (Philadelphia: Fortress, 1985), pp. 142–3. For the more immediate causes for Luther's writing, see Brecht, *Martin Luther: Shaping and Defining the Reformation*, pp. 142–50, and Prien, *Luthers Wirtschaftsethik*, pp. 73–80.

Economic ferment in central Europe, and the advent of what we now call early capitalism, had led to an increase in the number and impact of rich entrepreneurs. This was undermining the older feudal and guild systems, which, although they obviously had their share of injustices and abuses, had acted as sharp brakes on large land and profit accumulation,[2] and had promoted local self-sufficiency and mutual responsibility.[3] Many locales, particularly Wittenberg, now depended on trade with other areas for basic foodstuffs, frequently leading to scarcity and price rises, which local governments were powerless to regulate.

Economic and agricultural stagnation had resulted from the Black Death in the fourteenth century and was followed by enormous population growth, creating demand which the agricultural system (fragile from the effects of the plague) struggled to meet.[4] Swift and large price rises inevitably took place. Wages could not keep pace with the surges in price, with those on fixed incomes especially impoverished. These changes were especially pronounced in Luther's region, Saxony-Thuringia. For example, the price of grain doubled between 1519 and 1540.[5] This exacerbated a situation in which many peasants had been compelled to borrow in the cumulative wake of a series of severe crop failures from 1490 to 1519. They could not pay back what they had borrowed, and thus forfeited their property.

The discovery of the Americas and commerce with the Near East stimulated trade, but this seems to have done little to ease the acute need for everyday goods. Luther, with a typically medieval attitude to the sterility of money, perceived the international commerce in luxuries as a financial drain, increasing debt and wasting money which should have been spent on basic necessities. The great banking houses, such as the Fuggers from Augsburg, about whom Luther had complained in *An den christlichen Adel deutscher Nation* (1520), had attained massive sway, holding both secular and ecclesiastical authorities in thrall. Of course, the fact that they were 'zealous Romanists who supported Eck against Luther' can hardly have failed to further inflame Luther's ire.[6] Their clout with these authorities enabled them to quell attempts to regulate their business more strictly.

[2] Prien, *Luthers Wirtschaftsethik*, p. 215.

[3] A. G. Dickens, *Reformation and Society in Sixteenth-Century Europe* (London: Thames and Hudson, 1966), pp. 45–7; Robert Wuthnow, *Communities of Discourse: Ideology and Social Structure in the Reformation, the Enlightenment, and European Socialism* (Cambridge, MA: Harvard University Press, 1989), p. 29.

[4] Prien, *Luthers Wirtschaftsethik*, p. 32.

[5] Prien, *Luthers Wirtschaftsethik*, p. 32 and Steven E. Ozment, *The Age of Reform, 1250–1550: An Intellectual and Religious History of Late Medieval and Reformation Europe* (New Haven: Yale University Press, 1980), p. 198.

[6] LW v. 44, p. 155, n. 100. But Luther's opprobrium towards the Fuggers was by no means only a matter of opposing supporters of Rome—as the most wealthy and monopolistic banking house they merely typified their profession par excellence. Cf. his notorious comment that

The Christian tradition, represented by thinkers as influential as Jerome, Ambrose, and Augustine, and by councils as august as Nicaea, had believed for centuries that Scripture censured usury (i.e. the taking of *any* surplus on lending).[7] Closer to Luther's time, canonists, schoolmen, and councils had forbidden usury on pain of excommunication.[8] But this was difficult to enforce in a church which, like the civil government, was dependent on banking. In places, the church was deeply enmeshed in what was, by its own standards, commercial and financial malpractice, such as lending corn, livestock, and money at interest, and Luther's monastery was no exception.[9] The papacy relied on the banking houses and protected them, even enforcing payment of debts with the threat of excommunication.[10] The rise of the doctrine of purgatory offered hope in salvation even for the most flagrant of miscreants and so usury, instead of unequivocally meriting damnation, could now be atoned for.[11] Such atonement could be reduced through pious deeds such as almsgiving, prayer, and the purchase of indulgences.

The pawnshops (*montes pietatis*) run by the Franciscans to prevent the poor from having to resort to the exorbitant rates of the moneylenders unintentionally shifted the church's position. In sanctioning these institutions in 1516, the pope and the Fifth Lateran Council formally made the taking of interest permissible in certain circumstances. Despite the strict limitations on such permission, this concession opened the way for a wider acceptance of interest.[12] Various theologians, such as Tübingen scholars Johannes Eck (1486–1543), Conrad Summenhart (*c.* 1458–1502), and Gabriel Biel (d. 1495) argued openly for the rescission of the canonical prohibition on interest.

Thus, with events conspiring to exacerbate goods shortages and huge price escalations, the matter of lending at interest had become increasingly pressing. The traditional prohibition on usury was being eroded in both practice and theory. These are the circumstances in which Luther wrote.

'we must put a bit in the mouth of the Fuggers *and similar companies*' LW v. 44, p. 213 (emphasis mine); WA v. 6, p. 466, ll. 31–2.

[7] This is documented in David W. Jones, *Reforming the Morality of Usury: A Study of Differences that Separated the Protestant Reformers* (Lanham, MD: University Press of America, 2004), pp. 30–4. See also Benjamin Nelson, *The Idea of Usury: From Tribal Brotherhood to Universal Otherhood* (Princeton: Princeton University Press, 1949), pp. 3–5.

[8] See Jones, *Reforming the Morality of Usury*, pp. 25ff.

[9] Martin Brecht, *Martin Luther: His Road to Reformation, 1483–1521*, trans. James F. Schaaf (Philadelphia: Fortress, 1985), p. 96; Prien, *Luthers Wirtschaftsethik*, p. 42.

[10] R. H. Tawney, *Religion and the Rise of Capitalism: A Historical Study* (Harmondsworth: Penguin, 1938), p. 57.

[11] Jacques Le Goff, *Your Money or Your Life: Economy and Religion in the Middle Ages* (New York: Zone Books, 1988), pp. 65ff. and 92f.

[12] John T. Noonan, *The Scholastic Analysis of Usury* (Cambridge, MA: Harvard University Press, 1957), pp. 299–300.

THE GENRE OF THE *SERMON VON DEM WUCHER*

We should first note that Luther adopts the form of a sermon to address this issue. Understanding his perception of this genre will illuminate what he saw himself as doing.

Luther regarded preaching as God's indispensable means of self-communication to humanity. Early on, in the *Operationes in Psalmos* (1519–21), Luther commented on the importance of the preached word, in contrast to the written word:

> In the church, it is not enough to write and read books, but it is necessary to speak and to hear. Indeed, this is why Christ wrote nothing, but spoke everything. The apostles wrote very little, but spoke a lot. . . . The ministry of the New Testament is not engraved on dead tablets of stone; rather it sounds in a living voice.[13]

Through preaching, God speaks.[14] It carries God's authority in addressing his creatures. God uses the preacher to communicate, using human language to convey divine speech.[15] So preaching is not human speech about God, but 'God's own speech to human beings',[16] and it is not only authoritative, it is transforming: because it is God's speech, it effects what it proclaims.[17] By it, God is present and active in the hearts of his hearers to effect his purposes. Hence Fred Meuser comments, '[Luther] preached as if the sermon were not a classroom but a battleground . . . , an apocalyptic event'.[18] Preaching is a weapon of God in the cosmic battle against the devil. Therefore Luther assumes that he speaks for God in this particular situation.

By now, Luther is of course already a preacher and pastor. Addressing a pressing question of his time in a sermon is not strange on his part, but rather reflects his day-to-day duty. Some accounts of his moral theology emphasize the role of motivation within it to the exclusion of all else, because of his emphasis on the importance of spontaneously and naturally doing the

[13] See WA v. 5, p. 537. This translation is based on that of A. Skevington Wood, *Captive to the Word: Martin Luther, Doctor of Sacred Scripture* (Exeter: Paternoster, 1969), p. 90.

[14] For Luther, even Scripture is only the Word of God in a derivative sense, as it is formed from preaching, which is 'the basic form of the gospel' (Paul Althaus, *The Theology of Martin Luther*, trans. Robert C. Schultz (Philadelphia: Fortress, 1966), p. 72). Luther puts it thus in *The Freedom of a Christian* (1520): 'You may ask, "What then is the Word of God, and how shall it be used, since there are so many words of God?" I answer, . . . "The Word is the gospel of God concerning his Son"'. LW v. 31, p. 346; WA v. 7, p. 51, ll. 12–14.

[15] Oswald Bayer, *Living by Faith: Justification and Sanctification* trans. Geoffrey W. Bromiley (Grand Rapids: Eerdmans, 2003), pp. 48–9; Dennis Ngien, 'Theology of Preaching in Martin Luther', *Themelios* 28.2 (2003), pp. 28–48, esp. p. 32.

[16] Ngien, 'Theology of Preaching', p. 47.

[17] Bayer, *Living by Faith*, p. 46. See also Ngien, 'Theology of Preaching', p. 31.

[18] Fred W. Meuser, 'Luther as Preacher of the Word of God', in *The Cambridge Companion to Martin Luther*, ed. Donald K. McKim (Cambridge: Cambridge University Press, 2003), pp. 136–48, esp. p. 137.

right thing.[19] But it is obvious here that, far from presuming that right motivation is all one needs, Luther considers that his hearers need guidance to *recognize* right and wrong, and exhortation to *act* rightly. It is true that elsewhere Luther records his dislike for sermons which preach only about good deeds. Such sermons can only produce despair, as humans can never live up to them.[20] In such contexts Luther asserts that Christ must be preached first as *donum* or *sacramentum*, and only then as *exemplum*.[21] However, some commentators unfortunately therefore read this emphasis as all but excluding genuine moral guidance from preaching.[22]

Neither should this sermon be read in the light of Luther's concept of the theological use of the law, that is, upholding a standard which humans can never hope to meet in order to drive his hearers to despair of their own righteousness by demonstrating the depth of their inability to obey God, and thus to impel them to turn penitently to his mercy.[23] This simply does not fit the evidence of the sermon: Luther does not beseech his hearers to repent in order to be saved, but in order to amend their behaviour. Nor does it help to read this and similar sermons as predating Luther's concept of the *duplex usus legis* (on the basis that it is not explicit in his work until 1522). This does not

[19] The most influential exponent of this view is probably Ernst Troeltsch, *The Social Teaching of the Christian Churches* trans. Olive Wyon (Chicago: University of Chicago Press, 1976), v. 2, pp. 471f. This undoubtedly picks up a genuine thread of Luther's thought: his account of the renewing work of the Holy Spirit in the believer means that he thinks that they do God's will spontaneously. Yet this does not make him an antinomian, nor does it preclude all further need for disclosure of God's will. Rather, in general, the right thing to do is not shrouded in obscurity, but *meets us* concretely in daily life. He criticizes those who set up religious works in place of ordinary good deeds, since we are faced with ample opportunities to do good all the time: 'If you ask further whether they consider it a good work when a man works at his trade, walks, stands, eats, drinks, sleeps, and does all kinds of work for the nourishment of his body or for the common welfare, and whether they believe that God is well pleased with them, you will find that they say no, and that they define good works so narrowly that they are made to consist only of praying in church, fasting, and almsgiving'. *Treatise on Good Works* (1520), LW v. 44, p. 24; *Von den guten Werken*, WA v. 6, p. 205, ll. 14–19. His target is not the notion of divine commands, but the monastic ideal of religious life.

[20] See Ngien, 'Theology of Preaching', pp. 34–5.

[21] For an exploration of this theme, see Norman Nagel, '*Sacramentum et exemplum* in Luther's Understanding of Christ', in *Luther for an Ecumenical Age: Essays in Commemoration of the 450th Anniversary of the Reformation*, ed. Carl S. Meyer (St Louis: Concordia, 1967), pp. 172–99.

[22] Even some of the writers who have done the most to rehabilitate Luther's reputation as a thinker genuinely concerned with moral questions fall into this reductionism at times. For example, George Forell approvingly quotes Einar Billing's claim that one should 'never believe that you have a correct understanding of a thought of Luther before you have succeeded in reducing it to a simple corollary of the thought of the forgiveness of sins'. Einar Billing, *Our Calling*, trans. Conrad Bergendoff (Rock Island: Augustana, 1947), p. 7; quoted by George W. Forell in *Faith Active in Love: An Investigation of the Principles Underlying Luther's Social Ethics* (Minneapolis: Augsburg, 1959), p. 64.

[23] The first one being the civil use, that is, that the law secures earthly righteousness, although this is of no avail before God.

explain why he appended this sermon to a work in 1524, nor why later sermons are equally stringent.[24] Another attempt to explain away this anomaly is the suggestion that Luther advocated concrete moral positions purely for the sake of *civil* righteousness. This is not satisfactory either, because he specifically characterizes obedience to the commands of Jesus as *Christian* morality.

The conclusion must be that, in the name of their prior beliefs about Luther's ethics, such interpretative strategies essentially ignore his straightforward aim: to instruct people to live a certain way in the light of the gospel. His idea of the two uses of the law, and the distinction he employs elsewhere between law and gospel, are not rigid formulae, but dynamic, *dialectical* concepts used to interpret the same scriptural texts in several aspects. While Luther believes the law possesses a convicting role, and that obedience to it cannot establish a right relationship to God, this does not exclude its role in providing moral guidance. Some interpreters of Luther have argued on this basis for a third, moral, use of the law in his thought.[25] They claim that while the explicit phrase may be lacking from his work, the underlying concept is there. Others eschew the terminology of the uses of the law and describe this as a moral use of the *gospel*, emphasizing that for Luther the gospel is not morally vacuous but has particular moral implications.[26] The terminology is unimportant. What matters is that Luther indeed believes that Scripture conveys genuinely *moral* instruction. Even though his notion that Christ as *donum* is antecedent to him as *exemplum*, this shows that Luther still believes in Christ as a pattern. The sequence does not reject the imitation of Christ but explains it: being conformed to Christ's *exemplum* is an integral consequence of receiving him as *donum*, because it is he that one receives.[27]

[24] Indeed, 'as people used his message of forgiveness to excuse sinful living', Luther's zeal against usury grew more fevered. Meuser, 'Luther as Preacher', p. 139. Nowhere is this clearer than in the case of usury, as Hans-Jürgen Prien has shown by comparing Luther's earlier comments on usury to his later (*Luthers Wirtschaftsethik*, pp. 123ff.). See for example his 1540 treatise, *An die Pfarrherrn wider den Wucher zu predigen, Vermahnung* in WA v. 51, pp. 331–424, usefully summarized by Martin Brecht in *Martin Luther: The Preservation of the Church, 1532–1546*, trans. James F. Schaaf (Philadelphia: Fortress, 1985), pp. 259–60.

[25] For a discussion of this view, with rebuttal, see Gerhard Ebeling, 'On the Doctrine of the *Triplex Usus Legis* in the Theology of the Reformation', in *Word and Faith*, trans. James W. Leitch (London: SCM, 1963), pp. 62–78, esp. pp. 62–4 and 69–78. Ebeling rightly warns against seeking a later standardized pattern in Luther's writing ('On the Doctrine', pp. 70, 72).

[26] See, e.g., William H. Lazareth, *Christians in Society: Luther, the Bible, and Social Ethics* (Minneapolis: Fortress, 2001), pp. 34, 224.

[27] Simo Peura, 'Christ as Favor and Gift: The Challenge of Luther's Understanding of Justification', in *Union with Christ: The New Finnish Interpretation of Luther*, eds. Carl E. Braaten and Robert W. Jenson (Grand Rapids: Eerdmans, 1998), pp. 42–69, esp. pp. 60–2. Peura argues that the Formula of Concord influentially but mistakenly reduced the *donum* to faith—whereas for Luther the gift is Christ (p. 45).

THE CLAIM OF THE GOSPEL VERSUS THE CLAIMS OF ECONOMICS

This moral content of the gospel is the note on which Luther begins the sermon. He comments that, in recent times, greed and usury have come to operate through deceptive and covert means.[28] Crucially, he connects this with the fact that 'we regard the holy gospel as having no value'.[29] The solution he therefore advocates is to pay better attention to the gospel. This will train alertness as to the beguiling nature of financial practice.

Already we can identify a number of theological assumptions and their relevance for Luther's methodology. First, he assumes that the economic sphere cannot be approached with a basic orientation of trust. Economic practice is deceptive and opaque, and the gospel is lucid. Thus Luther's first methodological step is to hold up the gospel against contemporary practice for comparison. His second assumption is that the gospel has inherent moral import.

He begins *Von Kaufshandlung*, the treatise to which he later appended this sermon, with a similar theological account of what is happening: the gospel itself 'rebukes and reveals all the "works of darkness"'.[30] The gospel itself fights wrongdoing as part of its proper nature, whereas desire for money itself damages human flourishing (Luther cites 1 Timothy 6:9–10). Thus Luther construes part of his task as unmasking the true character of deeds in the financial sphere, which he assumes is deliberately obscure and duplicitous. The first step is therefore to scrutinize it using the gospel, which penetrates the obscurity to disclose the true character and motive of deeds within that sphere. This analysis cannot be neutral or empirical, but must be theological.

LUTHER'S USE OF SCRIPTURE

In the *Sermon von dem Wucher*, Luther's next step is therefore to outline what he calls 'the gospel' as it is particularly relevant here, in terms of 'three different degrees or ways of dealing fairly and righteously with temporal goods'.[31] These three norms are each taken directly from the teaching of Jesus in the Sermon on the Mount (Matthew 5:38–42): to relinquish goods freely when someone attempts to take them, to give freely without expecting return, and to lend without 'charge or interest'.[32] Again, the fact that he refers to this as 'the gospel' substantiates our claim that Luther does not draw a distinction between morality and gospel: the gospel has inherent moral substance.

[28] *Sermon von dem Wucher*, WA v. 6, p. 36, l. 7.

[29] LW v. 45, p. 273; WA v. 6, p. 36, l. 11.

[30] LW v. 45, p. 245; WA v. 15, p. 293, l. 1–2.

[31] LW v. 45, p. 273; WA v. 6, p. 36, l. 16–17.

[32] LW v. 45, p. 289.

Beginning with Scripture is not a particularly calculated step for Luther. He is preaching, and therefore begins with a Scriptural text. This is a reflexive move, but it is also born out of conviction. Scripture, rather than his own views, sets his agenda.[33] It possesses a critical edge against other claims of expertise such as church tradition and reason. His high account of the authority of preaching as the Word of God is noted above. This implies the preacher has great authority—yet it is a strictly delimited authority: the preacher speaks for God only insofar as he is expounding Scripture, since it is only thus that God speaks. Therefore, as Paul Althaus puts it, the 'form [of Luther's theology] is basically exegesis'.[34] The preachers can say nothing of themselves independently, but simply expound Scripture faithfully. Their authority is dependent on prior submission to Scripture.

Luther's method here is to lay out norms by which to judge potentially deviant practices later. These three ways of handling temporal goods are, he claims, the default standard, which he will then compare with other standards. Thus his ensuing analysis of the situation around him and the practical solutions he prescribes are dependent on the fundamental moral vision that he expounds from the teaching of Jesus.

We shall see that Luther is disputing the scholastic distinction between commands, the keeping of which was prerequisite for salvation, and the evangelical 'counsels of perfection', the keeping of which enabled one to attain beatitude more quickly.[35] It is essential for this to return to Scripture and prove that such a distinction is *exegetically* unsupportable. This demonstrates his view that Scripture is the 'primary authority in the church'.[36] Here we see him deploying a principle which pervades his work: the church fathers, councils, and creeds are valuable, and reason is indispensable, yet Scripture possesses a 'critical value' over and against them.[37]

In contradiction to the many caricatures of Luther's attitude, he by no means rejects tradition for the sake of it: 'I see some things that blessed Augustine did not see; . . . I know that others will see many things that I do not see. What recourse do we have but to be of mutual help to one another?'[38] This can be seen in his handling of the situation in Wittenberg in his *Invocavit* sermons in

[33] Cf. the parallel with the *Ninety-Five Theses* (1517), where Luther criticizes the priority given to preaching indulgences instead of the *verbum dei*, the Word of God (LW v. 31, p. 30; WA v. 1, p. 236, theses 53 and 54).

[34] Althaus, *The Theology of Martin Luther*, p. 3. It would be hard to better Althaus's summary of Luther's thought as a 'constant conversation with Scripture' (p. 4).

[35] This is discussed much more fully in the section entitled 'Luther's Method in Part One: Summary and Analysis'.

[36] Bernhard Lohse, *Martin Luther's Theology: Its Historical and Systematic Development*, trans. Roy A. Harrisville (Edinburgh: T & T Clark, 1999), p. 187.

[37] Lohse, *Martin Luther's Theology*, p. 187.

[38] LW v. 14, p. 285. Quoted in Bernd Wannenwetsch, 'Conversing with the Saints as they converse with Scripture', p. 131.

March 1522, when he opposed the overzealous reforms of Karlstadt and others, which had thrown the local population into consternation. He considers that these reformers were making reform into a law as strict as that which they replaced.[39] Tradition has a rightful place in maintaining order in Christian practice.[40] He also upholds the importance of human reason in its rightful place.[41]

[39] Already in *De Libertate Christiana* (1520) he comments, 'How much better is the teaching of the Apostle Paul who bids us take a middle course... they who neglect and disparage ceremonies, not out of piety, but out of mere contempt, are reproved, since the Apostle teaches us not to despise them.... As a man is not righteous because he keeps and clings to the works and forms of the ceremonies, so also will a man not be counted righteous merely because he neglects and despises them'. LW v. 31, p. 372; WA v. 7, p. 70, ll. 3–13. Brecht summarizes: 'There was a fundamental distinction between what was essential and what was allowable' (*Martin Luther: Shaping and Defining the Reformation*, p. 60). Tradition is not to be rejected *qua* tradition, but only if it does not fit with Scripture. See also Lohse, *Martin Luther's Theology*, p. 147.

[40] A useful illustration is Luther's later exposition of the relationship between Scripture and the councils which promulgated the creeds. In 'On the Councils and Church' (*Von den Konziliis und Kirchen*, 1539), he urges that conciliar statements only *defend* Scriptural teaching against heretical novelties, rather than declaring new articles of faith. The church has authority only to defend doctrine, not originate it. So, with respect to Nicaea, Luther comments: 'The council did not invent this doctrine [i.e. the consubstantiality of God and Christ] as though it had not previously existed in the churches, but rather defended it against the new heresy of Arius'. LW v. 41, p. 58; WA v. 50, p. 551, ll. 15–17. That is, he insists that the seemingly novel term *homoousios* is not the imposition of a foreign doctrinal category upon Scripture but a summary of its meaning: 'It thus became necessary to condense the meaning of Scripture, comprised of so many passages, into a short and comprehensive word'. LW v. 41, p. 83; WA v. 50, p. 572, ll. 25–7. Luther therefore argues that councils can make mistakes.

[41] Luther is certainly capable of sternly negative pronouncements on the blindness of reason following the Fall, e.g. his famous description of reason as the 'devil's whore'. Hence, reason is not neutral but partial, helping us construct 'our own image of God which corresponds to our own wishes and hopes'. Bernhard Lohse, *Martin Luther: An Introduction to his Life and Work*, trans. Robert C. Schultz (Edinburgh: T & T Clark, 1987), p. 160. Only if reason confesses its own inadequacy does it attain a true perception of reality. Then it is renewed in its divine vocation. On *this* basis Luther can be extremely positive about reason in theology, as in, for instance, his reported words at Worms (1521): 'Unless I am convinced by the testimony of the Scriptures or by clear reason... I am bound by the Scriptures I have quoted and my conscience is captive to the Word of God'. LW v. 32, p. 112; WA v. 7, p. 838a, ll. 4–7. This is only a report of what he said, but he expresses a similar idea in writing in 1517 in the *Ninety-five Theses* (LW v. 31, p. 27; WA v. 1, p. 234, thesis 18). These comments seem to give reason as much authority as Scripture. So clearly they are not in total opposition for Luther. Moreover, Luther is very positive about the role of reason in more human affairs: the gospel cannot teach someone carpentry or agriculture—but reason can. In the *Genesis Commentary* Luther distinguishes what humans can and cannot know using the trope of the four causes: humans retain some knowledge of their formal and material causes, but they have lost knowledge of final and efficient causes through the Fall, and thus their perception of truths pertaining to these causes is limited. See LW v. 1, pp. 124–5, 127; WA v. 42, pp. 93–5. For a full-length study, see B. A. Gerrish, *Grace and Reason: A Study in the Theology of Luther* (Oxford: Clarendon, 1962). Wayne Johnson argues that the crucial distinction for Luther is between reason as an appropriate tool of theological method, versus reason as an autonomous source of knowledge. See Wayne G. Johnson, *Theological Method in Luther and Tillich: Law-Gospel and Correlation* (Washington, DC: University Press of America, 1981), p. 74. This is also the judgement of Robert H. Fischer in his essay, 'A Reasonable Luther', in *Reformation Studies: Essays in Honor of Roland H. Bainton*, ed. Franklin H. Littell (Richmond, VI: John Knox, 1962), pp. 30–45.

He does not regard Scripture, tradition, and reason as *necessarily* antithetical. He is simply open to the possibility of their disagreement. If they do disagree, Scripture possesses primacy: reason and tradition are themselves authorized by Scripture and must be subject to it. Hence Luther is willing to juxtapose exegesis critically against Christian traditions of thought and practice. As he comments much later in the *Sermon von dem Wucher*, 'whether the practice be custom or not, it is not Christian or godly or natural, and no precedent can change that fact. For it is written: "You shall not follow a multitude to do evil [Exodus 23:2], but honour God and his commandments above all things"'.[42] Traditions and conventions must be open to revision in the light of God's commands.

Thus it is natural and necessary to begin with a passage of Scripture. However, it is not that he is setting out Scriptural principles to be *applied* to his situation, as it were. Rather, he sets out norms against which he will *weigh* the situation. His approach is: Scriptural exposition, followed by engagement and analysis, and then proscription and prescription based on the first two steps.

THE FIRST DEGREE: 'IF ANYONE WOULD SUE YOU AND TAKE YOUR TUNIC, LET HIM HAVE YOUR CLOAK AS WELL'

It is illuminating to explore how Luther handles each *grad* (degree) of handling temporal goods. We will briefly analyse his methodology with each degree, and then discuss various moves in more detail.

He begins with what he describes as 'the highest degree', that one should permit others to take one's property. This does not proscribe verbally rebuking a miscreant, as indeed Christ responded to Malchus and Pilate. A rebuke is even compulsory: even in the relationship between a malefactor and his victim, the victim bears a debt or obligation ('schuldig') to their neighbour because of their need, in this case a need for admonition. Even this relationship is to be characterized by a profound concern on the part of the innocent for the wrongdoer as neighbour: it is a duty to warn him, not to protect one's property, but *for the sake of the wrongdoer*, so that he might be reformed. Every interaction is subject to the demand of neighbour-love, and even in such an extreme circumstance, the other is a neighbour whom one is obliged to serve, and for whose well-being one is responsible. Their need creates an obligation.

[42] LW v. 45, p. 294; WA v. 6, p. 50, ll. 16–20.

This pattern is germane to Luther's discussion of right conduct towards a neighbour throughout the sermon. The later demand to forego one's rights, even to the point of allowing another to take one's goods unjustly, is made intelligible as a species of this obligation. This arduous duty is non-negotiable, because there is no relation that is exempt from the command to love one's neighbour.

A characteristic feature, therefore, is that Luther resists any attempt to minimize the demand or diminish the scope of this first degree. He enumerates a number of ways in which this diminution might happen, and it is instructive to observe his methodology in rebutting each. One attempt is the appeal to self-defence: 'Therefore, they hold that it is all right for anyone to take back what is his, and to meet force with force to the best of his ability and knowledge'.[43] Luther recounts the various arguments in favour of such a view: canon and civil law permit self-defence; so does proverbial wisdom; there are examples of self-defence in Scripture; and finally 'reason' argues that without self-defence, violence would rule. He adds a further attempt at evasion: the concept of readiness to relinquish property, being interpreted to mean that *only* readiness was necessary, and that it was not literally necessary to actually part with one's goods.

Luther's response is to reassert that, exegetically speaking, 'There is no evading it. This is simply a commandment that we are bound to obey'.[44] This is the core of his methodology here: to simply restate the absolute character of Jesus's commands on the basis of an exegetical engagement with the original text.

Let us examine the significance of this for Luther. He crucially assumes that morality is not something that humans may choose for themselves. Their role as creatures is to hear and respond to the demands which God makes of them. These demands are not arbitrary intrusions into human freedom for the sake of it; for the Luther of *De Libertate Christiana* (1520) the commands of God represent *freedom*—freedom not from all restraint, but freedom to live as God created humanity. Obedience is the consequence and embodiment of the liberation of the sinner from bondage to sin. Both champions and adversaries of Luther misunderstand him when they collapse his account of sanctification into his account of justification, and portray him as advocating merely a particularly forceful account of Christian moral psychology where motivation and spontaneity are all, with the Christian life being devoid of any real normative content. On the contrary, and as we see here, Luther understands the commandment to give shape and content to this spontaneous, joyful activity. While he emphasizes spontaneity in obedience, it is still *obedience*, that is, a response to a command which originated externally. The free-flowing works of the Christian need form, just as Adam in Eden needed a form for his

[43] LW v. 45, p. 275; WA v. 6, p. 37, ll. 28–30.
[44] LW v. 45, p. 277; WA v. 6, p. 39, ll. 3–4.

worship of God.[45] As Reinhard Hütter puts it, 'Christian freedom finds its appropriate *Gestalt* in being continuously addressed by the Decalogue'.[46]

Luther therefore asserts the primacy of Christ's command over temporal laws. These necessarily operate at a lower standard than that which God demands:

> It is of no consequence to God that laws—be they canon or civil—permit force to be resisted with force. And what precious things the laws permit! They permit public brothels, although they are contrary to God's commandment, and many other evil things which God forbids.[47]

Luther therefore thinks it absurd to argue that God permits self-defence simply because it is legal.[48] This illustrates another way in which, for Luther, Scripture possesses a critical quality not only against church tradition but against other claims too.

Self-defence is also dangerous because it employs the plaintiff in his own cause and is therefore untrustworthy. Scripture (Luther cites as examples Romans 13, Isaiah 1, and Psalm 82) indicates that punishment of wrongdoers must usually be executed by an impartial agency with independent proof:

> This [the punishment of wrongdoing] should be done in such a way, however, that no one would be the complainant in his own case, but that others, in brotherly fidelity and care for one another, would inform the rulers that this man is right and that one wrong.[49]

[45] 'We should think of the works of a Christian who is justified and saved by faith because of the pure and free mercy of God, just as we would think of the works which Adam and Eve did in Paradise.... Adam was created righteous and upright and without sin by God so that he had no need of being justified... but that he might not be idle, the Lord gave him a task to do, to cultivate and protect the garden. This task would truly have been the freest of works, done only to please God and not obtain righteousness'. LW v. 31, p. 360; WA v. 7, p. 61, ll. 2–11. Philip Watson has argued that the term *Gesetz* (law) for Luther always implies the possibility of a sanction. Therefore, the concept of a moral command which is not simultaneously law is quite possible for the Christian, who is no longer under the law. This does not imply they are no longer subject to God's moral commands, but that they are no longer under *sanction*. Watson, *Let God be God!*, p. 107.

[46] Hütter, 'The Twofold Center of Lutheran Ethics: Christian Freedom and God's Commandments', in *The Promise of Lutheran Ethics*, eds. Karen L. Bloomquist and John R. Stumme (Minneapolis: Fortress, 1998), pp. 31–54, esp. p. 44.

[47] LW v. 45, p. 277; WA v. 6, p. 39, ll. 5–9.

[48] On the basis of this section, Robin Gill misunderstands Luther as positing a dichotomy 'between the standards appropriate for the Christian and those to be required of the non-Christian' (Robin Gill, *A Textbook of Christian Ethics* (Edinburgh: T & T Clark, 1985), p. 178). This passage does not support such an interpretation: rather, it is simply that Luther recognizes that human justice cannot *enforce* obedience to the Sermon on the Mount, even if it is *morally* obligatory. For example, it is a binding moral obligation to have feelings of solicitude for one's enemy, but it is hardly possible to compel such feelings with coercive measures. But it is possible and legitimate to use such measures to discourage enemies from directly harming one another. Yet it does not follow that each set of standards applies to different groups of people: Gill's mistake is to transpose this from the political sphere to the individual one.

[49] LW v. 45, p. 278; WA v. 6, p. 39, ll. 26–9.

Acting in self-defence arrogates to oneself the authority delegated by God to the temporal government, and thus subverts the 'just and orderly way' of handling injustice provided by God.[50] Luther's response to the claim of self-defence is Scriptural reflection on temporal authority and earthly justice.

In order to grasp what Luther is doing here it is important to note the pedigree which the concept of self-defence had in Luther's context. On the basis of the concept of natural law, self-defence was considered not only permissible but indeed a strict duty. To take St Thomas as a reasonably representative example of this position, working from the premise that 'good is that which all things seek after', Thomas infers that, shared with all 'substances', human nature has an inclination towards:

> the preservation of its own being, according to its nature: and by reason of this inclination, whatever is a means of preserving human life, and of warding off its obstacles, belongs to the natural law.[51]

Thus, while Thomas vigorously maintains that, generally speaking, it is unlawful for a private individual to kill an evildoer (such as in ST 2a 2ae, q. 64, a. 3), the case of self-defence is different, since one does not intend the death of one's assailant, but only one's own preservation.[52] Thomas adds that 'one is bound to take more care of one's own life than of another's'.[53] One must not intend to harm another, but one has a duty according to nature to preserve one's own life. Yet Luther's engagement with the text of Scripture leads him to reject this established position. It is not that he opposed the notion of a natural law; indeed, he deploys it later in this very sermon. But for Luther the contents of the law of nature must be discerned in the light of Scripture, rather than operating primarily on the basis of the self-evidence of human nature. Such self-evidence, in Luther's opinion, no longer pertains because of the Fall, and so the judgements of human reason must be at least open to revision in the light of texts such as these which for Luther (at least at this stage in his career) prohibit self-defence.[54]

Given Luther's prohibition of self-defence, he therefore needs to rebut the objection that human society would degenerate if the command to relinquish temporal goods were heeded literally. Here one sees Luther wrestling with the exegetical material which is to grow into his so-called 'two kingdoms' concept.[55] Joan Lockwood O'Donovan and Oliver O'Donovan describe the 1524

[50] LW v. 45, p. 278. [51] ST 1a 2ae, q. 94, a. 2. [52] ST 2a 2ae, q. 64, a. 7.

[53] ST 2a 2ae, q. 64, a. 7. This topic is treated in detail in Thomas M. Osborne, Jr, *Love of Self and Love of God in Thirteenth-Century Ethics* (Notre Dame: University of Notre Dame Press, 2005).

[54] For Luther's more extended development of this theme, see his exposition of Matthew 5:38–42 in his commentary on the Sermon on the Mount in LW v. 21, pp. 106ff.

[55] The term *Zweireichelehre* is not Luther's but Karl Barth's, who coined it in 1922 in the context of his dispute with Paul Althaus as a critical appellation of the dualistic way in which the

treatise *Von Kaufshandlung und Wucher*, which incorporates this sermon, as containing 'illuminating applications of the earlier doctrine' contained in *Von weltlicher Oberkeit, wie weit man ihr Gehorsam schuldig sei* (*On Temporal Authority: To What Extent It Should be Obeyed*) (1523).[56] Yet one could reverse this insight and say that Luther's exegetical grappling with the issue in this earlier sermon partly shapes *On Temporal Authority*. This 'two kingdoms' idea is Luther's attempt to conceptualize a secure place in which Christ's commands can be obeyed, hence its relevance here.[57]

We will briefly consider this work now, since it will shed light on our exposition of the *Sermon von dem Wucher*, to see how the trains of thought which Luther is grappling with continue to develop.[58] In *On Temporal Authority*, he cites Scriptural passages such as Romans 13 and 1 Peter 2, which announce that secular government originates in divine providence: 'it is in the world by God's will and ordinance'.[59] Its purpose, according to Luther, is to uphold security and justice: 'Hence, it is certain and clear enough that it is God's will that the temporal sword and law be used for the punishment of the wicked and the protection of the upright'.[60] Coercive force employed by authority is for the sake of protecting others: this is not an arbitrary violence, but the upholding of justice within creation, and for the protection of God's creatures.

The second group of Scriptural instructions (such as are found in the Sermon on the Mount) enjoin non-resistance to evil: 'These and similar passages would certainly make it appear as though in the New Testament Christians were to have no temporal sword'.[61]

Because of these two groups of texts, a duality is unavoidable. As Oliver O'Donovan has expressed it, Christendom is inherently 'the doctrine of

idea had been used to 'justify Adolf Hitler and National Socialism' by demarcating the state as an autonomous entity (Robert Benne, 'Lutheran Ethics: Perennial Themes and Contemporary Challenges', in *The Promise of Lutheran Ethics*, eds. Karen L. Bloomquist and John R. Stumme (Minneapolis: Fortress, 1998), pp. 11–30, esp. p. 22. See also Lohse, *Martin Luther's Theology*, pp. 154–5, n. 18). The concept has been both savagely criticized and passionately defended. For a history of the interpretation of this controverted concept, see William J. Wright, *Martin Luther's Understanding of God's Two Kingdoms: A Response to the Challenge of Skepticism* (Grand Rapids: Baker, 2010), pp. 17–43.

56 Joan Lockwood O'Donovan and Oliver O'Donovan, *From Irenaeus to Grotius: A Sourcebook in Christian Political Thought 100–1625*, (Grand Rapids: Eerdmans, 1999), p. 584.

57 Of course, the concept did not emerge *ex nihilo* in Luther's writings. For an analysis of precursors to his fashioning of it, see David VanDrunen, *Natural Law and the Two Kingdoms: A Study in the Development of Reformed Social Thought* (Grand Rapids: Eerdmans, 2010), pp. 22–41.

58 A fuller analysis can be found in Brent W. Sockness, 'Luther's Two Kingdoms Revisited: A Response to Reinhold Niebuhr's Criticism of Luther', *Journal of Religious Ethics* 20.1 (1992), pp. 93–110, esp. pp. 94–9.

59 LW v. 45, p. 85; WA v. 11, p. 247, ll. 22–3.

60 LW v. 45, p. 87; WA v. 11, p. 248, ll. 29–31.

61 LW v. 45, p. 87; WA v. 11, p. 249, ll. 6–7.

the two'.[62] The question is how this duality is to be understood, how the groups of texts are to be interpreted in the light of one another. The prevailing explanation, to which we have already alluded, is here described by Luther: scholastic theology usually distinguished between commands, binding upon all, and voluntary counsels, to be followed by those who sought perfection, which would accordingly attain blessedness sooner. Under this interpretation, the duality is therefore posited at the level of groups of Christians, a division about which Luther complains:

> Of such commandments they make 'counsels' for the perfect. They divide Christian teaching and Christians into two classes. One part they call the perfect, and assign to it such counsels. The other they call the imperfect, and assign to it the commandments.[63]

Thus, those who hold positions of secular power are free to do so without breaking any commands. Such secular office is incompatible with the perfect life, and those who wish to attain the latter must withdraw from the world in order to observe the counsels of perfection.

This is unacceptable to Luther, again for exegetical reasons: the gospels make no such distinction. Luther insists that Jesus regarded his commands as commands, that is as binding on all:

> They fail to see that in the same passage Christ lays such stress on his teaching that he is unwilling to have the least word of it set aside, and condemns to hell those who do not love their enemies.[64]

His alternative is to shift the duality, from different ranks of Christians, to Christian and non-Christian:

> Here we must divide the children of Adam and all mankind into two classes, the first belonging to the kingdom of God, the second to the kingdom of the world.[65]

Yet the 'kingdom of the world' is not used in a simple pejorative sense, as in Augustine's delineation of the 'two cities'.[66] Rather, the duality corresponds to two God-given authorities, both of which God uses to combat evil.[67] For Luther this insight overcomes the claims made on behalf of the papacy

[62] Oliver O'Donovan, *The Desire of the Nations* (Cambridge: Cambridge University Press, 1996), p. 193.

[63] LW v. 45, pp. 87–8; WA v. 11, p. 249, ll. 9–13.

[64] LW v. 45, p. 88; WA v. 11, p. 249, ll. 14–17.

[65] LW v. 45, p. 88; WA v. 11, p. 249, ll. 24–5.

[66] See, e.g., Augustine, *City of God*, trans. Henry Bettenson (London: Penguin, 2003), xiv.28.

[67] Jürgen Moltmann helpfully brings out the importance of this 'apocalyptic' conception of the conflict between God and the devil for Luther's understanding of God's twofold rule. This agonistic struggle in turn dominates the world, and the life of the Christian (Jürgen Moltmann, *On Human Dignity: Political Theology and Ethics*, trans. M. Douglas Meeks (London: SCM, 1984), pp. 64–5).

to temporal as well as spiritual supremacy, because civil government is good in itself as an agent of God, without need of ecclesiastical authentication.[68] It fights evil in its particular, God-given way, namely of coercion:

> There are few true believers, and still fewer who live a Christian life, who do not resist evil and indeed themselves do no evil. For this reason God has provided for them a different government beyond the Christian estate and kingdom of God. He has subjected them to the sword so that, even though they would like to, they are unable to practice their wickedness.[69]

Given humanity's fallen state, it is necessary to subject non-Christians to God's will by force, for the sake of human preservation.

Christians are subject to God in a different manner: 'these people need no temporal law or sword'.[70] In them, God fights evil by liberating them from sin and the devil, and by conforming them to Christ:

> Christians have in their heart the Holy Spirit, who both teaches and makes them do injustice to no one, to love everyone, and to suffer injustice and even death willingly and cheerfully at the hands of anyone.[71]

Because Christians obey God and conform to his will because of his direct work in them by his Holy Spirit, compulsion is superfluous:

> 'The law is not laid down for the just but for the lawless.' Why is this? It is because the righteous man of his own accord does all and more than the law demands.[72]

So, at this stage Luther expects the believer to have virtually no need for coercive government.[73]

To bring together our discussion of Luther's exegesis of these two sets of passages in *On Temporal Authority*, it seems much better to summarize this aspect of Luther's thought as 'two governments' than as 'two kingdoms',

[68] In Luther's exposition of Psalm 82 (1530) he makes this very explicit: 'Once... popes, bishops, priests, and monks had such authority that, with their little letters of excommunication, they could force and drive kings and princes wherever they wished, without resistance or defense.... Now, however, the Gospel has come to light. It makes a plain distinction between the temporal and the spiritual estate and teaches, besides, that the temporal estate is an ordinance of God which everyone ought to obey and honor'. LW v. 13, p. 42; WA v. 31.I, p. 189, ll. 21–4 and p. 190, ll. 10–13. See also Heinrich Bornkamm, *Luther's World of Thought*, trans. Martin H. Bertram (St Louis: Concordia, 1958), p. 243.

[69] LW v. 45, p. 90; WA v. 11, p. 251, ll. 2–6.

[70] LW v. 45, p. 89; WA v. 11, p. 249, l. 36.

[71] LW v. 45, p. 89; WA v. 11, p. 250, ll. 2–4.

[72] LW v. 45, p. 89; WA v. 11, p. 250, ll. 9–11.

[73] For various reasons, especially his interaction with antinomians and more radical reformers and the events of the Peasants' War, Luther later came to see that even true Christians are very much affected by sin and frequently fall short of the standards required of them instead of consistently freely obeying God. He consequently concluded that coercion was in fact very much necessary for Christians too, in order to restrain that which is still sinful in them.

reflecting the two ways in which God rules his creation.[74] This term safeguards the fact that Luther does not imply a separation of the two: both are directed to the same end and relate to one another as distinct but not separate. Hence, for Luther the duality possesses an underlying unity in the fact that both governments are aspects of God's one rule over creation. For our purposes, the point to note is that therefore civil government is not independent of God's will and activity, but expresses and serves it, each form of divine rule working in its own way, each with its characteristic methods. To some extent, even the purposes of the two governments are distinct, in that one procures eternal salvation, while the other aims only at effecting a just and tranquil temporal order.

Yet according to the passages we have cited from this treatise, even this significant distinction should not be taken to suggest that the two governments correspond to a dualism of moral standards, as Robin Gill and Ernst Troeltsch suppose, since Luther is perfectly clear that in terms of immediately observable temporal effects, both governments produce very similar results, namely action in accordance with God's will.[75] Such an interpretation guards not only against the confusion of civil authority with the kingdom of the devil, which would lead to its denigration, but also against granting autonomy to civil authority, since despite their different proximate ends, both governments produce similar behaviour in the world.

Therefore, it is perfectly proper for a Christian to hold secular office and to execute its functions, even if this means utilizing force.[76] This befits its place in God's plan. Luther's famous dictum here is that one cannot 'rule the world by the gospel'.[77] Let us dwell on this much-quoted and oft-misunderstood phrase for a moment, as it is often read as a claim that civil government may or should apply a different (laxer) moral standard to that which God requires. Again, there is no suggestion in Luther's work that this is so. Rather, it refers to

[74] This is not to suggest that Luther himself uses the terms in a systematically distinct way. Lohse comments that the term *Zweireichelehre* ('doctrine of the two kingdoms'), 'is scarcely suitable... since it assumes a system and consistency in application that simply cannot be documented'. *Martin Luther's Theology*, pp. 154–5 (see also Heinrich Bornkamm, *Luther's Doctrine of the Two Kingdoms in the Context of his Theology* (Philadelphia: Fortress, 1966), pp. 16–18.) For example, the term 'reych' often refers to the distinction between the realm ruled by God and the realm of the devil, and at other times to the distinction between God's twofold government of creation. The crucial point is not to conflate them so that earthly government is misinterpreted as an aspect of Satan's rule rather than God's. Both governments are directed towards the suppression of the realm of the devil.

[75] See the quotation from Robin Gill on p. 18, and Troeltsch, *Social Teaching* v. 2, pp. 499–500 and 506ff.

[76] Thus Luther famously concludes, 'Therefore, if you see that there is a lack of hangmen, constables, judges, lords or princes, and you find that you are qualified, you should offer your services and seek the position, that the essential governmental authority may not be despised and become enfeebled or perish'. LW v. 45, p. 95; WA v. 11, p. 254, l. 37–p. 255, l. 3.

[77] LW v. 45, p. 91. See WA v. 11, p. 251, ll. 22ff.

a quite limited point, namely that civil government must not obey Christ's command not to resist evil with force. This indeed would, as Heinrich Bornkamm puts it, 'founder miserably in the world of reality.... Government without law and force would constitute, in effect, a charter enthroning evil'.[78] It would be deeply unloving, eschewing the duty of care which the ruling authorities bear towards their subjects. That is, the use of force is subsumed under the rubric of love and service to one's neighbour:

> Just as he performs all other works of love which he himself does not need... so he serves the governing authority not because he needs it but for the sake of others, that they may be protected and that the wicked may not become worse.... If he did not so serve he would be acting not as a Christian but even contrary to love.[79]

Thus, quite opposite to sanctioning a Christian dualism, for Luther this means precisely that love of neighbour must not be relegated to a private, individual sphere with a different standard of morality. Rather, there is but a single obligation (love of neighbour) which is exercised in different ways as appropriate to one's role in a given situation.[80] Hence George Forell concludes that Luther 'does not establish a secular source of ethics for society'.[81] With respect to Luther's *Dreiständelehre* (doctrine of the three stations or orders), Oswald Bayer comments that love is the 'general orientation', and action in the different institutions is 'its concrete expression, its embodiment'.[82] Nor does this imply that the gospel has no impact on the way in which one conducts oneself within a worldly office, a theme to which Luther in fact devotes considerable space in *Von weltlicher Oberkeit*.

With this point, we are approaching Luther's resolution of the seeming contradiction between these two groups of texts. This he does using the crucial notion of role or office. Using this concept, he argues that the two forms of divine rule are expressed in another duality, this time at the level of *each Christian*. The Christian is within both regiments, 'two areas of activity'.[83] This leads to Luther's infamous statement of this duality in terms of the Christian as 'two persons', perhaps an unfortunate turn of phrase, which has understandably elicited objections. The *locus classicus* for this concept is Luther's exposition of the Sermon on the Mount (*Reihenpredigten über*

78 Bornkamm, *Luther's World of Thought*, p. 244.

79 LW v. 45, p. 94; WA v. 11, p. 253, l. 33–p. 254, l. 4.

80 See LW v. 37, pp. 363–5, esp. p. 365: 'Above these three... is the common order of Christian love'. WA v. 26, p. 505b, ll. 11–12. Love is defined in these orders, but not exhaustively; it overrules them.

81 Forell, *Faith Active in Love*, p. 148.

82 Oswald Bayer, 'Nature and Institution: Luther's Doctrine of the Three Orders', *Lutheran Quarterly* 12.2 (1998), pp. 125–59, esp. p. 140.

83 Paul Althaus, *The Ethics of Martin Luther*, trans. Robert C. Schultz (Philadelphia: Fortress, 1972), p. 67.

Matthäus 5–7, 1530–32). Luther argues, with respect to the Beatitude, 'Blessed are the meek' (Matthew 5:5), that this refers only to the Christian *in one particular role*, namely, 'how individuals are to live in relation to others, apart from official position and authority'.[84] He goes on to say on this basis that:

> I have often said that we must sharply distinguish between these two, the office and the person. The man who is called Hans or Martin is a man quite different from the one who is called elector or doctor or preacher. Here we have two different persons in one man.... Once we are born, God adorns and dresses you up as another person.[85]

Thus, while Luther indeed speaks of 'two different persons in one man', it is quite clear from the context that such terminology does not imply some deep ontological dualism. The distinction is between a person as they act for their own sake and a person as they act in an official capacity, that is, a distinction of role or of *relations*. Luther makes this crystal clear when he returns to this theme later with respect to Matthew 5:38–42, the injunctions not to resist evil and to readily relinquish one's earthly goods, the latter of which he had earlier expounded in the *Sermon von dem Wucher*. It is instructive to see how he expounds this text a decade later. He summarizes, 'we are talking about a Christian-in-relation'.[86] The Christian relates to those around him or her both in themselves *and* in the roles or offices they bear, such as servant, parent, or magistrate. Insofar as it only harms them, they must not resist evil with force, or take others to court when they have been wronged in order to obtain restitution. But when they are responsible for others (such as parents for children, rulers for their subjects) the Christian may, and indeed must, resist evil with force within this role:

> we are talking... about this life and his obligation in it to some other person, whether under him or over him or even alongside him..., whom he is obliged, if possible, to defend, guard and protect.[87]

Here, then, is Luther's resolution: by allocating different commands to different roles, he is able to uphold the binding nature of both sets of biblical texts without having to moderate them. The command not to resist one's goods being taken by force need no longer be understood as a counsel of perfection: it is entirely binding on everyone with respect to their own possessions. At the same time, the divine mandate of rulers to protect those under their charge from unjust seizure of their goods is also upheld without compromise.

[84] LW v. 21, p. 23; WA v. 32, p. 316, ll. 10–12.

[85] LW v. 21, p. 23; WA v. 32, p. 316, ll. 15–21. There is some ambiguity concerning how accurately the text reflects Luther's own words (see LW v. 21, pp. xx–xxi), but the idea is clear enough.

[86] LW v. 31, p. 109; WA v. 32, p. 390, l. 33.

[87] LW v. 31, p. 109; WA v. 32, p. 390, ll. 34–6. See Bayer, 'Nature and Institution', p. 138.

Thus Luther is able to strongly affirm that Christians may be fully involved in worldly affairs without compromising their obedience to God, and without the need for a double standard. The concept of God's twofold rule is necessary for him to obstruct any abdication of responsibility for the worldly sphere *or* an abandonment of obedience to Christ's commands in their totality. Luther's stricture against 'ruling the world with the Gospel' therefore attempts to *uphold* radical Christian moral standards, by preserving a place in which they can safely be enacted.[88]

Returning to our discussion of the *Sermon von dem Wucher*, Luther ends his exposition of the 'first degree' with an example of a methodological motif which we will frequently notice in his work, namely the way in which his wider theological vision shapes his interpretation of a particular command. The unjust loss of temporal goods enjoined by this command is, according to Luther, instituted by God for the *anklebung* ('cleansing') of attachment to them:

> It would be impossible for us to become cleansed of our attachment to temporal goods if God did not ordain that we should suffer unjust losses, and thereby be trained to turn our hearts away from the false temporal goods of this world.[89]

Luther is adducing a broader theological point in order to illuminate this particular command: the command is not free-standing. Thus the loss of goods is not merely commanded and therefore non-negotiable, but commanded for a particular reason and therefore rational. Suffering injustice is configured as a purgative, to which the appropriate response is gratefulness to God, rather than insistence on one's due. The human heart is not capable of extricating itself from its enchantment with worldly goods: 'it becomes too deeply enmeshed in temporal things, and too firmly attached to them'.[90]

In Luther's particular context, particularly significant here is the notion that such suffering and cleansing are not works of deliberate renunciation, as in the mendicancy movement. Suffering is not meritorious, and poverty is not holy. Yet Luther does not ignore the possibility that impoverishment may, indirectly, effect the transformation of the sufferer. Such a transformation is significant in two crucial respects. First, it is not directly a transformation of moral character. Crudely, Luther does not suggest that losing one's goods unjustly will directly make one more generous, for example. Rather, by stripping away temporal goods God stultifies human reliance on them, and impels one to trust him. Thus what is increased is not one's moral goodness, but one's trust in God.[91] Second, this seeming misfortune is not a voluntary

[88] See Carter Lindberg, 'Theology and Politics: Luther the Radical and Muntzer the Reactionary', *Encounter* 37.4 (1976), pp. 356–71.

[89] LW v. 45, pp. 279–80; WA v. 6, p. 40, ll. 30–3.

[90] LW v. 45, p. 280; WA v. 6, p. 41, l. 10.

[91] Luther makes a similar point in the *Treatise on Good Works*, where he opines that the exercise of faith in the midst of suffering makes it stronger: 'Such works are to be done and such

achievement but something which is undergone. Suffering is not a mechanism for procuring God's favour, it is passive and involuntary, and it is God's role to bring forth good outcomes from it.

In order to clarify this, let us note a parallel in Luther's portrayal of marriage. In *Ein Sermon von dem ehelichen Stand* (1519) he states that marriage is a deliberate, consensual act of self-giving. It appears entirely voluntary: 'the estate of marriage consists essentially in consent having been freely and previously given one to another'.[92] At the same time, marriage is a work of God, who gives the husband and wife to one another, as in the archetypical example of Adam and Eve. Luther remarks:

> A wife is given by God alone.... In the case of Adam, God creates for him a unique, special kind of wife out of his own flesh. He brings her to him, he gives her to him, and Adam agrees to accept her. Therefore, that is what marriage is.[93]

On the one hand the partnership is contracted by an act of human will, but theologically speaking it does not depend on the particular performance of the spouses in question. This quasi-involuntary character is even clearer in Luther's observation that God uses marriage to subdue lust: 'In this way God sees to it that the flesh is subdued so as not to rage wherever and however it pleases'.[94] The couple need not intend this outcome, nor need they even be aware of it, in order for God to use marriage in this way. Also significant here is Luther's strong emphasis on God's presence and activity in the world independently of the church and of Christian faith. Just as it is not up to us to discern what is right, but to respond to God's commands, so it is impossible for us to be freed from sinful desires unless God does it. But God *is* present and active in the world at large in this way—a matter to which we shall return in Chapter 3, in the section entitled 'Eschatology Versus Creation as a Basis for Social Ethics'.

What is going on in Luther's claim regarding God's 'cleansing' of attachment to worldly goods is that Luther is asserting a theological vision of reality against a terminally earth bound imagination. The former broadens the presumption of what is possible. The latter is focused on the immediately perceptible. It therefore restricts action according to its proximate effects, while the New Testament vision of reality deployed by Luther liberates action in the light of eternity. Thus, while a conspicuous feature of Luther's method is to reassert that certain commands (such as the command to readily relinquish

sufferings endured in faith and in the sure confidence of God's favour, so that all works remain within the sphere of the first commandment and of faith, which exercises itself in these sufferings and grows strong'. LW v. 44, p. 79; WA v. 6, p. 249, ll. 7–10. The connection between *üben* and *stercken* in this treatise is discussed further in the section entitled 'The Second Degree: "Give to the One Who Begs from You"'.

92 LW v. 44, p. 11; WA v. 2, p. 169, ll. 11–12.
93 LW v. 44, p. 8; WA v. 2, p. 167, ll. 4–15.
94 LW v. 44, p. 11; WA v. 2, p. 169, ll. 3–5.

one's goods) are absolute, this does not mean that Luther treats them as if they are the only thing sufficient for rightly perceiving and acting. He reads and expounds the commands in the context of a much broader biblical-theological understanding of reality which illuminates and explicates the meaning of the command and its underlying rationality. Thus the commands are not arbitrary decrees, but cohere with and arise from claims about the way the world is. Therefore, in this case, Luther sketches an attractive picture of earthly and heavenly peace which comes through obedience to this command even to the point of losing one's earthly goods.

On the other hand, he also adds a smarting reminder of the opposite: those who do not allow themselves to suffer now will suffer eventually instead. To evade this command is a false economy: 'That is the perverted wisdom of the world; it fishes with golden nets, and the cost is greater than the profit'.[95] Thus the command to freely give up one's worldly goods is interpreted in the context of a wider account of the way things are which renders acts of sacrifice and martyrdom intelligible, even reasonable and, in an important sense, realistic. Divine commands are clearly indispensable components of the way in which God makes his will known—but for Luther they are by no means sufficient for this purpose on their own.

This illuminates further the critical edge which Scripture possesses against other sources of authority and perceptions of reality: it is not simply a matter of pitting Scriptural commands or propositions against those of the church and world. Scripture is not merely a list of commands; it also announces truth that goes beyond the limited possibilities of unenlightened human vision. In doing so it discloses the deficiency of other attempts to know reality. As we shall see, such deficiencies are themselves explained theologically, as originating in their prior, sinful, commitments. This insight overcomes the false interpretation of Luther's emphasis on spontaneity mentioned above, as if readiness to do God's will abolishes the need for moral theological reflection. Accurate description in the light of biblical depictions of reality and diligent attention to God's commandments are as necessary as the correct inward predisposition.

THE SECOND DEGREE: 'GIVE TO THE ONE WHO BEGS FROM YOU'

With respect to the second degree, Luther again stresses the binding nature of this command. It might be lower than the first degree, but it is still a very high standard. Once again, a major feature of his method is simply to acknowledge

[95] LW v. 45, p. 279; WA v. 6, p. 40, ll. 27–8.

the height of the standard, and to oppose all curtailments of it. However, first he continues the intriguing theme of the way in which obedience to these commands relates to the question of salvation.

That there can be such a relationship at all for Luther may on the face of it seem perplexing. Can Luther, of all people, be ascribing salvific merit to good deeds? Yet on closer inspection it is apparent that while he does not regard generosity as a *means* to salvation, Luther nevertheless regards one's treatment of the needy as crucially related to one's eternal destiny. In terms of understanding Luther's method, it is worth examining how these two core features of Luther's theological framework, namely justification by faith alone and the absolutely binding character of God's commands, are related.

The link is much easier to see if one simply reads the word 'faith' in terms of the word 'trust'. For Luther, one's disposition with respect to earthly possessions proceeds from one's disposition of trust or otherwise with respect to God. If one trusts God, one will trust him for temporal provision as much as for eternal salvation. If one does not, one will be perpetually seeking to provide for oneself, to procure assurance for the future. This inevitably results in hoarding worldly goods in case of future need. Thus greed originates in a lack of trust in God; hence it is incompatible with true faith. Since one is saved through faith—that is, through trust—one who does not trust God to meet one's present needs cannot be saved:

> They therefore fear that they would die of hunger or be ruined entirely if they were to obey God's command and give to everyone who asks of them. How then can they trust him to maintain them in eternity? . . . There is reason to fear that he who will not listen to this teaching and follow it will never acquire the art of trusting, and that those who will not trust God in little temporal things must at last despair also in those matters that are great and eternal.[96]

So, it is not that one earns merit by acting rightly with one's possessions. Rather, one's actions will display whether one trusts God for one's well-being.

Luther also particularly fears greed because, although it springs from a lack of trust in God, it also *feeds* unbelief, because attachment to possessions distracts the heart from God. Conversely, giving away one's property will as it were provide opportunities to exercise one in the art of trusting God. It will not secure one's salvation as a matter of reward, but it will help to foster that which does save, namely faith.

According to a study by Ricardo Rieth, greed is therefore not simply one sin among many: it wholly determines one's actions.[97] Lack of trust in God in the

[96] LW v. 45, p. 281; WA v. 6, p. 41, ll. 22–32.

[97] Alongside Rieth's monograph, *'Habsucht' bei Martin Luther*, see also Ricardo W. Rieth, 'Luther on Greed', in *Harvesting Martin Luther's Reflections on Theology, Ethics and the Church*, ed. Timothy J. Wengert (Grand Rapids: Eerdmans, 2004), pp. 152–68, esp. p. 159.

sphere of one's relationship with God takes the form of greed in the sphere of one's relationships with one's neighbours: 'Wealth's trust in mammon, by governing the heart, excludes faith and love'.[98] Just as faith for Luther is an active disposition which cannot but act in love (he was very fond of Galatians 5:6), so greed is 'a force or power inside the person that compels one to commit evil'.[99] Rieth shows that for Luther, because greed is not merely a habit or choice, but a profoundly narcissistic *enslavement*, no moral formula or system is sufficient for right action. It is not adequate to simply set out the right norms and follow them. The human must be liberated from the compulsive need to secure his own well-being. Such liberation can only come about through despair of one's own abilities to provide for oneself, forcing one to turn to God to meet one's dire need. Rieth's study therefore helpfully illuminates Luther's emphasis here on the involuntary character of the loss of temporal goods which we have mentioned.

One's attitude to earthly goods therefore has a disclosing function: how one handles one's property reveals the fundamental orientation of one's heart towards God. Avarice and stinginess disclose that even if someone somewhat complacently considers themselves to have faith in God, they lack authentic trust in him, faith being a deep, personal trust in God's fixed intention to care and provide for his creatures. So while this aspect of Luther's theological framework remains firmly distanced from the notion that one's good works can contribute towards one's salvation, neither does this lead Luther into a disregard for works. This resolves the apparent paradox as regards how Luther can consider one's handling of temporal goods as related to salvation. It is only paradoxical if one interprets faith as a purely mental subscription to a set of conceptual propositions, in which case it would be entirely compatible with greed, but it would not be faith as Luther conceives of it.[100]

We have therefore seen that all this has two implications. First, this trust in God's care shapes the way in which one handles one's temporal goods. Trusting God to meet one's needs liberates one from the neurotic compulsion to acquire more and more in order to be secure.[101] Faith therefore has concrete economic implications. Second, and conversely, what happens to one's temporal goods cultivates one's faith. Luther describes this educative function as a

[98] Rieth, 'Luther on Greed', p. 160. [99] Rieth, 'Luther on Greed', p. 161.

[100] The findings of the so-called Finnish school of Luther research substantiate this point in their contention that faith for Luther is union with Christ: it is by faith itself that Christ is present. Thus faith is of necessity morally transforming, since Christ becomes the subject of the believer's works. See, e.g., Tuomo Manermaa, *Christ Present in Faith: Luther's View of Justification*, trans. Kirsi Stjerna (Minneapolis: Fortress, 2005), pp. 16–19, 49–51.

[101] Faith is a different 'kind of having' (Oswald Bayer, 'Luther's Ethics as Pastoral Care', *Lutheran Quarterly*, 4.2 (1990), pp. 125–42, esp. p. 137). Greed isolates one in self-sufficiency; faith operates by receiving rather than acquiring, which breaks self-sufficiency.

training of the heart in the *Kunst* ('art') of trusting God.[102] There are parallels to this in *Von den guten Werken* (1520), where the need to exercise or practise (*üben*) faith is a theme.

It is worth pausing over Luther's tantalizing use of this verb. On one level, it simply means 'practise' in the sense of 'put into practice' or 'exert'. That is, faith is not inert or purely cognitive, but has concrete manifestations and effects. Yet, like the English words 'exercise' and 'practise', *üben* also seems to carry for Luther the connotation of improving a faculty by its exertion, as in practising a musical instrument or exercising a muscle. For example, faith is put into practice in prayer because it nurtures one's trust in God. In this context Luther twice places 'exercising' faith (*üben*) in apposition to 'strengthening' it (*stercken*). Addressing those who feel that God does not hear their prayers, Luther advises:

> You should thank God with all your heart that he thus reveals to you your weakness, through which weakness he teaches and admonishes you what your real need is, that is, to exercise (*üben*) and strengthen yourself in faith every day.[103]

This is exactly consistent with Luther's use of *üben* in this section of the *Sermon von dem Wucher*: obedience to Christ's command to give is a means of 'training' one's faith.[104] Thus, speaking of those who purport to have faith that God will grant them eternal salvation, but who do not display their trust by giving away their worldly goods, Luther comments with asperity:

> They even think that in this regard they have perfect trust in him; yet they will not heed this commandment of his by which he would train and drive them to learn to trust him in things temporal and eternal.[105]

It is God who is the subject of the verbs *üben* and *treiben*. This encapsulates the way in which obedience strengthens one's trust in God, yet, characteristically for Luther, the notion that God is the agent behind such activity is never far away.

Therefore, although faith is on the one hand the sole basis of once-and-for-all liberation from temporal angst, and thus a prerequisite for rightly handling one's goods, at the same time such handling can fortify one's faith. Yet this is

[102] WA v. 6, p. 41.

[103] LW v. 44, p. 61; WA v. 6, p. 234, ll. 18–20. A few paragraphs later he makes this connection again: 'No man is so heavily burdened with his work that he cannot, if the will is there, speak with God in his heart while he is working, lay his need and that of other men before him, ask for help, make petition, and in all this exercise and strengthen his faith'. LW v. 44, p. 62; WA v. 6, p. 234, l. 36–p. 235, l. 2.

[104] Although 'to train' is not the most obvious equivalent for *üben* ('practise' or 'exercise' would be more conventional), it is adopted frequently in Charles Jacobs's translation of the *Sermon von dem Wucher* in the LW edition, bringing out precisely this connotation.

[105] LW v. 45, p. 281; WA v. 6, p. 41, ll. 27–9.

not some kind of consciously adopted technique; it can be entirely passive, as explored with respect to relinquishing one's goods when they are unjustly expropriated. Either way, God is the agent behind one's growth in faith. Luther makes this explicit in *De Libertate Christiana*, where he comments that faith may grow through both suffering and good works: 'Your one care should be that faith may grow, whether it is trained by works or sufferings'.[106]

Luther developed these themes in 1524 in an exposition of Psalm 127. There, he assiduously separates human activity and divine provision. Humans are to work, and God will provide—but this does not mean that God's provision is dependent on one's work:

> The management of a household should and must be done in faith—then there will be enough—so that men come to acknowledge that everything depends not on our doing, but on God's blessing and support.... Man must and ought to work, ascribing his sustenance and the fulness of his house, however, not to his own labour but solely to the goodness and blessing of God.[107]

If one does not acknowledge God as the provider, in the words of the Psalm one will 'labour in vain', which Luther takes to mean that one's self-reliance will produce an incessant state of fear. Conversely, if one trusts God's abundant provision, one's work will be liberated from self-service and placed at the disposal of the needs of others.

Luther phrases his emphasis on involuntary suffering even more strongly here: God permits misfortunes to arise as an attack on unbelief, and to compel faith: 'This is why he permits such situations to arise in this world, as an assault on unbelief, to bring to shame the arrogance of reason with all works and cleverness, and to constrain them to believe'.[108]

This emphasis on the radical nature of greed plays into another aspect of Luther's understanding of the role of the worldly authorities to which he now comes: one cannot rely on individual human choices to secure just relations between humans.[109] Therefore, the authorities have a positive role in *counteracting* greed as well as restraining it.

Luther buttresses his argument for this with two commands given to the 'Jewish people' in Deuteronomy 15: that there should be no beggars among them (which Luther reads as an obligation rather than a promise), and that, rather contradictorily, since there will never cease to be poor people among them, they should give generously to the poor. It is worth noting another aspect of Luther's method in handling these biblical commandments. He does not regard them as ahistorical decrees but as given to a particular group at a

[106] LW v. 31, p. 371; WA v. 7, p. 68, ll. 31–4.
[107] LW v. 45, pp. 324–5; WA v. 15, p. 366, ll. 12–17.
[108] LW v. 45, p. 323; WA v. 15, p. 365, ll. 17–19.
[109] This is borne out by Luther's later advice in *Von Kaufshandlung* that the best way of ensuring just prices would be for the authorities to set them.

specific time. This is not then a 'divine command morality' whereby God's will is mediated through abstract, timeless stipulations. At the same time, Luther does not infer from his recognition that these commands are historically situated that they are devoid of moral significance for his own time. Knowing God's will for that people at that time helps to illuminate his will here and now. Indeed, for Christians these commands are intensified:

> Now since God gave this commandment in the Old Testament, how much more ought we Christians to be bound, not only to allow no one to starve or beg, but beyond that also to keep the first degree of this commandment and be prepared to let everything go that anyone would take from us by force.[110]

Luther is following Jesus's expository technique in the Sermon on the Mount: taking different Mosaic instructions, he intensifies them so that instead of regarding them as a pinnacle of moral achievement, they are far less than is required: 'This second degree is so small a thing that it was commanded even to the simple, imperfect Jewish people in the Old Testament'.[111]

Some details of Luther's historical context are relevant here. The mendicancy movements enabled chicanery whereby those capable of work made easy money from those who thought that almsgiving would atone for their sins.[112] Poverty was theologically and therefore socially acceptable; although almsgiving abounded, no sustained attempt was made to deal with poverty as such.[113] But because of his understanding of justification by faith alone, Luther has no need of the theological substructure on which some features of mendicancy had come to be based, opening the way for poverty to be treated as a social evil rather than a theological good. Poverty is no longer seen as a meritorious state, and therefore can and should be genuinely alleviated rather than perpetuated.[114]

What is also significant here is that, although Luther is often (and in some sense rightly) dubbed a realist for his insistence that the Kingdom of God can never be realized in this age through human effort, his expectations of what might be achieved are, at this stage at least, dramatically high: 'I think it would be more fitting if there were no more begging in Christendom under the New Testament than among the Jews under the Old Testament'.[115] His reputation as a realist or pessimist needs to be revised in the light of this extraordinarily

110 LW v. 45, p. 281; WA v. 6, p. 42, ll. 3–7.

111 LW v. 45, p. 281; WA v. 6, p. 41, ll. 33–4.

112 Lindberg, *Beyond Charity*, pp. 26–33.

113 Carter Lindberg, 'Luther on Poverty', in *Harvesting Martin Luther's Reflections on Theology, Ethics and the Church*, ed. Timothy J. Wengert (Grand Rapids: Eerdmans, 2004), pp. 134–51, esp. p. 139.

114 For a contemporary exegetical endorsement of his conclusion, by a Franciscan, see Leslie J. Hoppe, *There Shall Be No Poor Among You: Poverty in the Bible* (Nashville: Abingdon, 2004), esp. pp. 171–4.

115 LW v. 45, p. 281; WA v. 6, p. 42, ll. 9–11.

high level of expectation of what can and should be accomplished by spiritual and temporal authorities, who have a responsibility to ensure that nobody needs to beg.

Meanwhile, as with the first degree, a pivot of his method here is to reassert the unvarnished meaning of the command to give freely without asking for return, while training a critical eye on attempts to minimize the force of the command to give freely. He addresses three of these in turn.

First, he mentions the idea that one is more obliged to give to one's 'friends and to the rich and powerful who do not need then, but forget the needy'.[116] He replies that proximity is not the only thing which creates an obligation: so does need. This is a swipe at abuses of the notion of the *ordo caritatis* or *caritas ordinata*, namely the idea that one's charity (and thus one's almsgiving) is directed according to certain lines of priority. For example, St Thomas argues that some neighbours are to be loved more than others, according to the gravity of the sin one would commit if one failed to love them.[117] It would be more heinous to fail to love one's parents than it would be to fail to love a distant relative. Hence, one ought to love one's kindred more than those to whom one is not related, one's fellow-citizens more than citizens of other nations, and so on.[118] This system of ordering love according to proximity is later exhibited in Thomas's claim that one should give alms preferentially 'to those rather who are more closely united to us'—although he is careful to qualify this claim to prevent precisely the abuses which Luther complains of. Thus he adds:

> We must employ discretion. . . . For we ought to give alms to one who is much holier and in greater want, and to one who is more useful to the common weal, rather than to one who is more closely united to us . . . and who is not in very urgent need.[119]

So, one is obliged to give alms to the needy, if one's own dependents are reasonably well provided for. Thus this concept of ordered love functioned as a rough guideline in setting priorities in almsgiving, given one's limited resources.[120] Yet in Thomas's determination to uphold the idea that 'Nature is not done away, but perfected, by glory', he is according to Pope led to the perhaps disconcerting conclusion that it is more meritorious to give alms to a friend than a neighbour.[121] Yet Luther acknowledges the need to differentiate between classes of responsibility. He therefore draws a corresponding distinction, but he does so by distinguishing between offices or stations in life, rather than between different grades or levels of love. He regards the mistake as

[116] LW v. 45, p. 282; WA v. 6, p. 42, ll. 16–17. [117] ST 2a 2ae, q. 26, a. 6.
[118] ST 2a 2ae, q. 26, a. 8. [119] ST 2a 2ae, q. 32, a. 9.
[120] See Stephen J. Pope, 'Aquinas on Almsgiving, Justice and Charity: An Interpretation and Reassessment', *Heythrop Journal* 32.2 (1991), pp. 167–91, esp. pp. 173–4.
[121] ST 2a 2ae, q. 26, a. 13. See Pope, 'Aquinas on Almsgiving, Justice and Charity', p. 174.

subsuming one's duty to provide for one's family and keep civil luminaries in an appropriate manner under the rubric of almsgiving. He wishes to preserve charity as an unconditional obligation in itself.

It is Luther's method of scrutinizing contemporary customs and their underlying rationales *in the light of the command* that leads him to spot the abuse of the idea of ordered love as an excuse for restricting almsgiving to one's inner circle, or to conferring money on those who could return the favour. The underlying motive for such an arrangement is self-interest: seeking one's own honour or reward rather than serving the needy for their own sake.

Second, Luther responds to the customary view that one need not give to enemies. Again, his method is to restate the text of the command, pointing out that it makes no such qualification. It is an inevitable tendency of the fallen human heart to try and avoid God's commands, but Luther is frustrated to see this aided and abetted by teachers within the church. They argue that in forgiving one's enemy it is not really necessary to give up the *signa rancoris* ('the signs and outward tokens of wrath and bitterness towards one's enemy').[122] This is not necessary for salvation, and applies only if one wishes to be perfect.[123]

Thus Luther's method here is to reject the migration of Christ's command to the inward sphere, without requiring concrete action. In contrast to some accounts of Luther's ethics, which regard him as perpetrating precisely a split of inner and outer spheres, in which the inner sphere is classified as the authentically significant, it is vital to him to affirm that inner renewal must result in outward obedience—otherwise there cannot have been inward change.[124] His evidence for this claim is the character of God's forgiveness, which not only puts aside wrath, but also graciously *gives* to the forgiven one: 'You must forgive and forget, as you would that God should not only forgive you and forget, but also grant you even more kindnesses than before'.[125]

[122] LW v. 45, p. 283; WA v. 6, p. 43, ll. 15–16. Gabriel Biel, for example, argued that it was not necessary to change these external things, provided one's *intention* was proper. See Karl Holl, *The Reconstruction of Morality*, trans. Fred W. Meuser and Walter R. Wietzke, eds. James Luther Adams and Walter F. Bense (Minneapolis: Augsburg, 1979), p. 40.

[123] Holl, *The Reconstruction of Morality*, p. 39.

[124] Neither does this imply that Luther thinks that only outward actions matter, regardless of one's inner disposition. He regards any attempt to separate inner and outer by designating either as the one that really matters as an evasion of the command. Hence elsewhere he is equally adamant that forgiveness, for example, must not only involve proper conduct towards a wrongdoer but must include ceasing to hate them. See his expositions of the Fifth Commandment in *Von den guten Werken* (LW v. 44, pp. 100 and 102; WA v. 6, p. 265, ll. 28–33 and p. 266, l. 34–p. 267, l. 13) and *Der Großer Katechismus* in Theodore G. Tappert (trans. and ed.), *The Book of Concord: The Confessions of the Evangelical Lutheran Church* (Philadelphia: Fortress, 1959), p. 390; WA v. 30.I, p. 158, ll. 20–33). In the latter, he particularly comments on the way inward forgiveness *determines* right outward behaviour.

[125] LW v. 45, p. 283; WA v. 6, p. 43, ll. 26–7.

Luther's method here is literally theological: one learns the true nature of a deed through God's performance of it.

The third criticism Luther directs at contemporary practice is of what he regards as the diversion of financial support away from the needy to seemingly religious things such as church buildings and masses. The crucial methodological move he makes here is to analyse the origin of such activities. Giving to such causes proceeds from human desires, not obedience to Christ's commands:

> Giving has taken hold here, and the real stream of giving runs in the direction towards which men have guided it and where they wanted to have it. No wonder, then, that in the direction toward which Christ's word guides it things are so dry and desolate.[126]

That is, Luther detects two types of good works: those purportedly done for God, which in reality are performed by people for their own benefit, and those which are done for the benefit of neighbours who actually need them. George Forell summarizes this facet of Luther's thought as follows:

> Heretofore that had been called a good work which allegedly contributed to the eternal welfare of the person doing the work. Now Luther insisted that man did not have to do anything for God . . . in order to achieve his own salvation. . . . The good was no longer evaluated by what it did 'subjectively' for the doer but rather it was judged by what it could do 'objectively' for the neighbour.[127]

As in his objections to indulgences, he detects in human ostentation a devious means of assuring oneself of security—in contrast to what God really wants, which seems petty and ignoble, and has no earthly splendour or reward. As we shall explore further in the section entitled 'Luther's Method in Part One: Summary and Analysis', historian Carter Lindberg has particularly highlighted the way in which, because one's standing before God is for Luther determined by faith and not actions, he can reassert the priority of one's neighbour within the sphere of action, in place of devotion directed towards God.

Luther is not punctilious about this, and does not advocate ceasing to give money for the support of public worship. He concedes that church buildings are needed, and worship ought to be conducted properly, even 'in the finest way'.[128] But worship ought to be 'pure' rather than 'costly'.[129] The acid test is whether attention is diverted from what God has commanded, and whether God's command can be fulfilled without it:

126 LW v. 45 p. 284; WA v. 6, p. 44, ll. 1–4.

127 Forell, *Faith Active in Love*, p. 102.

128 LW v. 45, p. 286. This is perhaps a slightly strong translation of the phrase 'auff zierlichst' (WA v. 6, p. 44, l. 36). *Zierlich* could be translated 'decorative', but could simply mean, 'with decorum'.

129 LW v. 45, p. 268; WA v. 6, p. 45, l. 1.

> The pity—and the thing we are complaining about—is that we are diverted from God's commandments by such a stir and clamour, and that our attention is directed to things which God has not commanded, and without which his commandments can readily be kept.[130]

It is a question of priority: giving to the needy comes first because 'needy, living Christians' are more important than 'dead stone churches'.[131] Giving to the needy is true worship, because it is doing the thing that God *wants*.[132]

Luther next proceeds to outline his own suggestion as to how therefore obedience to this command should be accomplished: namely that each locality should support its own poor, thus obviating the need for begging. The people in each area have been committed to the care of the authorities of that area, and they must take responsibility accordingly. Luther does not regard almsgiving as located in a sphere of individualized moral decisions, where one is at liberty to give alms or not as one chooses, although generous giving to assuage need is certainly for Luther a matter of personal obligation. But here he also places it firmly in the sphere of public responsibility. Poverty is a matter which the community has an obligation to remedy. That is, the community is not merely to aid the particularly needy, but is obliged to ensure that the *need* for begging and almsgiving does not arise in the first place.

This is the foundation for the 'common chest' proposal which he here outlines, and which he later expands in his preface to the *Ordnung eines gemeinen Kasten* (1523). As well as providing for the relief of the poor (especially those who could not work due to age or sickness), the common chest was to support pastors, schooling, and civic and church buildings.[133] This local focus was to prove one of its central successful elements, since it ensured that charitable provision for the needy was accountable and effective, helping to break long-term dependence on alms of those who were capable of work, and preventing deceptive begging practices.[134] Yet the emphasis on locality was not to be taken as absolute: only those found to be idle or the fictitious poor were to be refused assistance. Hence newcomers to the area were to be assisted with loans and gifts from the chest, on the proviso that they use such provision to set themselves up in some kind of gainful employment. Thus begging could be completely banned, in the expectation that there would be literally no need to beg.

[130] LW v. 45, p. 286; WA v. 6, p. 45, ll. 2–5. [131] LW v. 45, p. 286.

[132] Vilmos Vajta, *Luther on Worship: An Interpretation* (Philadelphia: Muhlenberg, 1958), pp. 14, 166–7.

[133] See LW v. 45, pp. 188–91.

[134] Carter Lindberg, *The European Reformations* (Oxford: Blackwell, 1996), pp. 114–16. What worked at this time, of course, later became a serious problem. See A. M. C. Waterman, *Political Economy and Christian Theology Since the Enlightenment: Essays in Intellectual History* (Basingstoke: Palgrave Macmillan, 2004), pp. 145–6, 157–8.

It is striking that Luther subsumes the obligation upon local authorities to care for the poor in their district, under the rubric of the Christian command to give freely. Giving for Luther is not simply an act of individual decision. Rather, the existence of poverty is a public matter, and it is appropriate and necessary for it to be handled publicly. Aiding the poor should be, as it were, a legal requirement: each member of the community is compelled to contribute as they are able.[135]

Prima facie, this might seem to be in tension with Luther's dictum that one must not 'rule the world with the gospel'. This piece of evidence suggests that 'not ruling the world with the gospel' hardly implies that the authorities operate in an autonomous sphere untouched by theological considerations of morality. As we have seen, under the rubric of Christian love they have a responsibility to uphold social order and defend the weak using the sword. That is, this distinction is restricted to a special aspect of government, namely its use of force. Even this is an expression of neighbour-love. Therefore there is no difficulty with the idea that the command to give freely has implications for the authorities.[136]

Yet it is equally clear from the *Sermon von dem Wucher* and the *Ordnung eines gemeinen Kasten* that the authorities are not to operate with the free, almost naïve generosity that is to characterize the giving of individuals.[137] As we have seen, the authorities must ensure that the money they give is not squandered or given to those who do not need it. Thus, while the command to give impinges on earthly authorities, it does so in a way that is appropriate for them.

We might say that the common chest arrangement illustrates the *coherence* of Luther's supposed radical idealism and his so-called realism. It is realistic in that it has limited intentions, and it pays careful attention to the radically selfish character of humans and is thus sensible of the need for coercion and accountability. Yet Luther's grasp of the limits of what can be achieved by earthly justice does not lead him into a quiescent capitulation to the status quo, since his idealist emphasis on the unqualified character of God's commands drives him to call for a coordinated public response to what we might regard as the structural causes and symptoms of poverty. He is not seeking to

[135] The *Ordnung eines gemeinen Kasten* itself, while not directly written by Luther, was formulated with his support and advice, and published by him with a preface. In addition to voluntary gifts, it prescribes an annual tax to make up any deficit. Yet even voluntary gifts are not purely private, being solicited by officials when the parish gathers in church (LW v. 45, p. 182).

[136] Indeed, elsewhere Luther is quite explicit about the fact that civil authorities are bound by the same commandments as everyone else, as in *Against Hanswurst* (1541), LW v. 42, p. 247; WA v. 51, p. 557.

[137] For example, when one who has received money is unable to repay it despite valiantly trying, the administrators may after careful scrutiny cancel the debt (LW v. 45, p. 190). The individual to whom money is owed, on the other hand, is expected to cancel such a debt quite freely and without any qualification, as we shall see.

bring about the Kingdom of God through human means so much as trying to make the earthly kingdom all that Scripture says it can and should be, that is, a place in which there is no need for begging. Realism for Luther is not an excuse for disobedience to God's commandments, but an awareness of the steps that need to be taken so that they can be obeyed.

Returning to our examination of Luther's method in the *Sermon von dem Wucher*, the final attempt to circumvent this command that Luther identifies is the idea (sanctioned after a fashion by St Thomas and upheld by Luther's enemy Johann Eck) that one only has to give to those in extreme need.[138] Indeed, while Aquinas argues that almsgiving is a 'matter of precept', he does qualify this significantly: the command to give alms is a precept and not a counsel of perfection, but because of the limited nature of one's resources one is only obliged to give to those in *extrema necessitate*, and only out of one's surplus, after one's needs and the needs of one's dependents have been satisfied.[139] Moreover, this meeting of needs and the corresponding definition of surplus is not a matter of appeasing the bare minimum of human existence, but is relative to the status and dignity of the giver's position in the hierarchy of human relationships.[140] So, almsgiving is only a matter of precept with respect to those in dire need, and only applies to one's surplus. Giving in other circumstances is not obligatory: 'otherwise almsgiving, like any other greater good, is a matter of counsel'.[141]

[138] Holl, *The Reconstruction of Morality*, p. 39. The translated edition omits Holl's references to the primary sources which support his claims; they can be found in Karl Holl, *Gesammelte Aufsätze zur Kirchengeschichte* (Tübingen: Mohr Siebeck, 1927–8) v. 1, pp. 166–7.

[139] ST 2a 2ae, q. 32, a. 5. In his 1524 treatise *On Trade* (*Von Kaufshandlung*), which incorporated the *Sermon von dem Wucher*, referring to Luke 11:41, Luther comments that one is to give 'out of your surplus', and 'out of what you have left over', which was the typical interpretation of the Vulgate at the time (see LW v. 45, p. 259, esp. n. 38). This seems to correspond closely to Thomas's view in ST 2a 2ae, q. 32, a. 6. Yet differences remain, since Luther regards giving out of this surplus as compulsory whether the beneficiary is *in extremis* or not. Furthermore, Luther excludes self-interest as a factor in one's deliberations, stating that one's highest duty is to provide for one's family and servants, but not mentioning meeting one's own needs. Thomas by contrast regards meeting one's own needs as one's highest duty (ST 2a 2ae, q. 25, a. 4–5).

[140] ST 2a 2ae, q. 32, a. 6. It should be noted that Thomas makes an exception for cases of extreme need, when 'it would seem praiseworthy to forego the requirements of one's station'. Cf. Lindberg, *Beyond Charity*, p. 24, and John Witte, *Law and Protestantism: The Legal Teachings of the Lutheran Reformation* (Cambridge: Cambridge University Press, 2002), p. 6. Luther retains this after a fashion, but configures it under the rubric of his concept of the *Amt*. The ruler needs greater wealth than the labourer—but not for himself, but so he can discharge his office, for the benefit of all for whose sake the office of ruler exists. The splendour or dignity of the office-holder is derived from the office and not the individual (LW v. 21, p. 23; WA v. 32, p. 316). Thus, while a person with greater responsibility may indeed have correspondingly greater resources at his disposal, in an important sense they are not his. He has them not by virtue of his own illustriousness, but to enable him to discharge his office suitably. Predictably, Luther had little time for rulers who lived lavishly.

[141] ST 2a 2ae, q. 32, a. 5.

Luther argues that as soon as such qualifications enter in, opportunity is invariably given for further wrangling. On the notion of giving only to those in dire need, he waspishly comments: 'In addition, they have reserved to themselves the right to discuss and determine what extreme want is'.[142] Against this he sets the Golden Rule as an interpretative key to this command: since one would wish to be assisted long before one reaches the stage of desperation, it cannot be right to withhold relief from others simply because their need has not yet become sufficiently dire.

Luther's introduction of the Golden Rule shows the interrelated nature of Scriptural commands for him: they interpret one another, and together interpret a coherent moral reality, and human duty within it. The Golden Rule is an especially important heuristic tool, as it relates the command of God to its hearer: it involves one intimately and inescapably in the moral situations with which one is confronted. Thus, in order to understand the implications of this particular command more fully, Luther brings in this other, more general command in order to illuminate it.[143]

Yet the notion of need remains important. Returning to his theme of contrasting unwillingness to give to the needy with enthusiasm for church buildings and indulgences, Luther comments that monies given towards the latter have been 'taken from the needy to whom they properly belong'.[144] The language of ownership is significant: he is drawing on the patristic and scholastic tradition that need creates a quasi-right to aid, hence St Thomas's famous argument, citing Ambrose, that someone in dire straits who steals from one who has plenty has committed no crime.[145] Luther contrasts the current ecclesiastical practice of amassing wealth despite the existence of poverty, with the behaviour of Ambrose and Paulinus, who melted down the sacred metalware from their churches to help the needy.

Part of what Luther is doing is straightforward enough, as explored above: restructuring priorities. But he is also tackling a deeper issue. In the language of more recent theological movements, we might say he is exposing social or structural sin, that is, unjust aspects of human organizations and institutions. Luther identifies a number of ways in which, for its own ends, the church provided ideological sustenance for a state of affairs that perpetuated and exacerbated poverty. He regarded part of his duty as a preacher and theologian to unmask and challenge this: his method is not only to call for changes to personal actions, but also to institutional social arrangements.

142 LW v. 45, p. 287; WA v. 6, p. 46, ll. 5–7.

143 We analyse Luther's discussion of the Golden Rule further in the section entitled 'The Third Degree: "Do Not Refuse the One Who Would Borrow from You"', when he invokes it in his discussion of the 'third degree'.

144 LW v. 45, p. 289; WA v. 6, p. 46, ll. 32–3.

145 ST 2a 2ae, q. 66, a. 7.

THE THIRD DEGREE: 'DO NOT REFUSE THE ONE WHO WOULD BORROW FROM YOU'

With respect to the third and lowest degree, Luther sarcastically acknowledges that 'they' have at least not tried to turn this command (to lend without charge to whoever asks) into a counsel of perfection. That is, official teaching still technically forbade the taking of interest on loans. But again, he notices attempts to reduce the universal, unqualified scope of this command, for example in the claim that one is only required to lend to friends. This is so dangerous, as it deceives oneself into a false sense of assurance that by doing so one is fulfilling God's will. Once again, Luther adduces additional scriptural material in order to evaluate the legitimacy of such a restriction. In this case, he cites Luke 6:34–5, claiming that one is not to lend only to those who can return the favour, or to one's friends, because the command explicitly includes all.[146] His weary conclusion is that there is always 'trouble and labour' about doing what God commands. His method here is to push his examination of the motives of human action to an ever-deeper level, and expose what he regards as the partiality and stubborn self-deception which lurk behind so much human behaviour.

On the basis of this citation from the Third Gospel, Luther proposes a fresh definition of the very nature of lending: lending is only that which makes no charge and is thus without self-interest. According to him, anything else is by definition usury, because lending by definition expects nothing in return. The command to lend without charge defines the nature of lending per se:

> But if we examine the word of Christ closely, it does not teach that we are to lend without charge. There is no need for such teaching, since there is no other kind of lending except that which is without charge; if a charge is made, it is not a loan.[147]

Luther's method here is to first seek to understand something correctly (that is, in the light of Scripture), in order to know how to act rightly with respect to it. Biblical commands are not mere prohibitions or stipulations, but are themselves revelatory as to the nature of reality. He perceives descriptions of particular practices which he encounters, not as neutral or empirical, but as committed and proceeding from self-interest. The wrong description is itself capitulation.[148] Confronted with what he regards as a corrupted term, rather than eschew it Luther attempts to redefine it, filling it with meaning taken from Scripture—much as elsewhere he colourfully describes himself as

[146] LW v. 45, p. 290; WA v. 6, p. 47, ll. 24–36.

[147] LW v. 45, p. 291; WA v. 6, p. 47, l. 37–p. 48, l. 2.

[148] As Reinhard Hütter puts it, 'the description of a situation is everything; it is the situation itself. In describing a "situation" the morally decisive choices and moves are already made'. Hütter, 'The Twofold Center of Lutheran Ethics', p. 46.

bringing words to the bath.[149] Luther's emphasis on exegesis and expertise in classical and biblical languages means that his theological method can be highly grammarian, subjecting words and phrases to a rigorous, tenacious analysis in the light of reality as disclosed in and through Scripture.[150] Hence he concludes that the only difference between lending and giving is that in lending one *might* receive back what one lends. One should not count on *any* return, let alone anything supplementary. Thus part of his re-establishment of the obligation to lend without charging interest is his claim that this is inherent to the very act of lending.

In order to prove further the immorality of receiving back more than one lends, Luther adduces 'three laws'. Here we have an instance of *Gesetz* carrying for Luther the fully positive connotation of concrete moral guidance as an expression of God's will.[151] We will summarize these three laws, and then explore Luther's method in more detail:

1. The imperative in the gospels to lend without charge, as in the passage he has cited (Luke 6:35). This indicts any attempt to camouflage interest, for example by claiming the surplus is a gift given in gratitude rather than under compulsion, since what is forbidden is deriving any 'advantage' at all from a loan.[152]
2. Natural law, which Luther identifies with the Golden Rule.[153] Interest is thus 'contrary to nature', because one would not wish one's neighbour to profit at one's expense were the roles reversed. Natural law is therefore not for Luther an autonomous form of reason. Its content is disclosed in revelation, and it is binding on all.
3. The 'old and new law' of neighbour-love (Leviticus 19:18; Matthew 22:39). To profit from lending is to seek one's own good rather than that of one's neighbour. For Luther, self-interest in moral action is always excluded.

It is significant that these three laws all point to the same conclusion for Luther. Some interpreters have argued that Luther's distinction between

[149] This phrase occurs in *Die Promotionsdisputation von Palladius und Tilemann* (1537), WA v. 39.I, p. 229b, ll. 23–5.

[150] This theme is explored particularly well in the first three chapters of Gerhard Ebeling, *Luther: An Introduction to his Thought*, trans. R. A. Wilson (London: Collins, 1970). Indeed, Ebeling characterizes Luther's thought and impact primarily as one of 'linguistic innovation' (p. 13). See, for example, his analysis of Paul's phrase 'faith working through love' in Galatians 5:6 from his later Galatians lectures (1531) in LW v. 27, pp. 28–30; WA v. 40.II, p. 35b, l. 14–p. 37b, l. 25.

[151] See Gustaf Wingren, *The Christian's Calling: Luther on Vocation*, trans. Carl C. Rasmussen (Edinburgh: Oliver and Boyd, 1958), p. 199.

[152] LW v. 45, p. 292.

[153] See Johnson, *Theological Method in Luther and Tillich*, p. 4.

different forms of law points to an ultimate dualism between natural law, obeyed for the sake of worldly peace (and therefore one's own benefit), and a higher, Christian standard expressed in divine commands.[154] But here the content of these laws is clearly identical: the same demand is encountered in several ways. For Luther, the law of nature is written on the heart (Romans 2:15), but obscured by the deceitfulness of sin. It must therefore be revealed externally as well as internally. Thus the Decalogue, as well as being a particular code for a particular people at a specific time, is also an especially fine expression of natural law explicated as positive law. What is revealed is *natural* law, although in the relative form of stipulations addressed to the Jews. The distinction between kinds of law is therefore only epistemological, and does not refer to a dualism of standards.

Luther proceeds to elaborate his understanding of the Golden Rule, expounding it as the surest guide in matters of temporal goods. It particularly seems to function for Luther as a practical rule of thumb for concrete situations: it is not so much a formal explication as the Ten Commandments are; rather, it can be applied as a critical and heuristic tool for reviewing whom one's behaviour really benefits.[155] The Golden Rule eliminates any attempt to excuse oneself through ignorance, because one always has the means available to discern how one should act towards one's neighbour through this imaginative, empathetic consideration of the other's situation.

Luther traces the litigious culture he sees around him to the ignorance (both lack of awareness and deliberate disregard) of this command, and criticizes the readiness to be religiously observant, yet to disobey God 'in this matter, on which salvation depends'.[156] He reiterates:

> these wicked men . . . are altogether heedless and carefree, as if this commandment did not apply to them at all, although without it they cannot be saved even if they performed all the other works of all the saints.[157]

Much like the Hebrew prophets, Luther perceives that outward piety, even punctiliousness, is compatible with profound and deliberate wickedness.

[154] Althaus, for example, draws this conclusion by conflating 'natural law' with 'natural justice' (Althaus, *The Ethics of Martin Luther*, pp. 32–4). However, the latter term refers to the degree of earthly justice which is realistically achievable, rather than a normative standard. W. D. J. Cargill Thompson's exposition of natural law in Luther is more satisfying (W. D. J. Cargill Thompson, *The Political Thought of Martin Luther*, ed. Philip Broadhead (Brighton: Harvester, 1984), pp. 79ff.), although Antii Raunio has pointed out that he makes the more minor mistake of restricting Luther's understanding of natural law to temporal government (Antii Raunio, 'Natural Law and Faith: The Forgotten Foundations of Ethics in Luther's Theology', in *Union with Christ: The New Finnish Interpretation of Luther*, eds. Carl E. Braaten and Robert W. Jenson (Grand Rapids: Eerdmans, 1998), pp. 96–124, esp. p. 102). On the unity of law for Luther, see Johnson, *Theological Method in Luther and Tillich*, p. 4.

[155] Forell, *Faith Active in Love*, p. 103.

[156] LW v. 45, p. 293; WA v. 6, p. 49, l. 34–p. 50, l. 1.

[157] LW v. 45, p. 293; WA v. 6, p. 49, l. 34–p. 50, l. 3.

Outward indications of serving God can seductively masquerade as attempts to domesticate God's will and turn it into a manageable standard. Luther therefore warns his hearers of the bankruptcy before God of the practices by which they seek to assure themselves of God's favour.

Luther's method is then to discuss two objections to his line of argument. The first is that if money is lent, the profit which could have been made on that sum is lost. Some theologians permitted the making of a charge on lending, not as a charge on the loan itself, but as a notional recovery of the profit that might otherwise have been made. Luther overcomes this by pointing out that, given that lending is in any case the lowest obligatory way of handling temporal goods, if one's goods were forcibly taken or requested as a gift, one would be obliged to part with them entirely. There is therefore no reason to expect compensation for adhering to this lesser degree, since one's basic disposition towards temporal goods should be to relinquish them anyway.[158]

The second objection is that of precedent and example, especially that of the clergy and church, who both lent and borrowed in contravention of this command. Luther's response is characteristic: he restates that the location for discerning authentic Christian practice is not the church's practice, but the command of God. The church can claim no special divine warrant for its practice *except* insofar as it is commensurate with God's commands. As demonstrated above, it is not that Luther sets tradition against Scripture in permanent or necessary tension, but he does allow for the possibility of conflict, and acknowledges Scripture's critical power over tradition in such cases.[159] This extraordinarily high view of the role of Scripture by no means led to the assumption that the church had any claim to moral superiority to others—if anything, quite the reverse.

Methodologically, it is worth noting that the way he handles these objections makes something explicit that underlies what he has already been doing. Being mindful of the prevalent attitudes and the potential objections to his views, rather than simply demanding better behaviour, he uses his exposition to challenge these hidden attitudes and counter objections. Objections are not overcome primarily through conceptual argument, but by exposing the problematic inward disposition from which they originate. That is, he seeks to force his interlocutors to face up to their fear and greed. Indeed, only by being liberated from such things first can they reach a true theoretical framework.

Therefore he concludes his rebuttal of these two objections with the comment: 'If anyone finds, however, that these conditions make it hard for him to

[158] These facets of his method are discussed more fully in the subsequent section, Luther's Method in Part One: Summary and Analysis.

[159] Hence one recent in-depth study of the relation of Scripture and tradition in Luther's method concludes, 'it was not so much Luther's view of Scripture that changed as his perspective on the teaching of the Roman church'. Mark D. Thompson, *A Sure Ground on which to Stand: The Relation of Authority and Interpretative Method in Luther's Approach to Scripture* (Carlisle: Paternoster, 2004).

lend to his neighbour, it is a sign of his great unbelief; he despises the comforting assurance of Christ'.[160] Seeing one's actions in the light of God's commandment discloses one's inward disposition, which must be confronted and overcome through trust in the promises of Christ. This interrelation of promise ('*vorheyssung*') with command suggests that for Luther, even the promise of God has an inescapably moral content. It is not enough to believe in some abstract fashion—what one believes in is a promise which must guide one's actions. At the same time, moral action is not renewed through sheer demand, but by trust in the personal care of Christ.

LUTHER'S METHOD IN PART ONE: SUMMARY AND ANALYSIS

As we have seen, Luther expounds each of the three degrees or commands in a fairly straightforward pattern: he sets out each degree as an unqualified binding command, then he refutes what he sees as a proliferation of attempts to minimize this binding force. Having retraced these methodological steps, we will now examine in more detail some particularly interesting aspects of his method in this part of the sermon.

First, we have already found ourselves intrigued at how uncomplicated and brief Luther's exposition of the text of each command is. The meaning and practical consequences of each command are virtually self-evident for him. It is the attempts to circumvent the commands that are laborious to deal with.[161] Thus in each instance he spends just a few sentences outlining what he takes to be the plain meaning of the command. The bulk of the sermon is not exposition as such but a refutation of those who would minimize these commands. Discerning what is right is not necessarily inherently complicated, nor is moral theology a marginal activity for particularly perplexing situations. The right thing to do is often the obvious thing to do: 'a Christian man living in this faith has no need of a teacher of good works, but he does whatever the occasion calls for, and all is well done'.[162]

We have seen that some interpreters overstate this feature of Luther's thought, since he still clearly believes in the need for commandments to direct and shape action, despite his emphasis on the spontaneous readiness of the

[160] LW v. 45, p. 294; WA v. 6, p. 50, ll. 33–5.

[161] As Oliver O'Donovan puts it, it is the gospel which is 'in its essential features, luminous', and the 'political concepts needed to interpret the social and institutional realities around us' which are 'obscure and elusive'. Oliver O'Donovan, *The Ways of Judgment* (Grand Rapids: Eerdmans, 2005), p. x.

[162] *Von den guten Werken*, LW v. 44, p. 26; WA v. 6, p. 207, ll. 3–5.

Christian to do good works. Yet the actions which are called for are simple enough to discern in the light of the commands, and simple enough to do. The difficulty is in preventing people from wriggling out of obedience. His method of rebutting equivocations reflects this.

Another motif is his treatment of the degrees of how to handle worldly goods as an interrelated series. This is a pattern he also sees in the Decalogue. There, he reverses the conventional view that the First Commandment is fulfilled by obeying the others, that one loves God *by* obeying the lesser commands. Luther's position is the converse: only those who obey the First Commandment by placing their whole trust in God and in nothing else are those who do the will of God.[163] God primarily wants people's trust in him, not their good deeds, therefore this is true obedience.[164] Those who place their trust in anything else do not obey God, nor can they please him even if they formally adhere to the lesser commandments,[165] and those who do

[163] In his exposition of the First Commandment in *Der Großer Katechismus*, Luther puts it thus: 'This commandment . . . requires that man's whole heart and confidence be placed in God alone, and in no one else'. Tappert, *The Book of Concord*, p. 366; WA v. 30.I, p. 134, ll. 18–20.

[164] This point is made several times in *De Libertate Christiana*. See for example LW v. 31, pp. 350, 353. This develops Luther's earlier account of justification as the vindication of God's own justice, in which he asserts that the one who is justified before God is the one who agrees with his righteous judgement in condemning humanity by condemning oneself (F. Edward Cranz, *An Essay on the Development of Luther's Thought on Justice, Law, and Society* (Oxford: Oxford University Press, 1964), pp. 9–10). Even at this early stage, Luther's concept of faith is not purely intellectual but relational and affective. There is scholarly diversity on this point, and on the related question of the dating of the so-called Reformation breakthrough. Some scholars, such as Karl Holl, have regarded the *Dictata super Psalterium* as already fully reformed (Holl places the new insight between 1509 and 1511, arguing that Luther's own later statements on the dating are unreliable). Others, such as Ernst Bizer, have argued that they are wholly pre-Reformation. See the discussion in W. D. J. Cargill Thompson, 'The Problems of Luther's "Tower Experience" and its Place in his Intellectual Development', in *Studies in the Reformation: Luther to Hooker*, ed. C. W. Dugmore (London: Athlone Press, 1980), pp. 60–80. Tomlin argues that the *Dictata* have indeed moved on from the scholastic position, but do not yet fully articulate Luther's reformation insights. Therefore, within this period Luther's position can vary startlingly. He observes that in the early stages of the *Dictata*, Luther speaks of God humbling humans in order to bring them to his mercy, yet as late as the Romans lectures he suggests that forgiveness follows *self*-humbling (Graham Tomlin, *The Power of the Cross: Theology and the Death of Christ in Paul, Luther and Pascal* (Carlisle: Paternoster, 1999), p. 160). Newer insights break in piecemeal and only gradually work out more thoroughly since, after all, it is never Luther's concern to make them into some kind of comprehensive system.

[165] From *Der Großer Katechismus*: 'Wherever a man's heart has such an attitude toward God, he has fulfilled this commandment and all the others. On the other hand, whoever fears and loves anything else . . . will keep neither this nor any other'. Tappert, *The Book of Concord*, p. 409; WA v. 30.I, p. 180, ll. 27–9. David Yeago explains this as follows. For Luther, the law always condemns, even though some of its demands are in fact easy to keep, because it demands that human nature *exist* in a certain state, doing God's will freely and joyfully. That is, it is addressed to a subject who is simply no longer there. See David S. Yeago, 'Martin Luther on Grace, Law and Moral Life: Prolegomena to an Ecumenical Discussion of Veritatis Splendor', *The Thomist* 62.2 (1998), pp. 163–91, esp. pp. 171, 180–3.

God's will by trusting him will do his will in other ways too: good works flow out of faith.[166]

This is why faith fulfils the law: all the commandments inhere in the First Commandment, rather than vice versa. The First is *constitutive* of the others: they 'nest' in it, and *express* obedience to God and trust in him, rather than being means to the end of obedience.[167] Right activity towards one's neighbour flows out of a right posture towards God, which is what truly constitutes and defines the moral agent: 'The true radicalization that Jesus wrought in the commandment is shifting the focus of moral analysis from the typology to the psychology of action'.[168] Thus Luther does not expound the commands as a list of instructions, as a divine command theory of morality might have it. Rather, the commands publish a coherent vision of reality, and the moral agent is transformed by trusting God.

The 'nesting' is also seen in the way each commandment must be interpreted in the light of the others. For instance, within his exposition of the Fourth Commandment in *Von den guten Werken*, Luther observes that authorities must be obeyed, 'so long as it is not contrary to the first three commandments'.[169] Where an authority (a category which encompasses parents and church as well as civil government) demands something that would break the first three commandments, the authority is to be disobeyed:

> If such unbearable abuses are committed in the name of God.... we are certainly duty bound to offer appropriate resistance as far as we are able. We have to act as good children whose parents have lost their minds.[170]

He makes this principle explicit in the *Sermon von dem Wucher*:

> Christ teaches in the gospel that at God's command we must act even against father and mother, whom he has commanded us to honour. Yet the two commandments are not contradictory, but the lower is governed by the higher.[171]

So, there is a hierarchy within the Decalogue, although the distinction between lower and higher is not entirely static. Parents have authority over their children, but the Fourth Commandment does not grant them unlimited despotic power such that they could murder their offspring (obviously).

[166] A point made forcefully and frequently in *De Libertate Christiana*. For example: 'Behold, from faith thus flow forth love and joy in the Lord, and from love a joyful, willing, and free mind that serves one's neighbour willingly'. LW v. 31, p. 367; WA v. 7, p. 66, ll. 7–8.

[167] The term 'nesting' is from Bernd Wannenwetsch's article, 'You Shall Not Kill—What Does It Take? Why We Need the Other Commandments if We Are to Abstain from Killing', in *I Am the Lord Your God*, eds. Christopher R. Seitz and Carl E. Braaten (Grand Rapids: Eerdmans, 2005), pp. 148–74, esp. p. 148.

[168] Wannenwetsch, 'You Shall Not Kill', p. 151.

[169] LW v. 44, p. 81; WA v. 6, p. 251, ll. 2–3.

[170] LW v. 44, p. 90; WA v. 6, p. 257, ll. 23–8.

[171] LW v. 45, p. 278; WA v. 6, p. 39, ll. 18–21.

Their authority is still constrained and shaped by the other commands, which are interrelated and mutually shaping.

So there is a dual interrelation between the commands. The lower serve the higher. Yet, as explored above, fulfilment of the higher commands is *necessary* for obedience to the lower. Bernd Wannenwetsch has probed this in relation to the commandment not to kill, concluding: 'what does it take to keep the fifth commandment? The answer is: All the others ... plus the first'.[172] They are 'perichoretic'.[173] This overcomes supposed contradictions between the commands, since for Luther they are not a codification of distinct regulations but an organic, mutually illuminating unity. The command not to kill is not in itself an isolated expression of God's will, but meaningful in its interrelation to the other commands.

We mention this feature of Luther's thought because it illuminates the pattern here in the *Sermon von dem Wucher*. Luther interprets Jesus's three commands in Matthew 5:38–42 in *descending* order: instead of reading the first 'degree' as the zenith of right behaviour (an idealization to which one could hardly attain), he reads it as *definitive* for rightly handling worldly goods. It is primary in an analogous sense to the First Commandment. In the Decalogue, the other commandments 'hang' on the First: fulfilment of them flows from fulfilment of it. Here, all the right ways of handling temporal goods proceed from a fundamental posture of release and renunciation. In turn, the mandates to give and lend are not pinnacles of generosity and virtue, but already subordinate to a fundamental passivity towards temporal goods. The three degrees together are not the summit of a right attitude to temporal goods but its wellspring, its *sine qua non*.

This resonates with Luther's vigorous criticism of the dominance of a low-level baseline morality. It is commonly stated that his target is the so-called legalism represented by the slogan of the *via moderna*, *facere quod in se est*. This idea, as propounded by Gabriel Biel drawing on William of Ockham (*c.* 1288–1347), that humans could and had to reach a certain level of moral attainment as a preparation for God's grace, was encountered by Luther while being taught at Erfurt.[174] Karl Holl remarks that in his early period Luther does not 'hesitate to use the Nominalist formula "doing what one can" and the corresponding expression "congruent merit" on occasion'.[175] Recent, more sympathetic, accounts of Biel observe that he was reacting against the 'late medieval insecurity about salvation by directing the penitent to the objective guarantees of the sacramental life of the church'.[176] The movement required in

[172] Wannenwetsch, 'You Shall Not Kill', p. 174.
[173] Wannenwetsch, 'You Shall Not Kill', p. 173.
[174] 'Occam assumed that humans can fulfill God's commands on the basis of their natural powers'. Lohse, *Martin Luther's Theology*, p. 20.
[175] Holl, *The Reconstruction of Morality*, p. 23.
[176] Tomlin, *The Power of the Cross*, p. 135.

'doing what is in you' is an extremely small one—to 'flee to the sacraments of the church'.[177] This 'initial good act produced without the help of grace is accorded merit *de congruo*'.[178] Thus the obedience required was extremely small.

Luther opposes this reliance on human ability, but has a further objection. Counter-intuitively, he perceives that this seeming legalism also conceals a profound antinomianism: in attempting to make God's command *manageable* and realistic for human efforts, it ultimately results in a subversion and revision of God's commands. They must be adjusted to a level that humans are actually capable of keeping. As Holl comments, 'one *seems* to make one's task more difficult while actually making it easier'.[179] So, although Luther would have much sympathy with Biel's motive (offering assurance of salvation), it makes the basic features of the Christian life too minimal.[180] It fails to tackle the reason why humans do not obey God's commands (self-will), because if one only follows human prescriptions, one never 'encounters a will that crosses one's own desires'.[181] Thus Luther became highly suspicious of what he regarded as an achievable, self-chosen morality. Indeed, he saw it as a rebellious manifestation of self-assertion rather than a means to overcome it, particularly when the so-called good works it produces are directed at obtaining or assuring oneself of God's favour. Hence, in the *Sermon von dem Wucher* and *Von den guten Werken*, he offers a typology of two categories of good works, contrasting genuine good works, which are done 'so quietly and secretly that no one would notice it except God alone!' with religious deeds, 'all those works devised by men, the showy, far-flung works such as making pilgrimages, building churches, seeking indulgences'.[182] Holl comments: 'Whoever chooses something special for himself and expects to be rewarded by receiving preference from God assumes the role of a lawgiver . . . trying to impose one's own will on God. No matter how pious it may appear, this is in the final analysis nothing other than presumption and insolent self-exaltation'.[183]

This is closely related to Luther's polemic against the scholastic distinction between compulsory precepts and counsels of perfection, which also arose

[177] Tomlin, *The Power of the Cross*, p. 135.
[178] Tomlin, *The Power of the Cross*, p. 135.
[179] Holl, *The Reconstruction of Morality*, p. 101.
[180] Of course, some accounts of Luther's theology portray him in a similar light, with faith functioning as a minimal criterion. Such accounts assume that faith for Luther means intellectual subscription to doctrinal propositions, whereas faith as we have encountered it here is the wholehearted and unqualified movement of throwing oneself on God's mercy and trusting in his goodness. It believes not only that God exists, or even that he acts in Christ, but that he acts *pro me*. Althaus comments: 'This "for me" is the decisive and essential factor in justifying faith which distinguishes it from everything else which we otherwise call faith'. *The Theology of Martin Luther*, p. 230.
[181] Holl, *The Reconstruction of Morality*, p. 101. See also Luther's comments in *De Libertate Christiana*, e.g., LW v. 31, p. 359.
[182] LW v. 44, p. 99; WA v. 6, p. 264, ll. 8–9, 32.
[183] Holl, *The Reconstruction of Morality*, p. 65.

from concern regarding assurance. It was feared that the seeming enormity of God's demands could only produce despair. Thus nobody would ever even attempt to obey them and be saved. This distinction went as far back as Tertullian (*c.* 160–230), who drew it in relation to 1 Corinthians 7.[184]

The standard view became that it was only compulsory to adhere to prohibitions. Positive commands were 'only conditionally binding', for those who wished to reach a higher standard of righteousness.[185] If the prohibitions were observed, *one had not sinned* and therefore was not liable to divine punishment, even if one had not done anything actually positively meritorious.[186] Thus the possibility of salvation was recovered. As St Thomas puts it, 'the commandments of the New Law . . . have been given about matters that are necessary to gain the end of eternal bliss', but 'the counsels are about matters that render the gaining of this end more assured and expeditious'.[187]

Holl concludes: 'The result . . . was that the concept of morality became very flexible'.[188] It created a category of good actions which were not obligatory, only praiseworthy.[189] Luther, by contrast, clearly knows that humans will never obey perfectly, but this does not alter the obligation for him: he refuses to measure 'human duty by human powers'.[190] Thus he obliterates the distinction between a non-negotiable moral minimum and the perfect demands of the Sermon on the Mount. There is no category of optional but praiseworthy deeds: if something is good, it is compulsory.[191] The commands really are *commands*.

[184] 'The apostle, with regard to widows and the unmarried, advises them to remain permanently in that state . . . but touching marrying in the Lord, he no longer advises, but plainly bids. . . . The former springs from counsel, and is proposed to the will (for acceptance or rejection): the other descends from authority, and is bound to necessity'. Tertullian, *Second Book to his Wife*, chapter 1 [*c.* 200], trans. S. Thelwall, in *Ante-Nicene Fathers*, eds. Alexander Roberts, James Donaldson, and A. Cleveland Coxe (Peabody: Hendrickson, 1994), v. 4, p. 44. Of course, this passage is something of a special case, in that the distinction has an exegetical foundation which is absent elsewhere.

[185] Holl, *The Reconstruction of Morality*, p. 37. Holl's analysis is not flawless. He tends to portray all moral theology from Tertullian to the early Luther as entirely corrupted in this fashion, in the interest of differentiating Luther as the peerless recoverer of the authentic gospel. Hence, for example, even Augustine 'became a corrupter of Christian morality' (Holl, *The Reconstruction of Morality*, p. 38.) However, Oliver O'Donovan has shown that Augustine never minimizes the love command, and in order to preserve its full weight, at times he stretches his eudaemonism to breaking point precisely in order to do so: he 'sacrificed the coherence of his eudaemonism in order to speak of neighbour-love as the equal of self-love'. Oliver O'Donovan and Joan Lockwood O'Donovan, *The Problem of Self-Love in St. Augustine* (New Haven: Yale University Press, 1980), p. 117–18.

[186] Holl, *The Reconstruction of Morality*, p. 43.

[187] ST 1a 2ae, q. 108, a. 4.

[188] Holl, *The Reconstruction of Morality*, p. 44.

[189] Pope, 'Aquinas on Almsgiving, Justice and Charity', pp. 171–2.

[190] Holl, *The Reconstruction of Morality*, p. 46.

[191] This does not mean that Luther abolishes the sphere of the permitted. There is such a sphere, with respect to which one must resist an encroaching tyranny of moralism. He merely holds that actions which are praiseworthy cannot fall into this category: they are compulsory.

This is a frequent polemical theme in his work from this period. Because of this, he frequently points out that everyone is obliged to do far more than they ever could, without having to contrive additional religious deeds as necessary: 'a man has enough to engage all his strength to keep the commandments of God, and even if he neglects everything else, he can never do all the good work he is commanded to do'.[192] Other works are a distraction, absorbing time, effort, and money which God wishes to be used in the service of the neighbour. Indeed, they corrupt morality even further as they set out to *use* the neighbour to procure salvation. As he declares in *De Libertate Christiana*, 'in all these [religious works] we seek only our profit, thinking that through them our sins are purged away and that we find salvation in them'.[193] He perceives that in ascribing merit to good works, one makes them an end in themselves. As he claims in *Von den guten Werken*:

> All these people seek nothing beyond the work itself in their fasting. When they have performed that, they think they have done a good work.[194]

He utterly disagrees with this. In *De Libertate Christiana* he contends:

> A man does not live for himself alone in this mortal body to work for it alone, but he lives also for all men on earth; rather, he lives only for others and not for himself.[195]

Therefore the end of even seemingly inward disciplines, such as fasting, is ultimately the service of one's neighbour. Fasting is good, because it brings one's body under greater control, thus placing it more thoroughly at the disposal of one's neighbour: 'To this end he brings his body into subjection that he may the more sincerely and freely serve others'.[196] The same goes for meeting one's own physical needs: 'This is what makes caring for the body a Christian work, that through its health and comfort we may be able to work, to acquire, and lay by funds with which to aid those who are in need'.[197] Keeping one's body in good order is a good thing to do—insofar as this is oriented to the neighbour's benefit. Thus Luther rejects a private ethics of virtue in which the moral development of the individual (for their salvation) is the main goal.[198] For him, morality is always social and never self-interested.

[192] LW v. 44, p. 113; WA v. 6, p. 276, ll. 1–8.
[193] LW v. 31, p. 370; WA v. 7, p. 68, ll. 22–3.
[194] LW v. 44, p. 74; WA v. 6, p. 245, ll. 32–3.
[195] LW v. 31, p. 364; WA v. 7, p. 64, ll. 15–17.
[196] LW v. 31, p. 364; WA v. 7, p. 64, ll. 17–18.
[197] LW v. 31, p. 365; WA v. 7, p. 64: ll. 29–32.
[198] George Forell cites the system of Peter Lombard as an example of the ethics which Luther opposed. Lombard outlines a doctrine of 'ordered love' whereby first God is to be loved, then one's own soul, then one's neighbour's soul, and lastly one's body (Forell, *Faith Active in Love*, p. 96). It is tempting to wonder where care for the neighbour's physical needs is to feature. Forell relates this to the influence of Aristotle (see *Faith Active in Love*, pp. 75–81).

As Carter Lindberg has argued, this reconfiguration flows from and is enabled by Luther's understanding of justification.[199] Because he understands the human's relation to God as wholly determined by faith rather than action, action is free to be wholly dedicated to the service of one's neighbour. From *De Libertate Christiana* again:

> Man, however, needs none of these things for his righteousness and salvation. Therefore he should be guided in all his works by this thought and contemplate this one thing alone, that he may serve and benefit others in all that he does, considering nothing except the need and the advantage of his neighbour.[200]

As good works become penultimate, they can be put to penultimate ends: earthly justice and meeting human needs. Edward Cranz shows this by contrasting Luther's thought in the period of the *Sermon von dem Wucher* (along with *De Libertate Christiana* and *Von den guten Werken*) with his earlier work. In the *Dictata super Psalterium* (1513–15), human justice is the acknowledgement before God of one's sin, and is thus a 'real justice, valid before God'.[201] It is therefore essentially negative, a disavowal of any right to God's favour. In this sense, human justice is effective in the divine realm. It is oriented towards God, not neighbour. The more just one is, the *less* concerned about worldly matters one will be.[202] Hence perfection is 'most nearly realized in the monastic kind of life'.[203] Later, Luther comes to believe that human justice is utterly invalid before God. It can never justify *coram Deo*. But far from implying the bankruptcy of human justice in every respect, this frees it up for a positive role in the created realm, establishing justice in human society.[204]

This is borne out by an analysis by Lee Brummel of Luther's attitude to poverty. He adds that at first (1513–16) Luther understands poverty as essentially spiritual, the admission that one is spiritually and morally impoverished.[205] In the period 1516–19, he sees poverty as an earthly phenomenon to be treated by earthly means: it is a social evil perpetuated by self-love.[206]

[199] Among Lindberg's numerous publications, see his 'Luther's Struggle with Social-Ethical Issues', in *The Cambridge Companion to Martin Luther* ed. Donald K. McKim (Cambridge: Cambridge University Press, 2003), pp. 165–78, esp. pp. 166, 170.

[200] LW v. 31, p. 365; WA v. 7, p. 64, ll. 24–7.

[201] Cranz, *Luther's Thought on Justice, Law and Society*, p. ix.

[202] Cranz, *Luther's Thought on Justice, Law and Society*, pp. 12–13.

[203] LW v. 45, p. 83, n. 6.

[204] Cranz, *Luther's Thought on Justice, Law and Society*, p. 76.

[205] Lee Brummel, 'Luther and the Biblical Language of Poverty', *Ecumenical Review* 31.1 (1980), pp. 40–58, esp. pp. 42–3.

[206] Brummel, 'Luther and the Biblical Language of Poverty', pp. 44–5. Subsequent analysis in the article is less reliable, taking the trajectory of Herbert Marcuse's Marxist critique of Luther, and presenting a one-sided account of Luther's supposed change of heart following the Peasants' War. Yet after this Luther actively continued to promote support for the needy and oppose usury, not least in his treatise of 1524, *Von Kaufshandlung*, to which he later appended the

Carter Lindberg summarizes: 'The poor are no longer the objects of meritorious charity, but neighbours to be served through justice and equity'.[207] Luther makes this especially clear in *De Libertate Christiana*—the Christian must say to himself:

> Although I am an unworthy and condemned man, my God has given me in Christ all the riches of righteousness and salvation without any merit on my part... so that from now on I need nothing except faith.... Why should I not therefore... do all things which I know are pleasing to such a Father...? I will therefore give myself as a Christ to my neighbour.... I will do nothing in this life except what I see is necessary, profitable, and salutary to my neighbour, since through faith I have an abundance of all good things in Christ.[208]

In sum, we have seen that it is Luther's reconfiguration of the teleology of human action that enables his reassertion of the wide scope and obligatory nature of the commands. When the goal of works is salvation, God's commands must perforce be domesticated into achievable standards, and human action will no longer be available for the sake of the neighbour. But when salvation has already been received as a free gift, human action is liberated from self-interest and placed wholly at the disposal of others.

Thus two factors coalesce: a restatement of the enormity of God's commands, encompassing the whole of life, and a recovery of the neighbour as the beneficiary of action. Yet Luther is highly attuned to the subtle and manifold ways in which human hearers of the commands of God will attempt to justify their wilful evasions of God's will. Therefore, repetition of the bare command will not suffice: it must be combined with a strategy which constantly exposes these excuses so that ego's self-assertion is revealed and driven into submission.

Yet there is another, intriguing dimension to this story. It is tempting to assume on the basis of all this that Luther's rediscovery of justification *sola fide* was the motive for his polemic against substituting human standards for God's will, which is so frequent in his work at this stage. Chronologically speaking, the situation is the reverse. That is, Luther does not begin with a concept of the gospel and enhance his ethics to fit it. Rather, his recovery of the absolute nature of God's demands antedates and thus determines his understanding of the gospel. As Karl Holl has shown, *his renewed understanding of ethics drove his Reformation breakthrough*, rather than vice versa.

Sermon von dem Wucher. See Herbert Marcuse, 'A Study on Authority', in *From Luther to Popper*, trans. Joris de Bres (London: Verso, 1972), pp. 49–155, esp. pp. 51ff. See Prien's rebuttal in *Luthers Wirtschaftsethik*, pp. 193–4. On the Peasants' War see E. G. Rupp, 'Luther and the German Reformation to 1529', in *The New Cambridge Modern History: II. The Reformation, 1520–59*, ed. G. R. Elton (Cambridge: Cambridge University Press, 1962), pp. 70–95, esp. pp. 86–9.

207 Lindberg, 'Luther on Poverty', p. 141.

208 LW v. 31, p. 367; WA v. 7, p. 65, l. 36–p. 66, l. 6.

From his earliest writings Luther acknowledged the unconditional nature of God's command, and in his first lectures on the Psalms (1513–15) he had already rejected even the ethical eudaemonism of Augustine.[209] Action must be without 'ulterior thought of happiness or advantage', and in a state of 'warm devotion, passionate affection, supreme concentration'.[210] It must also be spontaneous, since an act which is forced is 'no real act of the will, and has no value at all in the eyes of God'.[211] Holl concludes: 'The question of justification could come fully into focus only after [Luther] had become aware of the extent of the moral demand'.[212] It was Luther's refusal to evade the enormous, non-negotiable demands of God which drove him to recognize in Scripture a radically alternative basis for God's acceptance of the sinner.

This seems to stand in contradiction to Lindberg's view that Luther's emphasis on justification liberates action from the need to merit God's grace, and thus enables full exposure to God's command without need for evasion. Yet it is possible to resolve the tension by acknowledging that Luther's focus on the absolute character of God's command is not *exclusively* a preparation for his doctrine of justification. It also affects Luther's thinking *beyond* justification with regard to how the justified sinner is to behave. He continues to uphold God's commands as absolute standards without despair on the one hand or evasion on the other.

PART TWO OF THE *SERMON VON DEM WUCHER*

Having spent over half the sermon on the exposition of Scripture, in this second part Luther turns to an analysis of contemporary practices regarding usury. He undertakes this in the light of his explication of the right degrees of handling earthly goods.

First, he observes that in addition to the Christian degrees for handling temporal goods given in the Sermon on the Mount there are other degrees, such as purchasing. In a limited sense these belong to a more neutral moral territory: 'By these methods no one becomes better or worse in the sight of God'.[213] Receiving something in, say, an inheritance or through work is neither meritorious nor blameworthy. This does not imply that dealings

[209] A useful discussion of this with full quotations showing Luther's development can be found in Forell, *Faith Active in Love*, pp. 93–100, although his characterization of Augustine is not entirely accurate, for which he relies too heavily on Anders Nygren's *Agape & Eros*, trans. Philip S. Watson (London: SPCK, 1982).

[210] Holl, *The Reconstruction of Morality*, p. 34.

[211] Holl, *The Reconstruction of Morality*, p. 34.

[212] Holl, *The Reconstruction of Morality*, p. 53.

[213] LW v. 45, p. 295; WA v. 6, p. 51, ll. 6–7.

such as buying and selling are an autonomous domain. God is concerned about right conduct in such transactions: they are still subject to 'temporal and spiritual law', as Luther's analysis here shows.[214]

THE *ZINSKAUF* AND LUTHER'S RESPONSE TO IT

The nub of this section of Luther's sermon is a penetrating analysis of a contract known as the *Zinskauf*. This arrangement supposedly constituted a purchase of money rather than a loan at interest. Luther's method is to examine this contract in the light of the Scriptural framework he has laid out, and he sets out his conclusion at the outset: the *Zinskauf* is not necessarily usury per se, but is often a disguise behind which usury hides—'this slippery and newly invented business very frequently makes itself an upright and loyal protector of damnable greed and usury'.[215] As he goes on he adduces a number of other moral theological arguments which militate against the practice of the *Zinskauf*, on the basis of which he argues that the contract is wrong whether it is *technically* usury or not: 'whether this contrast is usury or not, it accomplishes exactly the same thing that usury accomplishes'.[216] Rather than becoming bogged down in a minute theoretical discussion, his rhetorical strategy is not to leave any room for evasion.

Before exploring this further, let us sketch the historical circumstances of the *Zinskauf*. The taking of interest was still theoretically proscribed at this time, but that did not prevent its expansion in a number of ways. The *Zinskauf* was one such tactic, adopted essentially as a way around the prohibition. It was the purchase of a fixed annual income in exchange for a sum of capital, and was therefore claimed to be a sale rather than a loan and thus not usurious. Originally it was land-based: one paid a fixed quantity of yield, but in time it became almost purely monetary. Meanwhile, theologians of the Tübingen School considered revisions of the church's teaching and canonical prohibitions on interest. Biel and Summenhart argued that money was not solely a consumable, and that risk-free business was not necessarily usury: if it benefited the debtor as well as the creditor it was not necessarily wrong.[217] Eck defended a rate of 5 per cent, with certain exceptions to protect the vulnerable, although he was much vilified for being an opportunist and lackey of the bankers for his trouble.[218]

Luther's first point in response to the *Zinskauf* is to identify ways in which it can become a disguise for usury. That is, his assumption is that economic

[214] LW v. 45, p. 295; WA v. 6, p. 51, l. 6.
[215] LW v. 45, p. 295; WA v. 6, p. 51, ll. 17–19.
[216] LW v. 45, p. 297; WA v. 6, p. 52, ll. 17–18.
[217] Prien, *Luthers Wirtschaftsethik*, p. 64.
[218] Prien, *Luthers Wirtschaftsethik*, p. 67.

practice potentially operates under great subterfuge, and must thus be analysed in the light of Scripture in order to discern its true nature. But the opacity of economic practice does not originate in any epistemological difficulty of discerning God's will: the problem is not a lack of information about right and wrong. Rather, Luther is suspicious of the practices themselves, cognizant of the human propensity for self-deception and self-justification, which hampers one from admitting oneself to be in the wrong. The antidote is the command of God, which yields self-knowledge, overcoming this otherwise insurmountable refusal to acknowledge the truth of one's self-centredness.

Luther makes other moves as well, to establish that the contract is wrong even if it is not usury. For example, referring to 1 Timothy 4:1 he points out that the *Zinskauf* is an innovation, and hence likely to be a concealment for sin. This seemingly reactionary attitude is perhaps particularly distasteful to a modern perspective, and it is worth pausing on this aspect of Luther's method for a moment. Creativity and inventiveness are not automatically to be regarded as good things, since human desires in their corrupt state are far more likely to issue selfish and self-aggrandizing novelties than genuinely progressive ones.[219] It is not that he condemns innovation per se. But neither is it to be unhesitatingly accepted—rather, it should be critically evaluated.

One factor in such an evaluation is his observation that the *Zinskauf* serves the ends of wealth, reputation, and luxury. For Luther this means that it is prima facie hardly likely to be a path of service to one's neighbour. This illustrates a theme explored on pages 49–52—'good' works belong to one of two categories: those directed to the end of serving one's neighbour, and those serving one's own interests, which are not really good works at all. Here, therefore, a piece of seemingly innocent business is debunked, because it is concerned with one's own advantage rather than the welfare of one's neighbour.

Expanding our earlier point about Luther's twofold typology of good works, his method is to trace an action to its very deepest root, and assess the deed on the basis of whether its root is self-interest or neighbour-love. For Luther, self-interest and love are irreconcilably opposed and not susceptible of synthesis.[220] Any such integration is ultimately only a pretence for well-concealed self-interest, whereas Luther's understanding of the command to love one's neighbour as oneself actually *excludes* self-love. For him, the Golden Rule is

[219] Hence Luther of course claims that his Reformation views are not in the least novel, but a recovery of authentic Christian tradition.

[220] George Forell suggests that Luther's rationale for this is that genuine love of neighbour is 'modelled after the love of Christ', which is supposedly totally free of self-interest (*Faith Active in Love*, p. 95). But Simo Peura observes that this does not go far enough: such love is not free of self-interest merely because it imitates Christ's, but because it *is* Christ's love, which the believer receives by faith (Simo Peura, 'What God Gives Man Receives: Luther on Salvation', in *Union with Christ: The New Finnish Interpretation of Luther*, eds. Carl E. Braaten and Robert W. Jenson (Grand Rapids: Eerdmans, 1998), pp. 76–95, esp. pp. 93–4).

not only a heuristic indicator of the magnitude of love required, but demands the obliteration of self-love. Rejecting Augustine's careful integration of the two, Luther believes that self-love is always sin; there is no tolerable level at which it may remain.[221] Thus *all* commerce and contracts must be placed in the service of the neighbour.[222]

He applies this analysis here:

> Now in this contract the advantage of the buyer, or the receiver of the *zinss*, is invariably looked upon as greater and better and more desirable than that of the seller, or the payer of the *zinss*. This is a sign that the transaction is never made for the sake of the seller, but always for the sake of the buyer.[223]

Evidently, the buyer (creditor) seeks his own good, not that of his neighbour. The *Zinskauf* therefore violates 'natural law and the law of Christian love'.[224] The *Zinskauf* strives to evade this demand (doing as one would be done by) because the buyer would not want to be in the seller's place. Thus the contract is not mutually beneficial: 'the buyer would not want to be in the seller's place at all, as in the case of other purchase transactions'.[225]

Next, Luther makes an argument from outcome. We have already alluded to his claim that 'whether this contract is usury or not, it accomplishes exactly the same thing'.[226] Yet its consequences in terms of the ruin it brings are the same as those of usury. It is useful to see that, while Luther is obviously not a consequentialist in the recent sense of the word, his method still allows for the moral significance of consequences.[227] They can play a revelatory function in relation to the deed which produced them. This is best seen in the text he refers to, of which he was so fond: 'The Lord taught not that the fruit is known by its tree but that the tree is known by its fruit'.[228] It is not the consequences that make the deed right or wrong, but the *root* of the deed is unavoidably seen in its results. In this case the root is greed, evident in the fact that the purchasers of the contracts do not need the income, so their purchase must

[221] Bernd Wannenwetsch, 'Caritas fide formata: "Herz und Affekte" als Schlüssel zu "Glaube und Liebe"', *Kerygma und Dogma* 46.3 (2000), pp. 205–24, esp. pp. 215–16.

[222] If one is obliged to serve one's neighbour so utterly, one might then ask how Luther can permit any kind of profit at all. This he allows only to enable one to sustain oneself and thereby continue to be at one's neighbour's disposal. The very concept is defined in terms of service to the other. As Prien puts it, 'Luther understands property as an office [or duty] from which responsibility the Christian cannot dispense themselves, so that they must give their property to the needy and become a poor man themselves'. Author's translation of Prien, *Luthers Wirtschaftsethik*, pp. 189–90.

[223] LW v. 45, p. 296; WA v. 6, p. 51, ll. 31–4.

[224] LW v. 45, p. 296; WA v. 6, p. 52, ll. 5–6.

[225] LW v. 45, p. 297; WA v. 6, p. 52, ll. 15–16.

[226] LW v. 45, p. 295.

[227] This assumes the definition of consequentialism given in M. T. Nelson, 'Consequentialism', in *New Dictionary of Christian Ethics and Pastoral Theology*, eds. David J. Atkinson and David Field (Leicester: InterVarsity, 1995), pp. 253–4.

[228] LW v. 45, p. 297; WA v. 6, p. 52, ll. 21–2.

be driven by avarice. This is especially visible when *Zins* collected from one transaction is immediately reinvested in another.[229] He summarizes: 'This transaction gives free rein to avarice; therefore it cannot, as presently practiced, be of God'.[230] Indeed, endeavouring to hide the sin of greed from detection makes it doubly insidious.

Luther's next step is by now familiar: to counter objections to his rejection of the *Zinskauf*. One would be that canon law does not define such conduct as usurious and thus permits it. Luther retorts that the pronouncements of canon law are contingent, subject to a higher judgement. God requires more than the permitted minimum.

His treatment of the justification of *Zins* by the notion of *interesse*, a matter to which he now proceeds, is similar. This originated to prevent debtors from taking advantage of the fact that one could not be compelled to pay interest, and denoted compensation due by one who failed to fulfil the terms of a contract on time.[231] There were two titles to *interesse*. The first, *damnum emergens*, denoted *actual* loss incurred by late payment, the paradigm case being having to borrow money at interest oneself, to cover a shortfall caused by late payment or non-payment.[232] The other, *lucrum cessans*, was claimed to recover potential profit which had been missed through tardy payment.[233]

Sanction of these claims was by no means unanimous.[234] Yet from the thirteenth century it became gradually accepted that they were damages, not usury.[235] From this notion of interest as compensation rather than profit, interest in the contemporary sense emerged as an entitlement in principle whether actual loss was sustained or not. It was not considered usurious, because one was not making any more money than one could have had one deployed the money in trade.

Luther particularly scourges *lucrum cessans* as being carried out on a false basis. The term *interesse* was derived from the Latin *id quod interest*, 'that which is the difference'.[236] Drawing on this connotation, Luther contends that since the risks associated with productive labour are so manifold, the

[229] The notion of the lender's need enables Luther to authorize exceptions to his general prohibition of the *Zinskauf*. In such circumstances the contract is reciprocally advantageous and not exploitative. For example, those too elderly or sick to work, who have capital to invest, are permitted to purchase an income, subject to restrictions such as a low cap on interest rates (4–6 per cent). See Prien, *Luthers Wirtschaftsethik*, pp. 98–9.

[230] LW v. 45, p. 298; WA v. 6, p. 53, ll. 18–19.

[231] See Thomas F. Divine, *Interest: An Historical and Analytical Study in Economics and Modern Ethics* (Milwaukee: Marquette University Press, 1959), pp. 53–4.

[232] Noonan, *The Scholastic Analysis of Usury*, p. 109.

[233] Noonan, *The Scholastic Analysis of Usury*, pp. 109–10.

[234] For example, Aquinas argues that one is bound to pay compensation for a late payment, but he does not reckon that it should be as much as the amount of projected profit: 'A loss of this kind need not be made good in equivalent; because to have a thing virtually is less than to have it actually'. ST 2a 2ae q. 62, a. 4.

[235] Divine, *Interest*, p. 54.

[236] Noonan, *The Scholastic Analysis of Usury*, pp. 105–6.

difference could as easily be a loss as a profit: 'Thus the "interest" in the losses is as great as or greater than the "interest" in the profit'.[237] Obtaining a *fixed* payment from another on the basis that one has foregone an opportunity for income is therefore ludicrous: one has no way of knowing whether one would have made any such amount at all—incompetence, illness, poor yield, scarcity of raw materials, and many other factors could have prevented it. Furthermore, in business there are numerous periods during which money cannot be invested and must be idle. *Interesse* in reality involves loss as well as profit. Thus, 'Money engaged in business and money put out at *zinss* are two different things, and the one cannot be compared with the other'.[238]

This is the first time we see Luther take this particular methodological step: he (temporarily) enters into the inner logic of the practice, and probes it to see whether it is consistent with its own claims. Having examined its undergirding concepts, he concludes that it fails on its own terms. Although his analysis is still driven by his theologically informed polemic, it is striking to see that this by no means precludes an engagement with alternative positions on their own terms, attempting to understand them as they understand themselves. It is this moment of imaginative sympathy which supplies the appraisal that Luther delivers: he scrutinizes both ordinary trade and the *Zinskauf*, and is thus able to see the differences between them on their own terms:

> The latter has a base which is constantly growing and producing profit out of the earth without any fear of capital losses; while there is nothing certain about the former, and the only interest it yields is accidental and cannot be counted on.[239]

THE STERILITY OF MONEY

Luther's next step is to examine the difference between *Zins* and profit. This examination is predicated on a reassertion of the doctrine of the sterility of money, which had been taught in the church since the fifth century: 'You cannot make money just with money'.[240] More recently, St Thomas had buttressed the biblical ban on usury by drawing on the Aristotelian idea that money is a medium of exchange, not a productive thing. It is consumed through use.[241]

Luther's account of the sterility of money is slightly distinctive in the especially large emphasis it places on risk: 'It is the intervention of risk

[237] LW v. 45, p. 299; WA v. 6, p. 54, ll. 3–5.
[238] LW v. 45, p. 300; WA v. 6, p. 54, ll. 28–30.
[239] LW v. 45, p. 300; WA v. 6, p. 54, ll. 30–3. [240] LW v. 45, p. 299.
[241] ST 2a 2ae q. 78, a. 1. See also Joan Lockwood O'Donovan, 'The Theological Economics of Medieval Usury Theory', *Studies in Christian Ethics* 14.1 (2001), pp. 48–64, esp. pp. 55–6.

between capital and profit that defines the "sterility of money" for Luther'.[242] That is, practically speaking money can generate more money—but it is not *morally* sufficient to do so, because risk and work are necessary too. This conclusion is not drawn only from Aristotle, but also from Luther's understanding of the doctrine of creation. God has created and ordered the world in a particular way for its preservation and well-being. Humans are creatures, not free agents who are entirely at liberty to exist as they please, and their nature as creatures places them under certain unavoidable limitations and obligations. They are limited in knowledge and ability. They are subject to the many unpredictable exigencies of life.[243] And they are created to work for their livelihood, because God has created humanity to act as his cooperative agents in the work of sustaining and enriching that which he has made (although obviously not creating *ex nihilo* as he does). Based on these features of his theological account of what it is to be a human creature, Luther's method here is to set the *Zinskauf* alongside a counter-description of how money ought to be made, how one might honestly seek a profit without doing so to the detriment of one's neighbour.[244]

This account is what leads him to perceive that this contract operates through exploitation: in not using money in business on one's own behalf but receiving a fixed payment, one is exposing one's neighbour to the risk which one is avoiding. Such people are 'worse than usurers, . . . making their gains at the expense of other people's losses'.[245] Profit comes at an inevitable cost to the neighbour, who will lose money through the many pitfalls and dangers of business, while having to pay a fixed amount back.[246]

The attempt to avoid the fundamental risk involved in business is a further cause for opposition to this contract. Uncertainty is an inescapable aspect of human existence, and endeavours to artificially secure a life free of worry and difficulty by human methods constitute an attempt to abolish the need for ongoing trust in God's faithful provision and protection, and ongoing surrender to whatever comes from him.[247] It therefore represents a rebellion against 'the divinely ordained structure of humankind's relation to temporal goods'.[248]

242 Lockwood O'Donovan, 'The Theological Economics of Medieval Usury Theory', p. 63.

243 Lohse, *Martin Luther's Theology*, p. 242.

244 This is visible in Luther's version of the scholastic just price concept in *Von Kaufshandlung*. Against the maxim of the merchants that 'I may sell my goods as dear as I can', Luther asserts that prices should be set according to what will yield a sufficient wage for a 'modest living' ('*zymliche narunge*'). See LW v. 45, pp. 248–50, esp. p. 250; WA v. 15, p. 295, l. 20–p. 296, l. 36, esp. p. 296, l. 28.

245 LW v. 45, p. 300; WA v. 6, p. 54, ll. 14–16.

246 Lockwood O'Donovan, 'The Theological Economics of Medieval Usury Theory', p. 63.

247 '[Luther's] most urgent objection was directed against man's attempt to safeguard and guarantee by means of lending capital at interest what God has placed into the category of uncertainty and insecurity'. Bornkamm, *Luther's World of Thought*, p. 268.

248 Lockwood O'Donovan, 'The Theological Economics of Medieval Usury Theory', p. 62.

As discussed above, God wills that temporal goods be subject to uncertainty in order to prevent humans from idolizing them, and to train humankind to trust God instead of worldly things.

LUTHER'S SUGGESTIONS FOR REFORM

On this basis, and despite his despondency about the likelihood of reform, Luther makes a number of practical recommendations on how to govern the *Zinskauf* properly. A reformed practice of the *Zinskauf* could in certain circumstances be in keeping with the dictates of the Sermon on the Mount. Luther is notoriously aware that the gospel is not a utopian manifesto or a replacement of civil government, hence his opposition to both the revolutionary zeal of Muntzer and the plenipotentiary claims of Rome. Yet this does not exclude reforms which respect the genuine validity of earthly justice.[249]

So, for example, if money is lent, it must be secured on property, which must be itemized:

> It is not enough that the base of the contract actually exist and be named, but it must be clearly indicated, item by item, and the money and *zinss* specifically related to each piece.[250]

The reason for this is that the debtor should not be liable to pay a fixed amount: 'the *zinss* would then fluctuate or remain constant with its respective base'.[251] The amount the creditor receives is to be calculated according to the profit made on each enumerated item, not a fixed amount regardless of what the debtor can afford. Thus, if the debtor makes a loss, or only a tiny profit, they are protected from destitution. This is not usury—that is, a purely monetary loan repaid at a fixed rate of return—but an investment in a productive enterprise, in which the investor and borrower share the risk.

Servicing a debt cannot take priority over meeting one's needs, because one is entitled to access to the fruits of one's labours. Thus the lender has no right to any payment unless 'the payer of the *zinss*... can have free, adequate, and unhindered use of his own labour'.[252] This lending is startlingly oriented towards the advantage of the debtor, and Luther refers to the principle of *caveat emptor*. He is playing on the claim that the contract is a straightforward purchase. If so, the purchaser (creditor) should bear the risk, and only purchase a contract from one known to be scrupulous and solvent, rather than lending indiscriminately and relying on the courts to recover his money,

[249] Forell, *Faith Active in Love*, p. 159.
[250] LW v. 45, p. 302; WA v. 6, p. 56, ll. 10–12.
[251] LW v. 45, p. 303; WA v. 6, p. 56, ll. 27–8.
[252] LW v. 45, p. 303; WA v. 6, p. 57, ll. 2–4.

regardless of the consequence for the debtor. Luther dryly observes that scarcely anyone will wish to take out a contract under such conditions—which precisely demonstrates that the usual practice of the *Zinskauf* is a camouflage for making a profit without effort or risk.

LUTHER'S USE OF THE DOCTRINE OF CREATION IN ECONOMIC ETHICS

Thus one way to practise the *Zinskauf* non-usuriously is to ensure that the creditor shares the risk: if one wishes to have a stake in the profits, one must also share the losses. God's intention in creation is that risk be interposed between profit and capital: the creditor must be subject to unpredictability in order to remain open in financial matters to God's loving discipline of risk and loss. Relating the level of interest to the level of profit made by the debtor means that the creditor is once again exposed to 'death, illness, flood, fire, wind, hail, lightning, rain, wolves, wild beasts, and the manifold losses inflicted by wicked men'.[253]

The *Zinskauf* can represent an attempt to transgress the boundaries of human creatureliness in other ways too. For instance, it is beyond human ability to calculate how much profit would have been made if the money had been invested in business: 'Since it is not possible to define, compute, and calculate this other *interesse*, which is not within the power of man, I do not see how the *zinss* contract can stand up'.[254] It is based on a claim to know what cannot be known.

A further objection to this method of 'making' money is that it attempts to avoid work as well as risk. For Luther, this reveals the exploitative purpose behind the contract:

> There is in this contract a perilous intention, from which I fear none of the *zinss* buyers, or at least very few of them, are free, and that is the desire that their *zinss* and property be secure and assured. This is why they invest their money with others instead of keeping it and taking risks. They much prefer to have others do the work and take the risks, so they themselves can be lazy and idle, and yet remain or become rich. If that is not usury, it is mighty close to it.[255]

Work is not an option for a creature. It is both a created good and an obligation, a means of serving one's neighbour. In the later Genesis lectures, and the more contemporaneous exposition of Psalm 127, Luther clearly

[253] LW v. 45, p. 303; WA v. 6, p. 56, ll. 32–4.
[254] LW v. 45, p. 300; WA v. 6, p. 54, ll. 16–18.
[255] LW v. 45, p. 307; WA v. 6, p. 60, ll. 2–6.

regards the divine mandate to work as predating his punishment of sin.[256] Of course, after the Fall work becomes an oppressive burden, a curse, but this does not obliterate its positive role in God's benevolent order. Refusal to work is therefore a double rebellion, spurning an opportunity to serve others and revolting against rightful punishment. Althaus comments:

> Whoever does not work is a thief and robs his neighbour in two ways. First, he permits others to work for him and nourishes himself from their 'blood and sweat'. Second, he withholds what he ought to give his neighbour.[257]

Luther is cognizant that those unable to work (such as the housebound and the elderly) constitute exceptions to this precept.

LUTHER'S CONCEPTS OF WORK AND VOCATION

Luther's affirmation of work corresponds to his rejection of the notion that some ways of life are higher than others, and that the proper location for the fulfilment of the commands to love God and neighbour is the monastery.[258] He broadens the concept of *vocatio* or *Beruf* to include wider aspects of human existence: for him, *Beruf* indicates not a special setting apart into a religious community, but rather the situation in which one finds oneself, and its associated responsibilities, one's place within the concrete web of relationships that everyone occupies, whether daughter, parent, employee, merchant, or peasant.[259] One's particular situation mediates God's commands and discloses the appropriate place and way to serve him here and now.[260]

This theme is prominent in *An den Christlichen Adel deutscher Nation von des Christlichen standes besserung*, written not long after this sermon in the summer of 1520. There Luther lambasts the idea that the clergy are superior to or more spiritual than the laity, since it is faith alone which makes one spiritual: 'all Christians are truly of the spiritual estate, and there is no

256 For example, from the *Genesisvorlesung* (1535–8): 'It is appropriate here also to point out that man was created not for leisure but for work, even in the state of innocence'. LW v. 1, p. 103; WA v. 42, p. 78b, ll. 26 7.

257 Althaus, *The Ethics of Martin Luther*, p. 102.

258 See Karlfried Froehlich, 'Luther on Vocation', in *Harvesting Martin Luther's Reflections on Theology, Ethics and the Church*, ed. Timothy J. Wengert (Grand Rapids: Eerdmans, 2004), pp. 121–33, esp. pp. 123–4.

259 Jane E. Strohl, 'Luther's Spiritual Journey', in *The Cambridge Companion to Martin Luther*, ed. Donald K. McKim (Cambridge: Cambridge University Press, 2003), pp. 149–64, esp. p. 161; and Bornkamm, *Luther's World of Thought*, p. 271.

260 The dark side of this concept is well documented, namely the implication that one's worldly station is entirely static, and that one must remain in one's place permanently because it is one's calling. Certainly Luther had no affection for social climbers, but he encouraged people to step into a different role, if that was what service to others required (see LW v. 45, p. 95).

difference among them except that of office'.[261] On the basis of 1 Corinthians 12, he argues that the physical welfare of the community matters as well as its spiritual condition:

> Everyone must benefit and serve every other by means of his own work or office so that in this way many kinds of work may be done for the bodily and spiritual welfare of the community.[262]

The craftsman or labourer does not simply work in order to survive. They are called to assist their neighbour, meeting their neighbour's needs for such things as food and clothing.[263] Once again, self-interest is not the motive for behaviour but service of one's neighbour.

Yet Luther does not simply reject the monastic understanding of vocation. If anything, he reinforces it but broadens its scope. All Christians are called to be part of a community of interdependent neighbours who serve and provide for one another.[264] 'Monasticism was, so to speak, secularized'.[265] One might say that far from abolishing monasticism, Luther applies some of its features to everyone. As Karlfried Froehlich puts it, Luther 'did not eliminate . . . the priesthood. Instead he eliminated the laity!'[266] In this way, worldly work becomes spiritually significant.[267] Work is not something to be escaped, but to be willingly undertaken as an opportunity to benefit others, even if one does not personally need to. Consequently, refusal to work within one's situation is a refusal to assist one's neighbour.

Therefore, as well as forcing one's neighbour to bear all the risks and losses, the *Zinskauf* conscripts one's neighbour into working in one's stead. This is occluded by the Golden Rule: 'If you seek to take an advantage of your neighbour which you would not want him to take of you, then love is gone and natural law broken'.[268] Natural law (which for Luther is coterminous with the Golden Rule) forbids seeking one's own advantage at the expense of another.

The *Zinskauf* thus represents a threefold rebellion against humanity's creaturely status: it pretends to know what cannot be known, it attempts to avoid work, and it seeks to escape risk. These considerations explain why, for those who cannot work, Luther finds the *Zinskauf* acceptable, provided the creditor shares in the risk and the *Zins* is related to the actual profit made.

[261] LW v. 44, p. 127; WA v. 6, p. 407, ll. 13–15.

[262] LW v. 44, p. 130; WA v. 6, p. 409, ll. 7–9.

[263] See Karl Holl, *The Cultural Significance of the Reformation*, trans. Karl and Barbara Hertz and John H. Lichtblau (New York: Meridian, 1959), p. 33.

[264] Johannes Schwanke, 'Luther on Creation', in *Harvesting Martin Luther's Reflections on Theology, Ethics and the Church*, ed. Timothy J. Wengert (Grand Rapids: Eerdmans, 2004), pp. 78–98, esp. pp. 88–9.

[265] Tawney, *Religion and the Rise of Capitalism*, p. 107.

[266] Froehlich, 'Luther on Vocation', p. 127.

[267] Bayer, 'Nature and Institution', p. 133.

[268] LW v. 45, p. 307; WA v. 6, p. 60, ll. 7–9.

These exceptions have suggested to some scholars that Luther is simply contradictory, even rather unprincipled.[269] On closer inspection it seems that these exemptions are theologically governed, by the same considerations as his condemnation of interest.

LUTHER'S ASSESSMENT OF SELF-INTEREST

Luther's recognition that the goal of the contract is self-interest rather than neighbour-love is decisive for him:

> I am afraid that in *zinss* contracts we pay precious little heed to our neighbour's welfare, if only our own *zinss* and property are secure, though this is the very thing we ought not to seek.[270]

He therefore reaches the strident conclusion that, unless they conform to the standards he has set out, those who lend money through the *Zinskauf* are 'robbers and murderers, wresting from the poor man his property and living'.[271] This is because those who sell a fixed payment for capital usually do so out of *need*—and therefore they should be assisted through free loans and gifts. Elsewhere, Luther maintains that failure to help someone needy is equivalent to murder.[272] Similarly here, failure to aid one in need is to deprive them of their due, which is theft. Luther therefore stipulates that whenever the debtor is in need, the command of neighbour-love takes priority: 'God's commandment stands in the way and directs that the needy shall be helped by loans and gifts'.[273] The only exception is if the creditor is also in need. Then the contract is tolerable (hardly a ringing endorsement), provided interest is limited to between 4 and 6 per cent. The principle underlying this exception is again the Golden Rule: if the contract genuinely benefits both parties (one in need of capital, one in need of a regular income) then neither is taking advantage of the other. Even in such circumstances, Luther finishes, the lender should err on the side of caution and avoid overcharging, because the contract can so easily mask greed and laziness.

269 See for example Divine, *Interest*, pp. 68–70.

270 LW v. 45, pp. 307–8; WA v. 6, p. 60, ll. 9–11.

271 LW v. 45, p. 304; WA v. 6, p. 57, ll. 20–1.

272 For example, in his exposition of the Fifth Commandment in *Der Großer Katechismus* Luther argues, 'God rightly calls all persons murderers who do not offer counsel and aid to men in need and in peril of body and life'. Tappert, *The Book of Concord*, p. 391; WA v. 30.I, p. 159, ll. 19–20.

273 LW v. 45, p. 204; WA v. 6, p. 58, ll. 8–9.

REFORMS MADE BY GOVERNMENT AND PERSONAL ACTION IN LUTHER'S SOCIAL ETHICS

Despite this exception, Luther repeats that Christ's first three degrees of handling temporal goods take priority. The majority of contracts he witnesses are not mutually beneficial but exploitative, because they originate in the need of the seller (debtor). In such situations, obedience to Christ would drastically reduce such need and thus the practice of the *Zinskauf*. Thus for him right action is not only an individual matter of doing the right thing. It also has the potential to bring about wider changes in society.

The secular authorities also have a role to play. Luther ascribes three particular functions to them here. He first envisages that the authorities have a positive role in promoting good works and shaping right behaviour. Second, they have a role in discerning what is permissible and in which circumstances. For example, they must regulate the *Zinskauf* such that it is allowed in legitimate circumstances at an appropriately low rate of interest. Luther explicitly renounces responsibility for adjudging which circumstances a slightly higher rate may apply in: 'I leave it to the law to determine when the property is so good and so rich that one may charge 6 per cent'.[274] That is, while he insists that the authorities be guided theologically, there are questions which, although not morally indifferent, must be resolved by the authorities with their particular expertise, within the parameters furnished by theological considerations. Third and most familiar, the authorities have the role of opposing wrongdoing, such as prohibiting inflated interest rates outright, for the protection of 'the poor common folk'.[275]

These three roles illuminate Luther's understanding of God's two methods of rule. Although worldly authority has its own integrity, it is not an isolated sphere, unconstrained by the will and activity of God. The authorities should not minimalistically resist evil and avert disorder, but promote right behaviour. Not 'ruling the world with the gospel' does not imply that civil power has no role in enforcing a theologically informed moral vision. It must enforce natural law—the Golden Rule—which is known through revelation.

In short, economic ethics is not a thing of purely individual concern for Luther. He is interested in the attitudes and actions of particular individuals, but not solely so. Reform of civil authority and reform of individual behaviour do not exclude each other. Luther's method therefore involves a pincer movement, in which the plight of the needy is ameliorated through communal and individual action, and opportunities for exploitation therefore curtailed.

[274] LW v. 45, p. 305; WA v. 6, p. 58, ll. 18–19.
[275] LW v. 45, p. 305; WA v. 6, p. 58, l. 28.

CONCLUSION

This concludes the step-by-step analysis of Luther's moral theological method in the publication we have selected. This conclusion will now pick out some particularly fertile strands of Luther's method which seem to merit particular reiteration and attention for moral theology today. Thus, as well as acting as a summary of the preceding analysis, it will also be prospective, indicating potential areas of engagement in subsequent chapters.

First, against any claim for the autonomy of financial affairs as a sphere governed by its own laws and inner logic, Luther asserts the all-embracing moral implications of the gospel. The command of Christ to love one's neighbour extends to every aspect of life. Economic endeavour is not an autonomous field where they do not apply, or love is somehow suspended. His glad endorsement of the capacity of human reason in practical matters does not in any way imply that financial matters are a law unto themselves. Therefore, financial affairs should be regulated by the worldly authorities. Finance must be subject to the constraints of earthly justice.

Second, Luther asserts the need for individuals to obey Jesus's commands with regard to temporal goods. In the light of these commands, Luther perceives that many economic practices mask vested interest and avarice. Far from being a self-contained but empirically accessible system, financial matters tend to be *deliberately* obscure, and this opacity is a camouflage for duplicity. Luther regards the logic which justifies greedy behaviour as convoluted, while the commands of Jesus are refreshingly clear. The gospel has a revelatory power to unmask the truth. Trust in the gospel may appear naïve, but true naïvety would be an uncritical acceptance of economic claims. Economic claims must therefore be approached with suspicion. Preachers and theologians should use this vantage point to assist the temporal authorities in understanding the economic realities which confront them. Luther's primary move in engaging with economic affairs is thus a theological one: to pay better attention to the gospel, the gospel not being reduced to his account of justification by faith, but consisting of an account of reality with corresponding moral implications, including particular commands.

Third, self-interest is always wrong. Luther eschews all syntheses of self-love and neighbour-love. One must exist wholly for one's neighbour's benefit. Thus one's handling of worldly goods is wholly configured as an opportunity to serve others rather than make a profit. Even earning a living is to be done so one can benefit others. Whether one ultimately agrees with Luther's denial of a rightly ordered self-love, one may still appreciate the way in which this denial gives Luther an especial sensitivity to the way in which claims to synergize self-interest and the common good or the interests of others can mask greed and exploitation. Luther's absolute rejection of self-love is problematic, but his insight that there are many wrong forms of self-love which seek one's own advantage to the detriment of one's neighbour is highly salutary, as is his emphasis on the wilful self-deception to which humans are given.

Luther's solution is to expose people to the full force of God's commandments, which reveal and confront the depths of human recalcitrance. He refuses to accept evasions of Christ's command to freely part with one's temporal goods, because in order for people to be free to act in this way, their deep-seated avarice must be overcome. One cannot wholly blame injustice on social patterns; attempts to do so may themselves mask deep-seated personal sin. Yet this is not to deny a structural or public dimension to his thought: he also sees that greed can take structural forms, masked by beguiling ideological justifications. Luther's refusal to accept a fissure between private and public is evident in his concept of the *Amt* (office). This is not narrowly confined to officially recognized positions within government such as judge or soldier, but can apply to any situation where one has *responsibility* for another. It includes non-governmental offices such as teaching or parenthood, but even more widely can mean any situation where the need of another places them in one's care, a *Nächstenamt* purely by virtue of being a neighbour to someone in need of assistance, or to correct injustice.[276]

The structural dimension to Luther's thought flows from his concept of the twofold rule of God, which distinguishes between acting for one's own sake and acting for the sake of others. This offers Luther a theological rationale for earthly justice which neither seeks the hopeless goal of imposing the Kingdom of God on a fallen world by coercion, nor rests content with rampant injustice. His refusal to press for the enactment of the Sermon on the Mount by civil government is therefore itself a theological conclusion, not a capitulation to political pragmatism.

At the same time, his vision of the integrity of earthly justice yields far broader and higher standards than his disapproval of 'ruling the world with the gospel' might suggest, and his supposed realism does not prevent him from arguing fiercely for the enforcement of such standards. Thus his distinction between the two forms of God's rule does not derogate into a quietist surrender to the status quo, because the earthly form of God's rule is still precisely *God*'s rule.[277] Its purpose and calling are to govern in accordance with God's will, to secure justice, and to provide for the needy. Given the corruption of human nature it does this in its own properly coercive way. Indeed, it is his emphasis on the specially coercive character of earthly government which

[276] See Hans-Jürgen Prien, 'Wirtschaftsethik der Reformationszeit bei Martin Luther', <http://offenes-forum-wiesbaden.dike.de/wirtschaftsethik/Luther_wirtschaftsethik.htm>, [consulted 15 April 2006] and *Luthers Wirtschaftsethik*, p. 183.

[277] The charge of quietism is inter alia Reinhold Niebuhr's. See Reinhold Niebuhr, *The Nature and Destiny of Man: A Christian Interpretation* (New York: Scribners, 1953), v. 2, p. 187.

enables Luther to demand that existing wrongs be rectified and financial practices better regulated.

Furthermore, based on this theological account of authority, Luther argues that it has a proactive role in actively assisting the needy. Government's role is not construed minimally or solely negatively (to restrain wickedness). It also carries positive responsibility for doing and promoting good. Hence, care for the needy is not a private affair left at one's personal discretion, but a public, collective responsibility.

It is worth noting the effective practical implications of this aspect of Luther's thought in the common chest arrangements which he supervised. These reflect his so-called realism. Contributions were personal but mandatory. Recipients of disbursements were vetted to ensure they were genuinely impoverished. Money from the chest was usually given to alleviate short-term need, for example, if crops had been poor. Newcomers were given money to launch themselves in trade, or to tide them over while seeking employment. Recipients could not become perpetually dependent, unless they could not work for a strong reason such as age or illness. The intention was to foster a culture of local accountability, preventing abuses. The doctrine of the two governments therefore acts as a theological key to discerning not only the limits, but also the duties of earthly government.

This duty to give highlights Luther's emphasis on the way that involuntarily parting with temporal goods 'exercises' faith. Uncertainty compels one to trust God to provide—a compulsion which is deeply necessary given human contumacy since the Fall. Thus misfortunes such as theft, which would otherwise be met with horror and a quest for compensation, become reconfigured as joyful opportunities to be freed from worldly goods. Material loss can be perceived even as an act of God's mercy since it strengthens faith, without which one cannot be saved.

Conversely, it is faith (which for Luther means entrusting oneself to God's care in material matters as much as ultimate ones) which liberates one from the neurotic fixation on acquiring temporal goods in order to assure oneself of future security. Greed is to be totally engrossed with oneself, and as such is fundamentally incompatible with faith—hence Luther warns that the greedy person cannot be saved: the greedy person is by definition an unbelieving person. Far from being incompatible with Luther's doctrine of justification by faith alone, this view of greed is a corollary of this doctrine, since Luther understands faith precisely as a complete renunciation of one's own means of providing for oneself (in *all* matters), and confidently trusting in God's goodness. Luther's doctrine of justification thus gives a sharp impulse to moral reform.

Just as this doctrine has concrete economic implications, so too does the doctrine of creation, and Luther's thought is constantly shaped by this core doctrine. Humanity and its universe have been made a certain way by God, arranged according to his good purposes. Thus risk regarding temporal goods is inescapable, human knowledge is limited, and humans are obliged to work. These limitations are, of course, not alien to the well-being of God's creatures but rather ordered to it—but this is no longer obvious to humans in their corrupted state, and they perpetually rebel against such limitations. Luther's method in reasserting the doctrine of creation from Scripture is to furnish an intelligible rationale for acquiescing to life within these constraints. He renders human finitude coherent as a beneficial condition rather than as a bondage to be escaped at all costs, and he explicates the ways in which attempting to live beyond the boundaries of human creatureliness has deleterious effects on human flourishing, both personally and socially. Therefore, constraints are not necessarily antithetical to human freedom and to be overcome, but may be gratefully accepted as salutary.

Just as the boundaries of human creatureliness enable liberty rather than threaten it, so God's commandments give human freedom its shape. Luther has been notoriously misinterpreted as antinomian for his emphasis on Christian freedom—but when this theme is encountered in his writings, it is also precisely when he outlines the way in which the Christian has been set free *to serve* his or her neighbour. It is *because* the Christian is perfectly free that he or she is free to be a servant of all. The interrelationship of divine command and human freedom is no longer conspicuous to fallen humans, who therefore interpose a multitude of qualifications between themselves and God's commands. Against attempts to shirk their force, Luther constantly prods his hearers to recognize the absolute character of God's commands, and in doing so to find true freedom. Confronting people with the exceptionless, unqualified character of the commandments is vital in order to challenge human self-deception and self-will, to oppose attempts to supplant them in favour of more manageable, self-chosen virtues.

As we have seen, this emphasis on their non-negotiability does not mean that Luther treats the commands as bare instructions. Rather than simply marking certain things as off limits, they set out a vision of reality—a space in which to live, which of course includes limits. With respect to temporal goods, this space is fundamentally characterized by a posture of letting go. One's attitude is almost one of passivity. Giving and lending freely to the needy are therefore seen in the context of this default: this posture is necessary to enable such actions, and they flow from it.

So, this chapter has explored the different steps in Luther's moral theological method as exemplified in his *Sermon von dem Wucher*, and this conclusion has identified a number of especially fertile areas of his thought. We will return to these areas, among others, in Chapter 3, when we bring this close engagement with Luther's method into interaction with the approach of Arthur Rich.

2

Arthur Rich's Moral Theological Method in His *Wirtschaftsethik*

This chapter will briefly outline some of the biographical, intellectual, and contextual features of Rich's work, much as we did at the outset of Chapter 1 on Luther. We will also indicate some of Rich's intellectual developments, which culminated in the publication of *Wirtschaftsethik*, the major work on which we have chosen to focus. We will then set out some of the main methodological lines in Arthur Rich's project, as a preliminary to discussing them critically in Chapter 3 in the light of the earlier discussion of Martin Luther. It will therefore be primarily descriptive rather than analytic, leaving more detailed analysis for our final chapter, although in places we will indicate in a preliminary fashion some of the points of key dialogue with Luther. The chapter will conclude with a summary of Rich's conclusions with respect to economic ethics, which will be a key piece of evidence for our claim in the following chapter, that Rich fails to live up to his own desire for a radical Christian ethic.

THE CONTEXT OF *WIRTSCHAFTSETHIK*

Born in the early years of the twentieth century, in his youth Arthur Rich (1910–92) spent several years working in industry as an apprentice and then a mechanic in a factory, during which time he encountered Marxism and became disgusted with the pietistic faith of his upbringing because of the way it failed to challenge social injustice.[1] He was delivered from this brief

[1] This section draws on several sources. The first is a biographical sketch appended to a collection of Rich's writings, published to celebrate his 60th birthday: 'Biographische Notizen', in Arthur Rich, *Aufrisse: Vorarbeiten zum sozialethischen Denken*, ed. Hans ten Doornkaat Koolman (Zürich: Zwingli Verlag, 1970), pp. 231–5. The second is an article by Rich's successor as Professor of Systematic Theology at Zürich, Theodor Strohm, 'Arthur Richs Bedeutung für die Wirtschafts- und Sozialethik: Aus Anlaß des 80 Geburtstags von Arthur Rich', *Zeitschrift für*

atheistic spell by reading the works of Leonhard Ragaz, in which he discovered that Christian faith and socialism need not be perfectly incompatible—that Christianity could be concerned with politics and with helping the oppressed.[2] He therefore became involved with religious socialism and resolved to study theology.[3] He studied at night school in order to qualify for entrance to university. He studied theology in Zürich, under Emil Brunner, and Paris, where he also studied Marx's early writings. Rich was greatly impressed by Brunner's desire not to condemn the world, but to engage with it as it actually is.[4] But he came to fear that this gives Brunner's ethics too conformist and conservative a flavour.[5]

During Rich's student years (1932–4) he edited a monthly newsletter entitled *Nie wieder Krieg*, although he was not a pacifist as such, and he vigorously opposed the Swiss fascist movement, especially its anti-Semitism.[6] At this stage he was heavily influenced by Karl Barth, as is later evident in his acute awareness of the political as well as the theological danger of confusing nature and grace, which led to a utopian and therefore totalitarian view of human history. Barth also inspired Rich's attempt to ground his social ethics Christologically. He returned to the Swiss canton of his birth (Schaffhausen) just before the Second World War, becoming a pastor in a Reformed village church near the German border. During this time he began a doctorate on the Swiss reformer Zwingli (1484–1531), and he took his first academic post as the principal of the teacher training college of Schaffhausen in 1947.[7]

Rich's *Habilitationsschrift* on Blaise Pascal (1623–62) was an attempt to resolve the nature–grace dialectic which he had encountered in Barth, using Pascal's notion of *les verités opposées*, that is, of antinomical truths which must nevertheless both be simultaneously affirmed, without seeking to resolve either into the other.[8] Having qualified as a university lecturer, in 1954

Evangelische Ethik 34 (1990), pp. 192–7. The third is Harold Tonks, *Faith, Hope and Decision-Making: The Kingdom of God and Social Policy-Making; The Work of Arthur Rich of Zürich* (Frankfurt am Main: Peter Lang, 1984), pp. 29–40. One of the few items published in English on Rich, this draws on personal interviews with Rich, and Rich's own unpublished autobiographical self-portrait (p. 39, n. 3).

2 Rich, 'Biographische Notizen', p. 232.

3 Rich's mature views on Ragaz and religious socialism are explored in much more detail in the section entitled 'How Near is the Kingdom of God? Eschatology as Rich's Key Theological Theme'.

4 See Arthur Rich, 'Denken, das weh tut', in *Emil Brunner in der Erinnerung seiner Schüler*, eds. Werner Kramer and Hugo Sonderegger (Zürich: Theologischer Verlag, 1989), pp. 78–82, esp. pp. 80–1.

5 See BEE, p. 145; Rich, *Wirtschaftsethik I*, p. 148.

6 Tonks, *Faith, Hope and Decision-Making*, p. 31.

7 His thesis on Zwingli is published as *Die Anfänge der Theologie Huldrych Zwinglis* (Zürich: Zwingli Verlag, 1949).

8 Published as *Pascals Bild vom Menschen: Eine Studie über die Dialektik von Natur und Gnade in den 'Pensées'* (Zürich: Zwingli Verlag, 1953).

Arthur Rich returned to Zürich, where he taught until his retirement in 1976, succeeding Brunner as Professor of Systematic Theology. There, he also founded and directed an Institute for Social Ethics, which aroused controversy for siding with the trade unions in matters such as employee representation in industry.[9] Yet he was sought after as a consultant on this matter to both employers and trade unions, evidence perhaps of the judicious and even-handed temperament which manifests itself in his writing, as we shall see. He served as President of the Societas Ethica from 1971 to 1975. After retirement he remained active in teaching and research, as is amply shown by the fact that both volumes of the key work with which we will concern ourselves were published several years after he retired.

In terms of his wider social and intellectual milieu, we should briefly mention some other points, which will be expanded further at pertinent junctures in our exploration of Rich's *Wirtschaftsethik*. Rich writes in a pluralist society, in which Christianity remains part of the social fabric, but is no longer the dominant moral model. If Christian moral claims are heeded at all, it will not usually be because of any a priori assumption of their authority, but because they are convincing and beneficial.

Next, in Rich's and our time, economics is widely regarded in primarily scientific terms. That is, it is a discipline of enquiry which proceeds (or which we tend to assume proceeds) according to the methodology of the natural sciences, in which facts are objectively gathered, and hypotheses tested against the evidence of empirical observation. In some quarters it would be axiomatic that there is no such thing as a moral economics, still less a Christian economics, any more than there can be a moral biology or Christian physics, because economics is a neutral analysis of the facts.[10]

Finally, Rich writes in an industrialized capitalist society which, over the last few centuries, has witnessed and experienced a phenomenal transformation in terms of agriculture, industrial production, and technology. Coupled with the stability of liberal democracy and the establishment of the welfare state, this seems to have enabled unprecedented, even exponential, increases in length and quality of life for the vast majority of people living in such a society.[11]

[9] This issue is addressed by Rich in detail in his book, *Mitbestimmung in der Industrie: Probleme—Modelle—Kritische Beurteilung; Eine sozialethische Orientierung* (Zürich: Flamberg, 1973).

[10] Thus James M. Dean and A. M. C. Waterman ridicule the notion of Christian, Islamic, or even an atheist economics by a *reductio ad absurdum*: it would be as meaningful as a 'Christian botany'. 'Introduction: Normative Social Theory', in *Religion and Economics: Normative Social Theory*, eds. James M. Dean and A. M. C. Waterman (Boston: Kluwer, 1999), pp. 3–9, esp. p. 4. Yet in the same volume John P. Tiemstra observes that a Christian literary criticism, biology, and economics are exactly what the Kuyperian tradition calls for. 'Every Square Inch: Kuyperian Social Theory and Economics', pp. 85–98, esp. p. 87.

[11] See, e.g., Tomas Sedlacek, *Economics of Good and Evil: The Quest for Economic Meaning from Gilgamesh to Wall Street*, trans. Douglas Arellanes (Oxford: Oxford University Press, 2011),

Of course, much about the exact details of these changes remains hotly debated, in historical, political, economic, and moral terms, as does much about their causes and consequences. But in terms of Rich's situation, and our own, there is remarkable consensus on the one hand around the benefits of free market capitalism with some regulation, and on the other around the benefits of liberal society and the welfare state. The debates, fierce as they can be, tend to cluster around *how much* protective regulation the market can stand without impeding the growth we need it to deliver; or *how* welfare should best be allocated without making people dependent on handouts or overburdening taxpayers and therefore impeding growth; or *what* forms of free speech are legitimate; rather than *whether* all these things should exist in the first place. Part of our reason for selecting Luther as our first dialogue partner is that he wrote prior to this state of affairs and the consensus it has generated, in order to give us a vantage point from which to study how Rich handles this situation.

We will explore much of this in greater detail as we go, but for now let us summarize it. From Marx, Rich got his concern for the poor and oppressed, a fierce opposition to fascism, and an acute sensitivity to the way in which religion can ratify and nourish oppressive social structures. In Ragaz, Rich discovered a far more radical Christianity, which embraced rather than resisted socialism.[12] Barth taught Rich the need to ground social ethics in Christology, and the danger of identifying aspects of human history with the will of God. From the Reformation thought of Zwingli Rich takes the unbridgeable gulf between divine and human justice.[13] And from Pascal, he learned about theological dialectic. This point is crucial since, rather than becoming a mass of contradictions, Rich attempted to hold what he learned from each thinker *in tension* with the truths he gleaned from the others. Indeed, this becomes a hallmark of his method.

It is this method that Rich uses to engage with his pluralist, scientific, social democratic, and capitalist context. So, to anticipate our later observations, Rich's work is effectively a highly nuanced apologetic for this existing state of affairs, combined with a plea for continuing incremental reform and improvement. It is tempting to regard this as a rather conformist conclusion, as if Rich has simply adopted the majority view within his context. But it is important to remember that Rich writes at a time when communism still exists, not just in the USSR but in East Germany and Eastern Europe. Rich's early fascination with Marx, which to some extent remained with him, could not possibly

pp. 48–9; John Gray, *False Dawn: the Delusions of Global Capitalism*, new edn. (London: Granta, 2002), pp. 1ff.

[12] The quest for Christian radicalism was to remain with Rich all his life, but later he comes to define it in a rather unadventurous way. See his essays in *Radikalität und Rechtsstaatlichkeit: Drei Beiträge zur politischen Ethik* (Zürich: Theologischer Verlag, 1978). He revisits this theme in the work we are particularly studying (BEE, pp. 188–9).

[13] See BEE, pp. 228–9; Rich, *Wirtschaftsethik I*, pp. 229–31.

excuse the horrific evils perpetrated in Marx's name and the abject failure of the command economy as an economic system. Of course, communism was becoming increasingly discredited, even among its former adherents, but for a time it had seemed, to some at least, that there were genuinely two economic systems to choose from. Therefore, even at this late hour in the life of communism, Rich senses the need to oppose it, while seeking to rescue the seeds of something legitimate from within it.[14] These seeds are important, because Rich is not starry-eyed about capitalism either, and he is concerned about some of what he regards as the consequences of the capitalist economy, such as mass unemployment, environmental destruction, and rising levels of inequality. Rich wants a third way.[15]

We have now briefly introduced Arthur Rich, and explored some aspects of his intellectual and social context that are relevant to understanding his economic ethical method. Our next task is therefore to study that method in depth, and to this we now turn for the rest of the chapter.

RICH'S DESCRIPTION OF HIS OWN PROJECT

Rich begins his *Wirtschaftsethik* with several typologies with respect to ethics. First, he explores various definitions of ethics: descriptive, normative, and metaethics (*Wirtschaftsethik I*, pp. 20–4). He locates and defends his own project as one of normative ethics. Then he catalogues several schools of thought within normative ethics, and locates his project within one of these: the ethics of responsibility. Next, in order to explicate the scope of his own project, he enumerates possible fields of normative ethical enquiry according to different personal relationships: *Individualethik*, the responsibility of individuals to look after themselves, *Personalethik* (with *personal* carrying the sense of 'interpersonal'), the unmediated relation of one individual to another, and *Umweltethik*, the ethics of one's action as it impinges on one's environment. However, Rich is not concerned with these relationships per se, but with

[14] So much so that Rich worried that the second volume of his work, in which he extensively discusses the failings of a planned economy, had appeared too late. See Georges Enderle, 'Introduction to Arthur Rich's *Business and Economic Ethics*', in Arthur Rich, *Business and Economic Ethics: The Ethics of Economic Systems*, pp. xv–xxiii, esp. p. xv. Indeed, one of Rich's reviewers makes precisely this point. Joachim Wiebering, 'Rezension zu «Arthur Richs Wirtschaftsethik II»', *Theologische Literaturzeitung* 117 (1992), pp. 60–2, esp. p. 60.

[15] Strohm, 'Arthur Richs Bedeutung für die Wirtschafts- und Sozialethik', p. 195. In Britain this language immediately conjures to mind Tony Blair and his intellectual mentor Anthony Giddens, as in Giddens's book, *The Third Way: The Renewal of Social Democracy* (Cambridge & Oxford: Polity & Blackwell, 1998). But for a fuller historical and wider European picture, see Steve Bastow and James Martin, *Third Way Discourse: European Ideologies in the Twentieth Century* (Edinburgh: Edinburgh University Press, 2003), esp. ch. 1.

social ethics, which he characterizes as these three relationships not in themselves, but as they are affected by the mediation of institutions. He then devotes a section in turn in consideration of each of these relationships as they are institutionally mediated, that is, in terms of social ethics. Finally, he characterizes his own work ('business and economic ethics') as a particular subsidiary of social ethics.[16]

This is representative of Rich's systematic, orderly method of enquiry. He begins not with his own convictions, but with the most generous imaginable field of enquiry, and, step by step, narrows his focus and pinpoints his own project within that field, defending his rationale at each stage. This careful structure perhaps partly serves to make his ample volume credible to those whose own academic pursuits are structured in a rigorous and scientific way.[17] As we shall see, Rich is acutely conscious of the ways in which the work of an ethicist (and especially a theologian) may not be recognized in a post-Enlightenment, liberal, and scientific context, where economics is regarded as an empirical sphere of research, and where moral judgements may be regarded as inappropriate intrusions.

These opening steps therefore open up the *space* for Rich's moral comment on economic structures: he acknowledges that his is not the only necessary intellectual endeavour, and does not seek to displace other legitimate disciplines of thought while establishing his own. Similarly, he later takes some care to defend the legitimacy of including theological convictions in a work on economic ethics, lest he be accused of smuggling unprovable dogmatic assumptions into a supposedly neutral field. Theological motifs, biblical citations, and the like are certainly present, although they play a noticeably muted role compared to Luther. A key question for us to explore will be whether the more subdued tone of Rich's convictions necessarily makes them less substantively determinative for the moral content of his project.

THE 'BASIC ETHICAL QUESTION' AND THE UNIVERSALITY OF THE MORAL EXPERIENCE

So, what *is* this moral content? Even before Rich has delineated these main schools of ethical thought, at the outset of the whole work he begins with a

[16] 'Business and economic ethics' is how the English edition renders the term *Wirtschaftsethik* throughout, in order to convey the pluripotential connotation of the German term *Wirtschaft*, which could be translated as 'the economy', 'business', 'commerce', or similar, depending on context.

[17] Cf. Georges Enderle, 'Buchbesprechung: Arthur Rich, *Wirtschaftsethik: Grundlagen in theologische Perspektive*', in *Zeitschrift für Philosophische Forschung* 40 (1986), pp. 652–4, esp. p. 653.

consideration of what he calls 'Die ethische Grundfrage'—the fundamental or basic ethical question.[18] Our study of Luther suggested that the seemingly trivial semantics of a discourse are worth noticing, and in this case the singularity of the article in this oft-repeated phrase of Rich's gives the impression that such a question is ubiquitous: there is *one* basic ethical question rather than a dizzying array of incompatible and competing ones. This observation will be substantiated further in what follows.[19]

First, we should ask what this fundamental moral question which confronts all people is. Rich locates it in the widely attested experience of the gap that can arise between moral conventions and what we might call the transcendent demands of justice. He explores this by recounting the derivation of the Greek term *ethos*. It originally meant one's 'usual seat', and thus connoted habit and convention. Eventually it thus came to refer to morality as it is customarily perceived. Yet, beginning with Socrates, another meaning was introduced:

> 'Ethos' in the sense of 'you shall', . . . in the sense of a categorical imperative, however, is of a totally different kind. This is ultimately about a demand to which one does not become accustomed by growing up in society, which seeks instead to call one out from the customary and, in contrast to merely conventional 'law', seeks to challenge one to a new manner of conduct.[20]

The result of this process is that 'ethos is opposed to ethos, that which *I should do* to that which *one does*'.[21] Like Luther, Rich firmly believes that one can encounter goodness through customary norms, but that there is also an external and absolute moral standard which may find such received morality severely wanting:

> The basic ethical question was characterized just now as the question about the good or the just, which is more than morals, more than customary law, and more than civic legality.[22]

So, Rich would seem eager to evaluate moral conventions in the light of this uncompromising standard, rather than assuming the adequacy of their existing stipulations.

[18] BEE, pp. 11–15; Rich, *Wirtschaftsethik I*, pp. 15–19.

[19] Elsewhere Rich is acutely aware that there exists a monumental throng of divergent ethical questions. As he puts it in a lecture delivered in 1978: 'Ethics is unlike mathematics, physics, and the natural sciences generally, where one can speak of a common foundation. There is rather a plurality of ethics, which are totally different even in their approaches to motivation'. Author's translation of Arthur Rich, 'Sozialethische Kriterien und Maximem humaner Gesellschaftsgestaltung', in *Religiöser Sozialismus und Wirtschaftsordnung*, eds. Siegfried Katterle and Arthur Rich (Gütersloh: Gerd Mohn, 1980), pp. 10–30, esp. p. 10. Yet for Rich, it seems that a plurality of *ethics* might be compatible with an underlying unity of a single ethical *question* and common *experience*, namely of the tension between conventional and absolute ethos, as we shall see.

[20] BEE, pp. 11–12; Rich, *Wirtschaftsethik I*, p. 16.

[21] BEE, pp. 11–12; Rich, *Wirtschaftsethik I*, p. 16.

[22] BEE, p. 14; Rich, *Wirtschaftsethik I*, p. 18.

Yet Rich is perturbed by a potential implication of this dualism of absolute and customary morality. He sees the dangers in assuming that customary moral standards are inviolable, and affirms that the good can never be simply identified with received moral wisdom. On the other hand, he is nervous of the revolutionary potency of *ethos* in its absolute sense. Because it is inherently nonconformist, the ethical is inherently dangerous and revolutionary:

> It is no coincidence that Socrates, the first person really to raise the fundamental ethical question, was suspected by his countrymen of being a subversive and was finally sentenced to death.[23]

Rich sympathizes, if not quite with those who found Socrates guilty, then at least with Socrates's refusal to escape his sentence. While a mindset that is healthily critical of convention should be encouraged, one must beware the grave danger of ethical absolutism, which may veer into 'contempt' towards customs and laws—even to 'nihilism of values or laws'.[24]

So, 'the fundamental ethical question' is plunged from the start into a dilemma. If the second sense of *ethos* became regarded as absolute, to the detriment of imperfect human laws, political society would plummet into anarchy. And so Rich draws back from identifying the nonconformist sense of *ethos* with the basic ethical question. Ethics, precisely in order to be ethical, must respect convention—lest it undermine the basis of social life and thus the very possibility of meaningful action.

Therefore, Rich regards the basic ethical question as 'two-dimensional'.[25] Society needs laws. So, instead of opposing the two senses of *ethos*, they must be brought into interaction. The ethical consists not in absolute goodness, nor in custom, but in their interrelation. It is obliged to balance demand for reform with respect for convention:

> Discussion of the fundamental ethical question is not only concerned with the critique of the relative before the demand of the absolute; it is also about holding onto the law of the relative during genuine interactions with the absolute, without trivializing or completely hiding the difference between the relative and the absolute.[26]

This is suggestive, but we will have to wait to see more precisely what this means for Rich's method.[27]

[23] BEE, p. 13; Rich, *Wirtschaftsethik I*, p. 17.
[24] BEE, p. 13; Rich, *Wirtschaftsethik I*, p. 17.
[25] BEE, p. 14; Rich, *Wirtschaftsethik I*, p. 18.
[26] BEE, p. 14; Rich, *Wirtschaftsethik I*, p. 18.
[27] For a different and somewhat playful discussion of the dual meanings of *ethos* see Hans G. Ulrich, 'On Finding Our Place: Christian Ethics in God's reality', *European Journal of Theology* xviii (2009), pp. 137–44, esp. pp. 139ff. Instead of the contrast posited by Rich between custom and absolute demand, Ulrich, himself a student of Luther, distinguishes *ethos* as 'what is undoubtedly obligatory on everybody' from *aethos* as 'context' or 'habitat', which for Christian

Rich's contention, then, is that there is a universal human moral experience, and that the content of this experience is one of bidimensionality: the confrontation between absolute demand and customary morality. As examples of thinkers who were aware of this conflict, he adduces Jesus, Pascal, Socrates, and Kant.[28] He substantiates this claim later in the book, in a section entitled 'The experience of the totally other' (*Die Erfahrung des ganz Anderen*), in which he takes Karl Marx as a dialogue partner.[29]

Marx perceived there was an ultimate good which entirely transcended the profound evil that he saw. He did not have any historical experience of such a good, yet he somehow knew it. Such knowledge by no means vindicates Marx's thought as a whole, and Rich roundly takes him to task for expounding this good in terms of an idolatrous historicist ideology which flies in the face of experience.[30] Yet, despite being ensnared by ideology, Marx expressed something 'which coincides closely with the experience of Christian faith'—namely, the absolutely other.[31] Although this *ganz Anderen* is only fully historically present in Christ, in Rich's view it is somehow also accessible to human perception in some other, less full measure—more inchoate, but universal. Marx is *aware* of it, although he mislocates it so severely in history. Yet it *is* somehow there, standing against the structural evil of which Marx was so dramatically aware as an alternative possibility for human (and thus historical) existence. The precise degree and character of this universal moral awareness in Rich's thought will be explored further in what follows, and will have significant bearing on his method.

We have observed, then, that Rich believes there is a universal human moral experience, namely that human customary morality is in tension with an absolute, transcendent standard. We shall see that, for Rich, this transcendent standard must be explicated and distilled from a Christian theological position, and brought into critical interaction with received moral wisdom. Thus Christian theology has a seemingly important role to play in its definition. Yet *the notion itself of this tension and interaction* is not derived theologically, at least here. It is a universal feature of human moral experience. We will return to this observation.

We have also expanded on an important connotation of Rich's phrase, 'Die ethische Grundfrage': the singular definite article signifies for Rich that this question is uniform and universal. It will clearly also have much bearing on

ethics must be one of worship and the world of the Scriptures. An absence of this 'habitat' will, Ulrich claims, make ethics quintessentially 'homeless', and doomed to the fruitless foundationalist quest to ground *itself* (p. 143)—a claim which we will have reason to believe is borne out in the case of Arthur Rich.

[28] BEE, pp. 12–13; Rich, *Wirtschaftsethik I*, pp. 15–16.

[29] BEE, pp. 109–16; Rich, *Wirtschaftsethik I*, pp. 116–22.

[30] BEE, pp. 111–12; Rich, *Wirtschaftsethik I*, pp. 117–18.

[31] BEE, p. 112; Rich, *Wirtschaftsethik I*, p. 119.

Rich's method that he characterizes morality as a *question*. His point of departure is one of *enquiry*, one of ignorance and exploration, not one of definitive knowledge. Furthermore, because the question is fundamentally to do with the tension between the absolute demands of justice and the necessity for imperfect human rules to offer concrete guidance, it is a 'question that one cannot pacify with any definitive answer'.[32] Thus this *universal* human moral question is a fundamentally *unanswerable* one.

THE MAIN SCHOOLS OF ETHICAL THOUGHT, AND RICH'S PREFERRED OPTION

As mentioned above, having defended the concept of normative ethics, Rich sets out a typology of the 'main schools of thought in normative ethics in their internal problematic': empiricist ethics, norm or principle ethics, casuistry, situation ethics, and something he calls *Gesinnungsethik* (translated as 'the ethics of conviction', but defined later by Rich as 'an ethics of inner motivation').[33] He elucidates what he regards as problematic features of each type, and sets out his preference, *Verantwortungsethik* (the ethics of responsibility), an ethical approach which takes its cue from a lecture by Max Weber, 'Politik als Beruf'.[34] The distinctive element in this approach is taking account of the concrete consequences of actions: '[The ethics of responsibility] requires, in the process of finding the normative, also *including the consequences* of an action or decision justified by it and *accepting responsibility* for it'.[35]

Rich dryly observes that it is no accident that Weber originated this notion precisely in the context of political and economic ethics, where the decision maker has a special duty to consider the consequences of his actions:

> If his actions lead to terrible political and social consequences, he cannot excuse himself simply by saying that his motives were good. That would amount to pure irresponsibility in the real world.[36]

Rich is particularly appreciative of the way in which Weber explicitly contrasts the ethics of responsibility with an irresponsible debasement of Christian ethics. In the former, 'one is answerable for the (foreseeable) consequences

[32] BEE, p. 15; Rich, *Wirtschaftsethik I*, p. 19.

[33] 'In conviction ethics it becomes a question of conviction and, therefore, of the *inner motivation of the agent*'. BEE, p. 30; Rich, *Wirtschaftsethik I*, p. 34.

[34] BEE, p. 32; Rich, *Wirtschaftsethik I*, p. 36. See Max Weber, 'The Profession and Vocation of Politics', in *Political Writings*, trans. and eds. Peter Lassman and Ronald Speirs (Cambridge: Cambridge University Press, 1994), pp. 309–69.

[35] BEE, p. 32; Rich, *Wirtschaftsethik I*, p. 36. Emphasis original.

[36] BEE, p. 32; Rich, *Wirtschaftsethik I*, p. 36.

of one's actions'.[37] In the latter, 'The Christian acts rightly and leaves the outcome to God'.[38] Intriguingly for our purpose of comparing Luther and Rich, Weber may well be referring to Luther here: 'Although an exact source for these words (used on several occasions by Weber) has not been traced, the editors of the new *Gesamtausgabe* [of Weber's works] believe they allude to a passage in Luther's lectures on Genesis'.[39] Indeed, commenting on Genesis 32:6–8, Luther declares, 'Do your duty and leave the outcome to God'.[40]

Rich's concern, following Weber, is that this approach all too easily sanctions the negative consequences of inaction or obstructs positive action for the sake of keeping rules, leading to resignation or a 'sterile long-term protest' which, since the world cannot be made perfect, gives up on improving the world as it actually is.[41] That is, Rich's argument against the possibility of absolute rules is based on the unavoidable imperfection of the world.[42] Therefore, 'the question of the normative status of an action cannot be considered in isolation from its consequences'.[43] Indeed, assessment of the consequences of action in the light of human imperfection must '*take priority*'.[44]

To anticipate at this juncture one potential point of critique, we might ask whether Weber's antithesis between politically responsible action which takes account of its consequences, and action which trusts in divine providence, is a false one. As Raymond Aron points out:

> Weber more or less confused two sets of antinomies: . . . that of *political action* with its necessary recourse to ways and means always dangerous, sometimes diabolical, and that of *Christian action* as suggested by the Sermon on the Mount . . . : on the other hand, the antinomy of *thoughtful decision*, taking account of the possible consequences of the decision, and *immediate irrevocable choice* without any consideration of possible consequences. These two antinomies do not entirely coincide.[45]

This false antithesis rests on an ignorance of the way in which the theological tradition has taken account of the importance of considering consequences precisely under the aegis of trust in God's good ordering of the world. Indeed,

[37] BEE, p. 33; Rich, *Wirtschaftsethik I*, pp. 36–7.

[38] BEE, p. 33; Rich, *Wirtschaftsethik I*, pp. 37.

[39] Weber, 'The Profession and Vocation of Politics', p. 359, n. 51.

[40] LW v. 6, p. 105; WA v. 44, p. 78, l. 14: 'Fac tuum officium, et eventum Deo permitte'.

[41] BEE, p. 33; Rich, *Wirtschaftsethik I*, p. 37.

[42] BEE, p. 33; Rich, *Wirtschaftsethik I*, p. 37. Of course, the religious form is not the only form this conviction-based ethic may take. Also in Weber's sights were Kantian ethics and Marxist revolution. Weber argued that adherents of the latter were willing to embrace all kinds of disastrous consequences in order to enact a point of principle ('Profession and Vocation of Politics', pp. 360–1).

[43] BEE, p. 33; Rich, *Wirtschaftsethik I*, p. 37.

[44] BEE, p. 33; Rich, *Wirtschaftsethik I*, p. 37.

[45] Raymond Aron, 'Max Weber and Power-politics', in *Max Weber and Sociology Today*, ed. Otto Stammer, trans. Kathleen Morris (Oxford: Blackwell, 1971), pp. 83–100, esp. p. 97.

in the case of Weber's probable quotation of Luther, it is illuminating to examine more precisely what Luther actually says. The verses on which he makes this comment can be found towards the beginning of the story of Jacob and Esau's *rapprochement*. They recount Jacob's response to the news of Esau's approach with 400 men. Luther's interpretation is that the Christian must not despair even when circumstances seem dire, but trust God to act on their behalf. Yet trust in an active God, he adds, must not be confused with a presumption that causes us to neglect our own actions. Hence Jacob acts quite rightly in dividing his people and animals so that at least one group will escape the expected attack. He neither despairs by assuming all is lost, nor presumes on God's protection by neglecting to take legitimate precautions. Similarly, the doctrine of predestination should not become a pretext for neglecting the duty to preach, on the misguided basis that those who are to be converted will be converted anyway. Luther concludes that it is our duty to act, making use of the means God has given us, but to entrust the results to him.

THE SOURCE OF RICH'S METHOD IN THE THOUGHT OF MAX WEBER

It is worth pausing to consider Weber's thought more carefully, in order to discern how it has shaped Rich's method. It is not that Rich has adopted Weber's thinking as a whole, and there are points at which they diverge (as we shall see in our discussion of objectivity and value-neutrality in economics). It is Weber's *method* of ethical reasoning that Rich adopts, namely the ethics of responsibility, so it is important to understand Weber's method. *Verantwortungsethik* proceeds from a number of dimensions of Weber's thought.

First, although of course it is possible to overdraw Weber's pessimism, the vision of politics which he asserted against communists and others whom he regarded as naïve utopians is certainly a tragic and agonistic one.[46] Political and economic life necessarily takes the form of the struggle (*Kampf*) of self-interested parties for power.[47] Responsibility involves the clear-eyed recognition that one 'has no right . . . to presuppose goodness and perfection in human beings'.[48] Objective religious and moral interpretations of reality have, over centuries, been rationalized away, which is inimical to morality: 'the disenchanted world . . . creates conditions alien to brotherliness'.[49] Weber's solution

46 See, for example, Weber, 'Profession and Vocation of Politics', pp. 354–5.

47 Weber, 'Profession and Vocation of Politics', pp. 311, 330, 334.

48 Weber, 'Profession and Vocation of Politics', p. 360.

49 See Wolfgang Schluchter, 'The Paradox of Rationalization: On the Relation of Ethics and World', trans. Guenther Roth in *Max Weber's Vision of History*, eds. Guenther Roth and Wolfgang Schluchter (Berkeley: California University Press, 1979), pp. 11–64, esp. p. 55.

to this disenchantment is for the individual to take responsibility themselves, which Wolfgang Schluchter describes as the need for 'conscious world mastery'.[50] One cannot appeal to a transcendent source of moral meaning because there is none, and no absolute universal standard against which the competing claims of nations may be measured and adjudicated.[51] Such claims, where they conflict, must be settled by force.[52]

Second, actions might flow from quite legitimate values, but there are other values which are *equally legitimate*, but which *cannot be reconciled* with them.[53] Different values may be equally valid and meaningful, but may be simultaneously opposed to one another:

> The unified Christian value cosmos has been dissolved into a new polytheism.... There is irreconcilable conflict among the individual value levels and the different value spheres. The result is a value antagonism whose different positions are engaged in an 'irreconcilable deadly struggle' as 'between God and the Devil'.[54]

Indeed, even 'morality itself [is] one sphere of values among others'.[55] This is why political action is highly liable to produce unintended and profoundly unwelcome outcomes:

> It is a fundamental fact of history... that the eventual outcome of political action frequently, indeed regularly, stands in a quite inadequate, even paradoxical relation to its original, intended meaning and purpose [*Sinn*].[56]

In the perpetual conflict between values, what produces success according to one value may produce disaster according to another, although both are held with equal sincerity and conviction by the *same* politician.[57] This is the tragedy of political reality. Yet this value pluralism, to the point of value antagonism, is necessary: 'tensions between competing values are essential in order to prevent cultural stagnation'.[58] This meant that Weber believed that the struggle for success between nations was a crucial factor in their prosperity

[50] Schluchter, 'The Paradox of Rationalization', p. 58.

[51] Aron, 'Weber and Power-politics', p. 95.

[52] Peter Lassman and Ronald Speirs, 'Introduction', in *Max Weber: Political Writings*, eds. Peter Lassman and Ronald Speirs (Cambridge: Cambridge University Press, 1994), pp. vii–xxv, esp. pp. xiv–xv.

[53] See Max Weber, 'The Meaning of "Ethical Neutrality" in Sociology and Economics', in *The Methodology of the Social Sciences*, trans. and eds. Edward A. Shils and Henry A. Finch (Glencoe: Free Press, 1949), pp. 1–47, esp. pp. 17–18.

[54] Wolfgang Schluchter, 'Value-Neutrality and the Ethic of Responsibility', trans. Guenther Roth in *Max Weber's Vision of History*, eds. Guenther Roth and Wolfgang Schluchter (Berkeley: California University Press, 1979), pp. 65–116, esp. pp. 78–9.

[55] Aron, 'Weber and Power-politics', p. 94.

[56] Weber, 'The Profession and Vocation of Politics', p. 355.

[57] Hans Henrik Bruun, *Science, Values and Politics in Max Weber's Methodology*, new edn. (Aldershot: Ashgate, 2007), p. 53.

[58] Lassman and Speirs, 'Introduction', p. xviii.

and inner dignity.[59] This is why, for Weber, 'a thing can be beautiful not *although* but *because* it is evil'.[60] Even the tragic features of life can be harnessed to produce beneficial consequences such as nobility, eminence, and beauty. Indeed, the economic struggle was part of the contest for national supremacy, which Weber expresses as follows:

> We do not have peace and human happiness to hand down to our descendants, but rather the *eternal struggle* to preserve and raise the quality of our national species. Nor should we indulge in the optimistic expectation that we shall have completed our task once we have made our economic culture as advanced as it can be.... Our successors will hold us answerable to history... for the amount of elbow-room in the world which we conquer and bequeath to them.[61]

The politician absolutely must recognize and take account of this state of affairs, however uncomfortable. He must be willing to incur guilt and to go against his own conscience, if circumstances require.[62] The ethic of responsibility is thus not a resolution of the value conflict, since there is no objective resolution to it. It is a way of arriving at the best-case scenario, an exercise in damage limitation:

> The ethic of responsibility can effect a reconciliation neither among the various value positions and reality nor among the different values themselves. It can only establish the preconditions for facing up to the oppositions and for arranging a rational confrontation.[63]

It is therefore not sufficient to take principles alone into account when deciding on a course of action. It is not that a politician must entirely forego principles, lest politics be plunged into nihilistic despair and cynical self-service.[64] But what those principles are seems a matter of indifference to Weber. What matters is that the politician has some:

> He may be sustained by a strong faith in 'progress'... or he may coolly reject this kind of faith; he can claim to be the servant of an 'idea' or, rejecting on principle any such aspirations, he may claim to serve external goals of everyday life—but some kind of belief must always be *present*.[65]

59 See Wolfgang J. Mommsen 'The Antinomical Structure of Max Weber's Political Thought', in Wolfgang J. Mommsen, *The Political and Social Theory of Max Weber* (Cambridge: Polity, 1989), pp. 24–43, esp. p. 25.

60 Mommsen 'The Antinomical Structure of Max Weber's Political Thought', p. 25. This is a sentiment lifted directly from Nietzsche. See Bruun, *Science, Values and Politics*, pp. 39ff.

61 Weber, 'The Nation State and Economic Policy', p. 16. Emphasis original.

62 Weber, 'The Nation State and Economic Policy', p. 54.

63 Schluchter, 'The Paradox of Rationalization', p. 59.

64 Weber, 'The Profession and Vocation of Politics', pp. 354–5.

65 Weber, 'The Profession and Vocation of Politics', p. 355. Emphasis original.

But Weber equally warns against the politician who allows their principles to reign supreme, regardless of consequences. He foresees that principled conviction, if followed absolutely, can bring calamity. Therefore, how to *balance* conviction and responsibility, principles and consequences, is the essence of political judgement and the heart of political vocation for Weber.[66] This *is* the ethics of responsibility. The politician must, 'seek to reconcile, as best he can, the demands of principle and the likely consequences'.[67]

The goal of a Weberian politician is therefore an *optimization* of values within the constraints of the consequences of one's actions. As Weber scholar Wolfgang Mommsen puts it:

> Ethics deriving from a sense of responsibility... require the constant weighing-up of the possible consequences of one's actions, with a view to the optimal possible realization of whatever ideal values one has, and if necessary employing the rational knowledge available to the actor about their possible consequences or their unintentional side-effects.[68]

Optimization, then, means acting to secure the maximum possible realization of justice (or whichever value) in the circumstances, without the consequences of the course of action undermining that value more than the consequences which realize it. It is an equilibrium of values and rational efficiency which refuses to elevate either above the other. This *strategy* based on values and rationality is what matters. It is the heart of the political-ethical vocation for Weber.

It is not that Weber considers this approach applicable to all persons. Rather, it is pertinent to those who bear public office. Indeed, immediately prior to propounding his notion of *Verantwortungsethik*, Weber explicitly contrasts political ethics with the Sermon on the Mount. This is particularly intriguing for our purposes, given the importance of this text to Luther's method. For Weber, the two are mutually exclusive. Either one may live wholeheartedly by the Sermon on the Mount, and try to be a saint, or one may be involved in politics. It is not possible to do both: 'we must accept [the Sermon on the Mount] in its entirety *or* leave it entirely alone'.[69] It is not that Weber is opposed to the ethics of the Sermon on the Mount, or that its adoption in the political sphere would be recklessly irresponsible (although it would), but because he respects it so much that he wants to safeguard its purity:

[66] Bruun, *Science, Values and Politics*, p. 272.

[67] Lassman and Speirs, 'Introduction', p. xxiii.

[68] Wolfgang J. Mommsen, 'Politics and Scholarship: The Two Icons in Max Weber's Life', in Wolfgang J. Mommsen, *The Political and Social Theory of Max Weber* (Cambridge: Polity, 1989), pp. 3–23, esp. p. 19.

[69] Weber, 'The Profession and Vocation of Politics', p. 358.

> It is not to be taken frivolously.... It is not a hired cab which one may stop at will and climb into or out of as one sees fit. Rather, the meaning of the sermon (if it is not to be reduced to banality) is precisely this: we must accept it in its entirety *or* leave it entirely alone.[70]

The impossibility of fusing the Sermon on the Mount with responsible political ethics for Weber is particularly noticeable in relation to Luther's method of deriving economic ethics from it very directly. If Weber is correct about this incommensurability, one question we shall have to put to Rich is whether it can be coherent for a Christian to adopt the ethics of responsibility.

RICH'S CONCEPT OF SOCIAL ETHICS

We are now in a position to make some connections between aspects of our study. Rich begins with the contention that the universal, fundamental moral question is how one is to mediate between the absolute demands of justice and the inherently flawed possibilities of its formulation in human history. Weber provides Rich with his core methodological *strategy* in response to this question, namely that one cannot act according to a set of pre-prescribed norms, or out of a noble and righteous motivation. Rather, the consideration of the possible consequences of actions must play a vital role in social-ethical deliberation, in order to optimize the realization of values. It is to this social-ethical dimension which we shall now turn in our exposition of Rich's method.

Rich's work is unabashedly social ethics. Not that he claims other aspects of ethics to be unimportant; merely that he leaves them aside. As we have seen, Rich defines social ethics as the ethics of relationships as they are affected by and exist through the mediation of institutions. Relationships have individual, unmediated aspects (as in a friendship between two persons), and mediated aspects (as in the relationship between employee and manager in a workplace, or between members of a political society). Social ethics is concerned with the latter:

> Social ethics ... is the theory and practice of the responsible existence of human persons in relation to their fellow human beings and to the environment, in so far as this relation does not have a direct character but is instead mediated by social institutions.[71]

The basic question of social ethics is therefore *how institutions should be structured.*

[70] Weber, 'The Profession and Vocation of Politics', p. 358.
[71] BEE, p. 65; Rich, *Wirtschaftsethik I*, p. 71.

It is worth considering why Rich is particularly concerned about social ethics. It stems from a healthy concern to guard against indifference towards those with whom one has no direct, unmediated relationship. That is, it is readily conceivable that one might seek to evade one's duty to care for certain others under the pretence that they are not one's responsibility. Rich counters that

> the human person . . . is also responsible, in so far as he is indirectly affected in all of that [that is, other people and the environment] by the structures of the social institutions within which his life concretely takes place.[72]

The inelegant English here ('affected in all of that') reflects the translation difficulty in giving the exact sense of 'betroffen wird', which could perhaps be better rendered as, 'is touched by'. For Rich, the fact that people are *affected by* their surroundings seems to mean that they are *responsible* for them. The individual may on the one hand be constrained by the society in which they live, but they cannot shrug off responsibility for the consequences which that society produces:

> We cannot simply talk our way out of [responsibility for social injustice] by saying that it has to do with a *force majeure* that transcends the realm of human responsibility.[73]

Why cannot one excuse social or structural injustice this way? According to Rich, the forces which condition us may seem permanent and inevitable, but are ultimately the outcome of particular human actions, however manifold and collective they may be. That is, it is possible to change the behaviour of societies and not just individuals. Next, some matters (such as environmental breakdown) can only really be adequately addressed collectively, due to the enormity of their scale and significance. To neglect a collective remedy would amount to 'a self-castration of the ethical'.[74]

Furthermore, the structures of human society are not only shaped by human action, but in turn themselves affect it, to the point where, Rich claims, unjust social structures can actually eliminate the possibility of an individual acting ethically. He gives the example of a conscientious manager who assiduously endeavours to treat his workers well, but who is prevented from doing so because 'the corporate structures are authoritarian and notoriously thwart his good will'.[75] It is important to emphasize the strength

72 BEE, p. 52; Rich, *Wirtschaftsethik I*, p. 57.

73 BEE, p. 53; Rich, *Wirtschaftsethik I*, p. 57.

74 BEE, p. 59; Rich, *Wirtschaftsethik I*, p. 63.

75 BEE, p. 60; Rich, *Wirtschaftsethik I*, p. 65. Elsewhere, he claims that questions of individual conduct are 'meaningless' (*sinnlos*) unless the social structures permit responsible individual action. In an ultra-competitive economy, an entrepreneur would either be driven to compete by making life difficult for his or her workers, or give up. Both courses of action are irresponsible (BEE, p. 645; Rich, *Wirtschaftsethik II*, p. 369).

of Rich's claim here: he is not stating the truism that social structures may *hinder* right action, but arguing that they can generate circumstances in which it is no longer a coherent possibility—another reason why social ethics in particular is fraught with such a tragic dimension for Rich, as we have already seen. Thus, for example, 'someone affected by self-alienation in work can only cope with his fate in terms of individual ethics . . . when structures of production are developed through which work can be humanized'.[76]

Similarly, calling on an individual to act in an environmentally responsible manner will only 'really make sense' if the economy as a whole has been ordered in such a way first.[77] Indirect, mediated forms of relationships have a far greater impact, quantitatively, than direct ones; it is they which 'actually determine the quality of our existence and, therefore, are of crucial importance'.[78] Therefore it is crucial that 'the human person himself is responsible for the institutional ordering of his society and, therefore, must also accept responsibility collectively for its structural consequences on individual, personal and environmental behaviour'.[79]

So, although individual ethics clearly matters, because institutional structures have such a dramatic effect on human behaviour and conditions, social ethics is in a sense the senior partner. Social ethics is for Rich the location of the *integration* of human responsibility, because good social structural conditions promote good individual behaviour: 'Human responsibility is integrated into a whole only in social ethics understood in this sense'.[80] That is, individual ethics must be integrated *into* social ethics: 'the ethics of the immediate must integrate itself into the ethics of the mediate'.[81] Social ethics is the matrix from which individual ethics is to derive its significance and coherence: 'Thus, it can be said . . . that "*all* ethics is finally and ultimately 'social' ethics"'.[82]

[76] BEE, pp. 60–1; Rich, *Wirtschaftsethik I*, p. 66.
[77] BEE, p. 61; Rich, *Wirtschaftsethik I*, p. 66.
[78] BEE p. 58; Rich, *Wirtschaftsethik I*, p. 63.
[79] BEE, p. 53; Rich, *Wirtschaftsethik I*, p. 58.
[80] BEE, p. 53; Rich, *Wirtschaftsethik I*, p. 58.
[81] BEE, p. 59; Rich, *Wirtschaftsethik I*, p. 63.
[82] BEE, p. 61; Rich, *Wirtschaftsethik I*, p. 67. Rich is here quoting Heinz-Dietrich Wendland, *Einführung in die Sozialethik* (Berlin: de Gruyter, 1971), p. 7. Emphasis Wendland's. Rich has much in common with Wendland in several areas. For a summary in English of his thought, see H. D. Wendland, 'The Theology of the Responsible Society', in *Christian Social Ethics in a Changing World: An Ecumenical Theological Enquiry*, ed. John C. Bennett (New York: Association Press, 1966), pp. 135–52. For further analysis, see Carl-Henric Grenholm, *Christian Social Ethics in a Revolutionary Age: An Analysis of the Social Ethics of John C. Bennett, Heinz-Dietrich Wendland and Richard Shaull* (Uppsala: Verbum, 1973), esp. ch. 3.

ECONOMICS WITHIN ETHICS

Having set out his methodological strategy of value optimization, it is logical enough for Rich to consider exactly *how* one is to take consequences into account in ethical reasoning. That is, what is the relationship between social ethics and the social sciences, that group of academic disciplines to which one might look for social analysis and thus for predictions as to the possible outcomes of political decisions?

Naturally, in order to honour the methodological arguments he has set out so far, Rich must place a strong emphasis on empirically accessible, objective data regarding economic outcomes. This is accordingly the subject of his next chapter. At the same time, he must address the question on a seemingly different front: how can theological ethics play a role in social-scientific reasoning, given the assumption of some that particular moral convictions should not play a role in its discourse, lest they cloud its proper neutrality and therefore render it useless precisely as an empirical science?

Of course, it is no coincidence that it was Weber who advocated the ethics of responsibility, and Weber who advocated the ethical neutrality of sociology.[83] In entering the world of the ethics of responsibility, with its rejection of the ethics of pure *Gesinnung* (conviction), Rich has entered a world in which moral convictions, like any values, cannot be regarded as absolute:

> Since the time of Max Weber there has been a prevailing tendency in the social sciences to divorce social scientific-correctness from human justice, in order to make it (as much as possible) 'value-free.' That is, I believe, correct up to a point.[84]

Yet Rich also defends a continuing interrelationship of ethics and social science. Indeed, he detects within Weber's thought a resource to overcome their alienation: by holding values in tension with one another one can preserve the integrity of each. Thus Rich concludes that one should subordinate neither ethics to economics, nor economics to ethics—that truly would separate the two spheres. What he seeks is a 'methodological reconciliation of economic rationality and ethical reason'.[85] Whether Rich succeeds in this will be addressed in Chapter 3.

[83] Unsurprisingly, the relationship between Weber and *Wertfreiheit* is rather hotly debated. See Paul Oslington, 'Review, *Divine Economy: Theology and the Market* by D. Stephen Long', *Journal of Markets and Morality* 4.1 (Spring 2001), pp. 136–41, esp. p. 138. For a broader analysis of the concept's history, see Douglas Vickers, *Economics and Ethics: An Introduction to Theory, Institutions, and Policy* (Westport, CT: Praeger, 1997), pp. 62ff. For a discussion of Weber and value-freedom, see Talcott Parsons 'Value-freedom and Objectivity', in *Max Weber and Sociology Today*, ed. Otto Stammer, trans. Kathleen Morris (Oxford: Blackwell, 1971), pp. 27–50.

[84] BEE, p. 67; Rich, *Wirtschaftsethik I*, p. 73.

[85] BEE, p. 432; Rich, *Wirtschaftsethik II*, p. 173.

In any case, Rich begins with a ringing endorsement of the importance of the empirical work of economics: social ethics requires the *support* of social-scientific expertise.[86] In order to *be* social ethics, it must take into account predictions regarding the likely consequences of particular actions. Rich introduces a genial analogy here, that of building a bridge.[87] Scientific methods of construction are entirely empirical and, in one sense, morally neutral. Yet to neglect the objective laws of engineering would be irresponsible and dangerous. Scientific ignorance in this case would be morally indefensible. Responsible action must therefore be scientifically correct, because 'scientifically incorrect conduct . . . would be directed ultimately against human persons, and consequently, against human justice'.[88]

So, justice that is divorced from reality is not really justice. Yet the opposite is also true—supposed economic 'facts' which are opposed to justice cannot really be true in the deepest sense. Rich summarizes this in the following dictum: 'That which is not economically rational cannot really be humanly just; and that which conflicts with human justice cannot really be economically rational'.[89] The key term here, *das Sachgemäß*, has, as Georges Enderle points out,

> no precise equivalent in English. Literally it says, 'in accordance with the matter'. It means what is 'objectively' required, based on theoretical knowledge and/or practical expertise of the field of the application of ethics.[90]

Thus the term is usually rendered by the translators as 'the economically rational'.[91] As Rich later expresses it, economic reality has the 'right of the operational'.[92] It is the objectively discerned means by which economic ethical goals are to be accomplished. The importance of this for Rich can be seen by comparing his list of 'criteria for human justice' (a concept we will explore further in this section) as found in *Wirtschaftsethik I*, to those which appear in his earlier work. In the earlier iterations, a commitment to 'economic rationality', or 'faithfulness to the facts', was one criterion among many.[93] In *Wirtschaftsethik*, it has become a governing principle which supervises and permeates the others.

An example will help. Rich believes that the fundamental purpose of the economy is 'service to life' (*Lebensdienlichkeit*). It follows that efficiency is an essential feature of a just economy, since efficiency serves life better than

86 BEE, pp. 65–6; Rich, *Wirtschaftsethik I*, p. 72.
87 BEE, p. 70; Rich, *Wirtschaftsethik I*, p. 76.
88 BEE, p. 70; Rich, *Wirtschaftsethik I*, p. 76.
89 BEE, pp. 74–5; Rich, *Wirtschaftsethik I*, p. 81.
90 Enderle, 'Introduction to Arthur Rich's *Business and Economic Ethics*', p. xvi.
91 Enderle, 'Introduction to Arthur Rich's *Business and Economic Ethics*', p. xvii.
92 BEE, p. 433; Rich, *Wirtschaftsethik II*, p. 174.
93 For example, in Rich, *Mitbestimmung in der Industrie*, pp. 59–61.

inefficiency.[94] Competition is therefore beneficial to justice, because it acts as a stimulus to efficiency.[95] A business must make a profit, else it cannot give people worthwhile work or pay them a fair wage.[96] That is, an economy must be effective *qua* economy in order to be just. Justice should not be sacrificed for economic expediency, but neither should economic necessity be ignored in the name of justice: that would make it unjust.

Taking into account an economic necessity (such as efficiency or profit) and its corollaries (such as competition) is thus not a concession, but is *constitutive* of human justice:

> Conversely, human justice is also to be understood in such a way that it takes into account objective necessity in the economy, which is not simply identified with so-called inherent constraints, and to which economic efficiency belongs.[97]

Hence, as we have said, economic ethics must be economically sound in order to be authentically ethical. Indeed, the term Rich uses to denote justice is *das Menschengerechte*, human justice: not justice in some pure, abstract sense, but, as Georges Enderle has it, 'to do justice to humanity'.[98] Just action is action that *corresponds* to humanity, to the way that humans actually *are*, which includes economic requisites as much as it encompasses high-minded moral verities. Thus, to take an example from later in the book, Rich argues that employees must be treated as responsible subjects rather than the means of production analogous to raw material or machines, since responsible subjects are what they *are*.[99]

Rich later offers a theological explanation of this, drawing on the notion of *agape* love. For him, it is the nature of *agape* to be conversant with the world as it is, rather than as one might prefer it to be, because real love loves humanity in its fallen, decidedly non-ideal condition. Only in this way can *agape* make a genuine difference to the real world: 'Someone who flees from the present will be incapable of true love'.[100] The alternative is an escape into utopian fantasy which, although its contemplation is more pleasant, will not actually improve anyone's lives:

[94] BEE, p. 398; Rich, *Wirtschaftsethik II*, p. 140.

[95] BEE, p. 72; Rich, *Wirtschaftsethik I*, p. 78.

[96] One must bear in mind the Aristotelian distinction between an end which is a means to something else and an end which is an end in itself. So, one might regard an economic end (e.g. human prosperity and material well-being) as a final end in itself—or one might recognize that even this end should in fact in a sense be a means to something else: virtue, obedience to God, eternal life. According to Rich, the 'fundamental purpose' of the economy is the service of human life and the meeting of human needs. See BEE, pp. 275–7.

[97] BEE, p. 399; Rich, *Wirtschaftsethik II*, p. 142.

[98] Enderle, 'Introduction', p. xvi.

[99] BEE, p. 595; Rich, *Wirtschaftsethik II*, p. 323.

[100] BEE, p. 101; Rich, *Wirtschaftsethik I*, p. 107.

> What he is then capable of loving is at most an idealized picture of the human person, not the human person as he presently is.... This genuine person is instead abandoned.... Genuine love, however, always has to do with the present, actual person, who is not at all ideal, but rather is often enough repulsive.[101]

Thus, while at times it will be necessary to insist that love has its own rationality which transcends common sense and overly cautious prudence, one must not throw out reason altogether since at other times, 'the deeper love is found in reason'.[102]

This point is elsewhere accredited by a reading of Philippians 1:9–10, in which Paul speaks of his prayer that his readers' *agape* would increase in knowledge (*epignosis*) and insight (*aisthesis*), to the end that 'you may be able to discern what is best'.[103] Clearly, love and knowledge need not be antithetical, although it may be stretching Paul's point to read knowledge in this context as technical investigation of facts and probabilities. Yet, for Rich, in the final analysis love does not play a role in social-ethical decision making:

> The criterion here... is not *agape*-love itself (which should be heeded precisely, because otherwise the danger of a social-ethical utopia would be evoked). It is, rather, the critical authority, which, according to its own criteria of course, must examine critically what in given situations, conditions and processes best understands how to satisfy the demands of the humanly just and what for that reason matters in the formation of ethical judgement and decision.[104]

Thus, we discover, it is the very nature of love to be self-effacing as a criterion of action. *Agape* bows out graciously, ceding centre stage to 'die kritische Instanz'. An English equivalent for this is hard to find: the translators give us the slightly vague 'critical authority'. *Die Instanz* can indeed refer to an authority, but the context suggests more the connotation of a court, so perhaps the best rendering is 'critical judgement'.[105] In any case, what is striking is that this critical process of judgement is to take place ostensibly without being formed in detail by *agape*, lest it descend into utopianism. As Rich says, this critical judgement functions 'according to its own criteria'.

Yet as we have seen, Rich's dictum is intended to cut both ways. Economics cannot be *subordinate* to ethics. But neither may ethics become a 'mere supplementary function in its relation to economics'.[106] It must remain genuinely

[101] BEE, p. 101; Rich, *Wirtschaftsethik I*, p. 107.

[102] BEE, p. 122; Rich, *Wirtschaftsethik I*, p. 128.

[103] BEE, pp. 165–6; Rich, *Wirtschaftsethik I*, pp. 168–9. See also Tonks's discussion in *Faith, Hope and Decision-Making*, pp. 228–35.

[104] BEE, pp. 165–6; Rich, *Wirtschaftsethik I*, pp. 168–9.

[105] This is borne out by the fact that Rich likens it to the biblical Greek term *kritēs* (judge) in BEE, p. 166, n. 90; Rich, *Wirtschaftsethik I*, p. 168. See Friedrich Büchsel '*Κριτής*', in *Theological Dictionary of the New Testament*, eds. G. Kittel and G. Friedrich, trans. Geoffrey W. Bromiley (Grand Rapids: Eerdmans, 1964–76, repr. 2006), v. 3, pp. 942–3.

[106] BEE, p. 431; Rich, *Wirtschaftsethik II*, p. 172.

normative. Economic science cannot provide moral principles—so it cannot exclude an ethical dimension which is, in a sense, not inherent to itself.[107]

This means that Rich by no means advocates a naïve and uncritical attitude towards claims made by economic science. He wants to uphold the laws of economic science as analogous to the laws of sound construction in objectivity and accuracy, yet remain sensitive to the possibility of their masking injustice. If social structures are purely scientific, the discipline of social ethics is entirely unnecessary. Yet earlier he emphasized the responsibility of humans for their social structures. Hence he affirms, on the one hand, 'the economy . . . is an historical, cultural product'.[108] An economy is a human creation and as such under our control. At the same time, some features of economic life 'are economic necessities related to the rational structure of man and his economic activities'.[109] Elsewhere he says they are 'factual necessities . . . similar to natural laws'.[110] Hence they *cannot* be opposed to justice, although Rich is quick to point out that while this may be true of laws such as efficiency and competition *in themselves*, it is by no means true of 'every form' of them.[111] Rich therefore draws a distinction between *die Sachnotwendigkeiten*, which are the given necessities of a case that cannot be overcome, and *die Sachzwängen*, which he defines as practical constraints that are contingent and circumstantial. The latter must not be invoked as a camouflage for remediable injustices: 'one must distinguish between genuine and merely putative economic laws'.[112]

So, some aspects of a given economy are objectively determined, others are mutable. But the fact that these latter are historically and not naturally conditioned does not mean that they are easily altered: the experience of the economy as an 'objective force' (*sachliche Gewalt*), which constrains actions within very narrow limits, is a familiar one.[113] Yet this objectivity 'is of a kind different in principle from the objectivity of natural laws'.[114] It is not a natural but a historical law—a law in the sense that it compels humans, but not in the sense that it is absolute. Hence, although it may not be easy, it may be morally imperative to change such laws.[115]

Thus, for example, there is all the difference in the world between the objective necessity of profit as a gauge of and healthy stimulus to efficiency and competition (which *cannot* contradict human justice), and an insatiable

[107] BEE, p. 66; Rich, *Wirtschaftsethik I*, p. 73.
[108] BEE, p. 71; Rich, *Wirtschaftsethik I*, p. 77.
[109] BEE, p. 72; Rich, *Wirtschaftsethik I*, p. 79.
[110] BEE, p. 646; Rich, *Wirtschaftsethik II*, p. 369.
[111] BEE, p. 73; Rich, *Wirtschaftsethik I*, p. 79.
[112] BEE, p. 74; Rich, *Wirtschaftsethik I*, p. 80. See Theodor Dieter, 'Fundamentals of the Economic Ethics of Arthur Rich', in *Worship and Ethics: Lutherans and Anglicans in Dialogue*, eds. Oswald Bayer and Alan Suggate (Berlin: de Gruyter, 1996), pp. 202–31, esp. p. 207.
[113] BEE, p. 71; Rich, *Wirtschaftsethik I*, p. 77.
[114] BEE, p. 71; Rich, *Wirtschaftsethik I*, p. 77.
[115] BEE, pp. 73–4; Rich, *Wirtschaftsethik I*, pp. 79–80.

lust for acquisition coupled with an aggressive drive for market dominance and the annihilation of one's competitors (which will *always* contradict human justice). Of course, the cult of materialism may disguise itself as economic rationality.[116] But precisely in its injustice, such an economy would be by definition *irrational*: an unjust economy must be questioned on the grounds of economic as much as of moral correctness since it will, in the long run, self-destruct.[117] Insofar as an economy is just, it will also be rational, and vice versa.

Thus, while Rich has carefully stated the case for the partition of economic rationality and social ethics (in order to preserve the integrity of each), at the same time the two remain in an interrelationship of the utmost proximity. Just as economic justice includes economic necessities such as competition and efficiency, so the notion of economic reason encompasses that which is in accordance with justice, since for Rich the very purpose of the economy, from which its rationality is derived, includes humane, social, and ecological considerations.[118] Hence, as we have said, Rich speaks of a *reconciliation* between ethics and economics.

Thus we have highlighted two key moves of Rich's here: his definition of the relationship between the disciplines of ethics and economics; and his distinction between objective economic necessities (natural laws, which social ethics must accept), and contingent historical instantiations of these natural laws (which only *seem* fixed). If social ethics deems these latter to be unjust, it may call for their alteration, although of course the question of whether one should attempt to alter them would clearly be one for the ethics of responsibility, given Rich's caution regarding the potential for such changes to produce graver injury than they inflict. Therefore, the following question must be put to Rich in Chapter 3: how often is injustice actually strong enough to outweigh the potential negative consequences of overturning established historical laws?

So, we have seen how Rich defends the role of economic facts in social ethics. Now he must make the opposite case: for the inclusion of social ethics within economic thought. This is the subject of our next section.

ETHICS WITHIN ECONOMICS

Having staked his claim for the indispensability of economic expertise to social ethics, Rich sets out to explain how the discipline of economics should take account of moral convictions, without compromising its scientific purity.

116 BEE, p. 74; Rich, *Wirtschaftsethik I*, p. 80.
117 BEE, p. 76; Rich, *Wirtschaftsethik I*, p. 82.
118 See BEE, pp. 275–90; Rich, *Wirtschaftsethik II*, pp. 21–35, *passim*.

The first point Rich makes is that morality cannot be established in an equivalent scientific manner: 'It is impossible to ground human justice as a materially-definite norm in the sense of a scientifically-objective, universally-valid rationality'.[119] But certain accounts of morality do claim to be neutral and verifiable by all. Rich turns the tables on these approaches by suggesting that insofar as they claim to be objectively verifiable, to that extent they are in fact dogmatic: 'Behind attempts of this kind ultimately stand rationalized conviction- or experience-certitudes of a confessional character'.[120] There is no neutral and empirical method for establishing moral truths which can secure universal agreement—as is evident from the plethora of alternative moral conceptions which exist.

In particular, Rich considers the attempt to ground morality scientifically as dangerous, because such a procedure can only rely on an analysis of the way things actually *are*. Manifestly, the way things are is far from ideal. For example, the notion of human rights is established on an indicative description, as in the form 'humans are equal, so they must be treated as such'. This runs into terrible difficulties for Rich, given the objective gap between the ways things are and the way they should be: 'There exists, therefore, a gap between the historical-social reality of [humanity's] true nature and the concept of nature in the idea of natural law'.[121] Indeed, 'gap' is too tame a rendering of the German *Kluft*, which can literally refer to a ravine or chasm. Given this rift, Rich is worried that monstrous things may be *observed* about human nature as it exists, and mistakenly regarded as normative, such as the domination of the weak by the strong, slavery, and even mutually contradictory things such as private property and common ownership.

Yet Rich's opposition is not to the natural law tradition as such, but its forms that tend to legitimate injustice under the guise of neutrally inspecting human nature. It is when natural law *overstretches* itself that it becomes problematic:

> So far as the conception of natural law seeks to provide an objective foundation for human justice, reasonable to every rational or scientifically-thinking person, and not merely to bring to light the fact that positive law, valid in state and society, must always orient itself to a norm of the just that transcends itself, it will hardly be able to withstand critical examination.[122]

[119] BEE, 93; Rich, *Wirtschaftsethik I*, p. 100.

[120] BEE, 93; Rich, *Wirtschaftsethik I*, p. 100. For a useful discussion of the inescapability of theological presuppositions, see Roy A. Clouser, *The Myth of Religious Neutrality: An Essay on the Hidden Role of Religious Belief in Theories*, rev. edn. (Notre Dame: University of Notre Dame Press, 2005), e.g. pp. 3–4, 91.

[121] BEE, p. 79; Rich, *Wirtschaftsethik I*, p. 85.

[122] BEE, p. 80; Rich, *Wirtschaftsethik I*, p. 86.

Thus it is the pretence to ahistorical objectivity that Rich finds objectionable: it can have a positive role in articulating what, as we have seen, Rich regards as the universal fundamental ethical experience of the gap between customary law and transcendent justice. Rich finds Hegel's historical idealism equally problematic: one cannot assume the passage of history in its dialectical fluctuations will unfold a true concept of justice.[123] Both forms of idealism idealize their own access to empirical truth, and this self-confidence is now widely discredited, as in the critiques of Karl Popper and Hans Albert, who sought to replace the guise of impartiality as a gauge of truth with the criterion of falsifiability.[124] As no ethical theory can be proven or falsified scientifically, this would seem to lead to their elimination, or at the very least to their isolation from the sphere of the rational.[125] This presents a quandary. Rich wants social science to make space for moral convictions, in a way which does not compromise its objectivity. But he recognizes the impossibility of grounding or specifying such standards in scientific method.

Rich's solution is to draw a distinction between certitude (*Gewißheit*) and certainty (*Sicherheit*).[126] He finds a congenial spokesman for this in the figure of the social scientist Gerhard Weisser. On the basis of Weisser's work, Rich draws a distinction between moral convictions (which may or may not be theological), which he variously describes as 'experience-certitudes' (*Erfahrungsgewißheit*), or 'value premises' (*Grundwertentscheidungen*), and 'dogmatic' principles.[127] The former cannot be established or assessed empirically, but that does not mean they are downright arbitrary. They may not be scientifically verifiable, but neither are they placed dogmatically beyond question: they are 'critically revisable certitudes, capable of self-reflection'.[128] Such convictions need not fall afoul of Popper and Albert's strictures against dogmatism.

Weisser appeals for such value judgements to be explicitly included in social-scientific reasoning. Indeed, just as ethics needs to take account of what economics tells it is possible in order to be methodologically true to itself, so social science needs to pay overt attention to ethical convictions because they are constantly deployed in social-scientific work anyway, but

[123] BEE, p. 83.

[124] BEE, p. 84. Ironically, others have made a case for the admissibility of theological considerations in economic matters on the same grounds, namely that a lack of falsifiability is quite proper to the character of theological claims (see Paul Oslington, 'A Theological Economics', *International Journal of Social Economics* 27.1 (2000), pp. 32–44, esp. p. 35). Rich's concern would be that this might make theological claims seem arbitrary, or attempt to hermetically seal them from criticism.

[125] BEE, p. 86.

[126] For our purposes it is satisfying to note that Luther noted a similar distinction—between existential *assurance* of one's salvation and a cocksure sense of one's *invulnerability*.

[127] BEE, pp. 92–4; Rich, *Wirtschaftsethik I*, pp. 99–101.

[128] BEE, p. 94; Rich, *Wirtschaftsethik I*, p. 101.

covertly and ad hoc.[129] *Candid* inclusion of values enables them to be considered critically, rather than masquerading as assured fact.[130] Thus the inclusion of value judgements in social science is not inimical to its scientific integrity, but essential to it.

This, then, is Rich's case for a meaningful relationship between ethics and economics: one takes two sets or systems of propositions—one confessional, one scientific—and one draws 'conclusions from both groups of axioms'.[131] Yet there is a further, related question which Rich now needs to address. To what extent can social ethics, which aims at garnering consent and thus seeks structural implementation in a pluralistic society, be theological ethics?

HUMANITY AND REVELATION

As we have seen, Rich considers that morality is not objectively perceptible like the laws of engineering or economics. But he is unyielding in his conviction that Christian belief must play a role in public debate, without first having to be flattened into a common moral language.[132] But he is aware that the specificity and exclusivity of such convictions may consign the Christian to irrelevance in a society where many do not share them. How, then, can normative claims be normative, in a field which will be characterized by many significantly different claims? Rich, after all, therefore seeks to make space for a universal human moral experience. We saw earlier that he characterized this as one of bidimensionality: recognition of the validity of conventional norms *and* an absolute standard against which such conventions fall short. Here, Rich regards this experience as more concrete than this, such that particular experience-certitudes can be tested or legitimated at the bar of this general experience:

> Although the persuasiveness of such normative certitudes is subjective and not universally valid, they nevertheless aim . . . at least possibly, at general evidence and, consequently, at universal obligation. . . . In short, it is a matter of certitudes

[129] BEE, p. 89. Rich gives examples in BEE, p. 431.

[130] BEE, p. 91.

[131] BEE, p. 90.

[132] Rich is not being paranoid. It is worth pointing out just how adamantly some economists maintain that theological considerations must not be permitted to play any part in the pursuit of a better understanding of economic matters. Others simply maintain that such considerations are inherently *irrelevant*: As Paul Heyne puts it: 'I find no insights relevant to economic understanding in the belief that the world was created by God rather than by chance' (Paul Heyne, '"If the Trumpet Does Not Sound a Clear Call . . ."', in *Religion and Economics: Normative Social Theory*, eds. James M. Dean and A. M. C. Waterman (Boston: Kluwer, 1999), pp. 141–51, esp. p. 144.)

> that seek to prove themselves to be certain in their tendency for other persons as well.[133]

If they are truly convictions about humanity per se and not just private religious standards, moral norms will prove themselves in practice to those who do not share the underlying theological convictions.

So, Rich does not want to compromise the importance and uniqueness of Christian revelation. But he wants to do justice to 'the horizon of general human experience rooted in faith, hope, and love' (*Der allgemeinmenschliche Erfahrungshorizont von Glauben, Hoffnung, Liebe*).[134] This experience *precedes* Christian revelation:

> After all, non-Christians also know about faith, hope, and love in their own, indeed elementary, way. When these words are used, non-Christians do not encounter them with a complete lack of understanding.... If that were not true, the Christian experience-certitude expressed by them could not be communicated.[135]

Faith, hope, and love are obviously not the exclusive preserve of Christianity: all have some awareness of them, although this may be 'elementary'. Faith, hope, and love do not come into being with the advent of Christianity, but are integral to what it means to be human: 'there is no specifically Christian humanity, only a human humanity'.[136]

For Rich, this conclusion resolves the dilemmas of theological involvement in a scientific world on the one hand and a pluralistic one on the other. First, it guards against the seduction of theological arrogance. Christianity does not have a monopoly on moral thought, nor on faith, hope, and love. Rich fears that theology can easily become self-important and disdainful of external insights.[137] Hence it should not reflect exclusively on its own internal material:

> Christian faith ... will not simply reflect on its humanity contained in its experience-certitude ... without accounting for what is encountered as human in some other way, or still claims to be human, no matter how controversial the form in which it may appear.[138]

Thus this conclusion serves to keep theology properly humble and open.

Second, it enables Christian moral thought to be expounded and heard among a plurality of other ways of thinking, since it is already in tune with a more universal experience of the moral. Theological engagement in the public sphere is endorsed, even required. Christian convictions may be heeded *safely*,

[133] BEE, p. 94; Rich, *Wirtschaftsethik I*, p. 101.
[134] BEE, p. 99; Rich, *Wirtschaftsethik I*, p. 105.
[135] BEE, p. 99; Rich, *Wirtschaftsethik I*, p. 105.
[136] BEE, p. 122; Rich, *Wirtschaftsethik I*, p. 127.
[137] BEE, p. 121; Rich, *Wirtschaftsethik I*, p. 127.
[138] BEE, p. 122; Rich, *Wirtschaftsethik I*, pp. 127–8.

without their making a bid for hegemony, since a theological explication of justice cannot be something alien to humanity because it is *human* justice. Thus Rich ensures that theological data will not seem like an other-worldly intrusion into the human quest for self-understanding and right action. Thus this conclusion serves to keep theology properly accessible.

Third, this conclusion safeguards the idea that Christian convictions apply to everyone. As Oliver O'Donovan has put it, 'Christian moral duties' are not 'analogous to such ecclesiastical house-rules as respect for the clergy or giving to the church, duties which presuppose membership of the church community and lay no claim on those outside it'.[139] If a theological anthropology describes *anthropoi* as such, not a particular subset, one cannot opt in or out of it according to individual preference. Thus this position serves to keep theology universally applicable to humanity and so properly normative.[140]

RICH'S ROOTS IN KARL MARX

Having considered Rich's mature view of the relationships between ethics and social science, and between theology and general human experience, it is worth noting the roots of these aspects of Rich's method in his lectures on Marx, given in Zürich in 1975.[141] Rich believed that many of Marx's criticisms of religion were, in a sense, right on target. Yet, unbeknownst to Marx himself, their target was not real Christianity, but its degenerate, oppressive form.[142] Thus Rich makes a distinction between real faith and degenerate, or ideological, pseudo-faith. Faith is an 'autonomous and non-derived event on its own plane'.[143] But, because of this non-derived character, humans are sorely tempted to seek props for faith, things which one has at one's own disposal

[139] Oliver O'Donovan, *Resurrection and Moral Order: An Outline for Evangelical Ethics*, 2nd edn. (Leicester: Apollos, 1994), p. 16.

[140] As Roelf L. Hann puts it, it is not only God, but also humanity itself, whose true character must be discovered through divine revelation (Roelf L. Hann, 'Man and Methodology in Economic Science: About Abstraction and Obedience', in *Social Science in Christian Perspective*, eds. Paul A. Marshall and Robert E. Vandervennen (Lanham, MD: University Press of America 1988), pp. 219–54, esp. p. 220). This resonates well with Luther's thought: he grew fiercely impatient with theology that was only speech about God. This he regarded as abstract and speculative; it did nobody any good. Real theology concerned the existential matter of the redeeming God and fallen humanity *in their interrelation*: 'The proper subject of theology is man guilty of sin and condemned, and God the Justifier and Saviour of man the sinner. Whatever is asked or discussed in theology outside this subject, is error and poison'. LW v. 12, p. 311; WA v. 40.II, pp. 328b, ll. 17–20.

[141] These lectures remain unpublished; our acquaintance with them depends on the extended discussion in Harold Tonks, *Faith, Hope and Decision-Making*, pp. 97–136.

[142] Tonks, *Faith, Hope and Decision-Making*, p. 112.

[143] Tonks, *Faith, Hope and Decision-Making*, p. 109.

such as the Bible, rigid orthodoxy, or spiritual experience. These things are perfectly legitimate in their proper place, but when they are claimed as keys to the ultimate, as objective and circumscribed repositories of all necessary knowledge, conveniently packaged in manageable form, they are distorted, and faith becomes ideological. Of course, ideology need not be religious, and Rich is equally scathing about secular ideologies of reason and humanity.[144]

Thus Rich seeks to avoid what he regards as an obscurantist, biblicist approach to faith. The claims of faith must be made in dialogue with those of science:

> [Faith's] understanding of the world is, therefore, nothing ultimate, but derived, secondary, historical, always arising out of the confrontation between faith and a knowledge of reality [disclosed in] the never-completed results of the empirical sciences.[145]

Therefore faith's apprehension of reality can never be final, and therefore neither can its moral stipulations.

We should note a parallel conclusion of this train of thought. A self-critical humanism, of a Marxist or other stripe, if also shorn of prop-grasping ideology, and which eschews ideological claims to absoluteness, can have a close alliance with theological ethics. Rich is keen for dialogue with this form of humanist (or, simply 'humane') thought:

> The hoping love of faith will, therefore, never ignore what reason has to say regarding what is just in society. It must . . . consider reason's insights seriously.[146]

Hence, Rich feels free to adopt insights from, and enter intellectual coalitions with, ostensibly non-theological thinkers. We have already seen him do so with Marx, Weber, and Gerhard Weisser—although he often offers modifications to their ideas—and he also does so in relation to John Rawls and Adam Smith.[147]

[144] Tonks, *Faith, Hope and Decision-Making*, p. 109.

[145] Quoted in Tonks, *Faith, Hope and Decision-Making*, p. 111.

[146] BEE, p. 204; Rich, *Wirtschaftsethik I*, p. 207.

[147] On Rawls, see the following chapter. For Rich's interpretation of Adam Smith's thought, see BEE, pp. 492–6; *Wirtschaftsethik II*, pp. 229–33. Rich quite rightly joins recent scholarship by reading Smith in his context as a moral philosopher and not through the lens of Milton Friedman and Ayn Rand, on which see Keith Tribe, 'Natural Liberty and *Laissez Faire*: How Adam Smith Became a Free Trade Ideologue', in *Adam Smith's* Wealth of Nations*: New Interdisciplinary Essays*, eds. Stephen Copley and Kathryn Sutherland (Manchester: University of Manchester Press, 1995), pp. 23–44, and the essay by Heinz Lubasz in the same volume, 'Adam Smith and the "Free Market"', pp. 45–69. Of course, even if the 'left wing' reading of Smith is correct, that does not necessarily mean that Rich is right to be so enthusiastic about yoking Smith's project to Christian social ethics. On the problems of interpreting Smith, see James R. Otteson, 'The Recurring "Adam Smith Problem"', *History of Philosophy Quarterly* 17.1 (2000), pp. 51–74 and Kelly Rogers (ed.) *Self-Interest: An Anthology of Philosophical Perspectives* (London: Routledge, 1997), pp. 81–2. Knud Haakonssen argues for the coherence of Smith's

RICH'S CHOSEN METHOD: DIALOGUE

Now we have seen him use it several times, Rich's pattern of argumentation feels familiar. Economic science and social ethics must take account of one another. So must theological ethics and self-critical humanist ethics. Each time, his arguments cut both ways. So, when he argues that theological convictions must be included within public social ethics, he adds that such convictions must be tested at the bar of general human experience. Indeed, he adds that these theological convictions must be *shaped* by dialogue with a wider vision of humanity:

> [Christian faith] must expound the normative content of its humanity, which it is first necessary to determine more closely, not dogmatically-apodictically, but dialogically-argumentatively.[148]

The translators have added the term 'dialogically' to give the sense of the adverb *argumentativ*. This term here does not bear the connotation of quarrel or disagreement, as its English homonym does, but signifies presenting one's arguments persuasively: explaining and demonstrating them rather than simply asserting them without room for dissent or discussion. Hence, Christian faith is obliged to 'account for' perceptions of humanity external to Christian

thought in his essay, 'Introduction: The Coherence of Smith's Thought', in *The Cambridge Companion to Adam Smith*, ed. Knud Haakonssen (Cambridge: Cambridge University Press, 2006), pp. 1–21.

148 BEE, p. 122; Rich, *Wirtschaftsethik I*, p. 128. This is the first of a number of parallels between Rich's work and that of Reinhold Niebuhr. Anna Robbins characterizes Niebuhr's social-ethical method (especially as it influenced the World Council of Churches) as a 'study-dialogue method' (*Methods in the Madness*, pp. 167–9). A more recent parallel might be drawn with the work of Malcolm Brown, who advocates what he calls 'dialogic traditionalism' as a social-ethical method (see for example, Malcolm Brown, *After the Market: Economics, Moral Agreement and the Churches' Mission* (Bern: Lang, 2004), p. 23 and *passim*). Brown is working from within the 'middle axiom' tradition established by J. H. Oldham, which seeks to formulate moral axioms intelligible to all through dialogue with those outside the church (hence 'dialogic'). Brown also wishes to incorporate insights regarding the integrity of the church's own theological-moral beliefs which he finds in the work of thinkers such as Michael Banner, Alasdair MacIntyre, John Milbank, and Stanley Hauerwas (hence 'traditionalism')—although he vigorously castigates them for what he perceives as their inability to communicate and work together effectively with those outside the church, especially on economic questions. His evidence for this is what he sees as the tendency of Banner and Hauerwas to concentrate on sexual and medical ethics—that is, on seemingly 'private' matters, in which individuals and communities can adhere to counter cultural standards without the need for wider social consensus (Malcolm Brown and Paul Ballard, 'Plurality and Globalization: The Challenge of Economics to Social Theology', *Political Theology* 4 (May 2001), pp. 102–16, esp. p. 112). Hence for Brown, the economy is a 'test case for a public theology' (see Malcolm Brown and Paul Ballard, *The Church and Economic Life* (Peterborough: Epworth, 2006), pp. 7ff.). For a brief summation of the 'middle axiom' tradition, see Duncan Forrester, 'The Scope of Public Theology', *Studies in Christian Ethics* 17.2 (2004), pp. 5–19. The connection to Oldham is noteworthy, since Rich describes the 'middle axiom' approach as close to what he means by his term, *Maximen* (BEE, pp. 222–3, n. 3; Rich, *Wirtschaftsethik, I*, pp. 223–4, n. 3).

experience-certitudes, and to prove itself to them.[149] Thus his claim, quoted above, that 'there is no specifically Christian humanity, only a human humanity', refers not only to the universally binding character of Christian reality, but also to the idea that human nature can and should be discerned and interpreted through attention not just to Christian experience, but to wider human experience. Such experience may not necessarily be explicitly Christian, but it is still in a sense *theological*, because, Rich claims, humanity-in-Christ is not alien to humanity-as-such, even in its fallen state. Elsewhere Rich speaks of a *convergence* between the 'humanity from faith', and 'secular humanity'.[150]

What this means in practice is that what distinguishes Christian morality from other humane perceptions of justice is not at all a matter of their respective *contents*:

> One of the greatest misunderstandings is that Jesus brought a new morality, in the sense of a new order of values, into the world. He no more brought a new order of values than he brought a new religion.[151]

Rich therefore forbids that the particularity of Christian faith be 'played off' against general human experience—that would be 'theological hubris', a trivialization of human experience and thus of humanity itself.[152] Carl-Henric Grenholm summarizes Rich's view as follows:

> Rich holds that the maxims which are formulated within the framework for a Christian social ethics are not specifically Christian. They are humane and can be understood even by those who are not Christian. Nor are the social-ethical criteria which motivate these maxims specifically Christian in the sense that they are completely different from those criteria which can be accepted by human beings with another philosophy of life.[153]

Hence Rich comments that, while the Christian notion of humanity is rooted theologically in the resurrection *for Christians* ('beim Christen'), nevertheless 'in its ethical concretion, it is not tied exclusively to Christianity as a religious confession'.[154]

Furthermore, precisely because of their universal normative status, Christian convictions must make themselves accessible to those who do not share the Christian account of human nature. They should be promoted on the basis

[149] BEE, p. 122; Rich, *Wirtschaftsethik I*, p. 128.

[150] Author's translation of Arthur Rich, 'Das «Humanum» als Leitbegriff der Sozialethik', in *Humane Gesellschaft: Beiträge zu Ihrer Sozialen Gestaltung; Zum 70. Geburtstag von Heinz-Dietrich Wendland*, eds. Trutz Rendtorff and Arthur Rich (Zürich: Furche/Zwingli, 1970), pp. 13–45, esp. pp. 39–40.

[151] BEE, p. 181; Rich, *Wirtschaftsethik I*, p. 184.

[152] BEE, p. 116; Rich, *Wirtschaftsethik I*, p. 123.

[153] Carl-Henric Grenholm, *Protestant Work Ethics: A Study of Work Ethical Theories in Contemporary Protestant Theology* (Uppsala: Acta Universitatis Upsaliensis, 1993), p. 212.

[154] BEE, p. 121; Rich, *Wirtschaftsethik I*, p. 127.

of arguments which those who do not share the basic Christian beliefs can understand. Rich cites 1 Corinthians 14:19, on the basis of which he comments:

> This means that the humanity originating from faith, hope, and love, in so far as it is precisely a matter of the normative, must strive to make itself perceptible also to those who have different basic beliefs. The prerequisite for this is a way of argumentation that meets the conditions of rational thinking and judging, and that consequently is available to everyone.[155]

So, despite Rich's earlier recognition of the impossibility of an objective universal apprehension of moral claims, he does believe that there is some kind of 'rational' standard for moral discussion, which *is* 'available to everyone'. Christian convictions must meet the conditions of this standard for discussion. In the section entitled 'Humanity and Revelation', we saw that Rich makes a general case for the inclusion of theological norms in social ethics by arguing that theological norms should be judged at the bar of general human experience. Here, he has made a theological case for the same thing: theological apprehensions of what it is to be human will by definition appeal beyond the confines of their own founding convictions. As he puts it later in the volume:

> In so far as these criteria prove to be principles of Christian existence, a specifically Christian character naturally befits them. But in so far as Christian existence seeks to be nothing other than genuinely human existence, they must legitimate themselves simply as human criteria, as criteria for true humanity in general.[156]

Yet previously we noted that Rich recognizes the immense plurality of moralities and the impossibility of grounding ethics in a universal, objective way. In an essay published in 1970, he notes the huge diversity of interpretations of humanity, and readily affirms that true human nature is 'not at all self-evident'.[157] Later, he seeks to resolve this tension as follows:

> [The] criteria of human justice, since they are oriented towards the absolute of Christian faith-conviction, are not established by scientific rationality, although they are supported by a degree of evidence, which makes them capable of communication at the level of reason.[158]

That is, Christian social ethics can be shaped by dialogue with other humane traditions, and communicate its findings 'at the level of reason', without pretending to be grounded in some neutral, pre-theological reason. One

155 BEE, p. 122; Rich, *Wirtschaftsethik I*, p. 128.
156 BEE, p. 169; Rich, *Wirtschaftsethik I*, p. 172.
157 Rich, 'Das «Humanum» als Leitbegriff der Sozialethik', p. 14.
158 BEE, p. 432; Rich, *Wirtschaftsethik II*, p. 173.

question that we will therefore put to Rich's method in Chapter 3 will concern the extent to which he evades the force of his own strictures against the possibility of empirical, universally accessible criteria for justice, and the derivation of norms of justice from the way things are.

To sum up this section, theological contributions to social ethics are for Rich to be doubly determined by what he regards as a common or general human experience: in their formulation (because Christian ethics is not distinctive in its contents), and in their promulgation. The universality of human nature configures not only its normativity, but also the *method* by which its content is apprehended and subsequently advocated: not dogmatically but dialogically. The particular content of Christian social ethics is not distinctive: this it shares with other humane and humble experiences of what it is to be human. What, then, *is* distinctive about it? What distinctive contribution does Christianity have to make to the field of social ethics?

THE DISTINCTIVENESS OF CHRISTIAN SOCIAL ETHICS FOR RICH

We have observed that Rich believes that theological social ethics must be shaped in dialogue with thinkers motivated by general humanist impulses. Yet he certainly also believes that there is a specifically Christian contribution to social ethics. In what does this consist, since it is not found in the contents of such ethics?

The Anamnetic Role

As we have seen, Rich argues that Enlightenment attempts to ground ethics in a 'timeless, ahistorical concept of nature and norms' fail—although at least they bear witness to a *general* awareness of a transcendent standard of justice.[159] This restates his contention that there is a ubiquitous human moral experience, of the tension between imperfect conventional moral standards and a higher, absolute standard. Yet, in his own particular context, this moral apprehension is also partly a fruit of the presence of Christianity in the soil of the Enlightenment: behind human rights there is a 'confessional

[159] BEE, p. 80; Rich, *Wirtschaftsethik I*, p. 87. Cornel West makes a similar point regarding the ahistorical character of many defences of free enterprise (Cornel West, 'Neo-Aristotelianism, Liberalism and Socialism: A Christian Perspective', in *Christianity and Capitalism: Perspectives on Religion, Liberalism and the Economy*, eds. Bruce Grelle and David A. Krueger (Chicago: Center for the Scientific Study of Religion, 1986), pp. 79–89, esp. p. 81.)

certainty', whether in terms of Christian faith (all humans are created in God's image), or in the Enlightenment's conceptualization of humanity, 'where such beliefs live on in a secularized form'.[160] Behind Enlightenment idealism is not objectivity but a Christian conviction, a 'certitude that is not rationally grounded, but rather (although this is not admitted) has the character of a confession or conviction'.[161] Therefore, part of the contribution of theology is to draw attention to the beliefs which gave rise to contemporary notions of justice:

> The universal recognition of traditional human rights . . . continues to exist only to the extent that the declaration of belief in humanity behind it [that is, Christianity] stands up for itself effectively and gains recognition.[162]

Thus, one role for Christian ethics is to remind contemporary society of the beliefs which have shaped its moral presuppositions, lest the latter be jeopardized.

The Radical Role

More importantly, the distinctness of Christian experience is that it is situated within faith in the resurrection. For Rich this essentially means that Christian faith empowers and enables ethics to be deeper and stronger, which is what Rich means by 'radical'. Faith in the resurrection furnishes Christianity with robustness: general human trust, hope, and love are liable to 'shatter easily at the experience of evil, or even change into their opposites'.[163] The Christian peers of faith, hope, and love cannot be so easily shipwrecked, because they are animated by a vital and authentic experience of the trustworthiness *of God*. Furthermore, the experience of the resurrection is an experience of the *certainty* of the coming Kingdom of God:

> Ultimately [the distinctiveness of Christian social ethics] lies in the fact that the humanity of faith with its ethics is never merely ethics, never merely a reflected 'ought' . . . *but is instead a given 'is' that stems from what is coming.*[164]

That is, Christianity does not merely issue imperatives (which are impotent to effect change), but experiences an approaching reality *out of which* transforming action takes place. This furnishes Christian social ethics with an especial *relentlessness* in its search for justice, a refusal to be satisfied with the way things are. Rich regards this as particularly important given the pessimism

160 BEE, p. 80; Rich, *Wirtschaftsethik I*, p. 86.
161 BEE, p. 83; Rich, *Wirtschaftsethik I*, p. 90.
162 BEE, p. 80; Rich, *Wirtschaftsethik I*, p. 86.
163 BEE, p. 117; Rich, *Wirtschaftsethik I*, p. 123.
164 BEE, p. 242; Rich, *Wirtschaftsethik I*, p. 243. Emphasis original.

which the collapse of Enlightenment expectations of progress left in its wake. Christian faith has a vital role to play in revitalizing hope for change without lapsing into naïve optimism.[165]

Again, this is not a matter of concrete content: Rich cites with approval his fellow social-ethicist Martin Honecker's view that one must refrain from deducing from the Kingdom of God 'any concrete standards for the shaping of the world'.[166] What really matters is one's existential attitude, in this case the particular power (*Kraft*) which is specific to the Christian experience. Elsewhere, however, he chides Honecker for claiming that 'faith does not bring any increase in ethical knowledge', but only motivation.[167] Yet this seems very close to Rich's own position, as we have just documented it.

How should this seeming discrepancy be understood? It seems that Rich believes that theological convictions should shape Christian social judgements *within intramural Christian ethics*. But his upbeat appraisal of the general accessibility of moral reality means that he expects moral judgements that proceed from very different conceptual backgrounds to nevertheless cohere with one another. This enables him to reach a nuanced position that allows for the way in which Christian faith can add to the ethical knowledge of Christians, without claiming to be the exclusive source of such knowledge in the world. Similarly, Christians need not be differently *motivated* (non-Christians too may be motivated by hope, faith, and love), but they will be differently *empowered*.

RICH'S ROOTS IN JOHN RAWLS AND THEIR CONSEQUENCES FOR HIS SOCIAL ETHICS

Having set out Rich's opinion that Christian social ethics should develop and communicate itself in dialogue with other humanist moral traditions, it is worth exploring how Rich does this in practice, namely by adopting the approach of John Rawls:

> Rawls' second principle of justice provides . . . *a rational means, which can be adopted by the humanity originating from faith, hope, and love,* of bringing the criterion of participation in its essential concerns closer to the concrete world . . . without limiting its claim to universal validity.[168]

165 BEE, pp. 117–18; Rich, *Wirtschaftsethik I*, pp. 123–4.
166 Cited in BEE, p. 129.
167 BEE, p. 167, n. 94; Rich, *Wirtschaftsethik I*, p. 170, n. 94.
168 BEE, p. 216; Rich, *Wirtschaftsethik I*, p. 218. Emphasis original.

We will explore what Rich means by 'the criterion of participation' in the section entitled 'The Criteria for Justice', but for now it is sufficient to note that this is one of Rich's core theologically derived principles. It has a universal authority about it, but it would appear that it is too general in itself. It needs to be brought nearer to actual situations, to *dem Konkreten*. For Rich, this is not done through further theological deliberation, although he does not say whether this is because theology is not capable of such specific work or because being theologically specific about such matters would make Christian social ethics unintelligible to others. In any case, John Rawls's second principle of justice is doubly congenial: it can be used to apply ethical principles more specifically, and it is 'rational', that is, comprehensible beyond the theological circles.

Yet as we have shown, Rich is no rationalist. Indeed, in his earlier case against attempts to access moral norms through an objective, universal rationality, Rich explicitly disagrees with Rawls.[169] Yet, this theoretical rejection of rationalism notwithstanding, it is existentially imperative that moral consensus be sought, lest social paralysis ensue. Yet it is impossible for everyone to agree on fundamental beliefs. Therefore Rich hankers after a way to build consensus, without requiring everyone to abandon the particularity of their convictions. In this respect Rawls is highly valuable:

> The humanity originating from faith, hope, and love is, therefore, directly and seriously interested in rational theories of justice, such as that of John Rawls, because and provided that they are useful for the intended finding of consensus.[170]

It is not, then, that Rich after all believes that one can derive social morality from a timeless model to which all persons must perforce subscribe insofar as they are rational, and which guarantees accurate moral knowledge. Rather, Rawls's method is a useful heuristic device for identifying and clarifying what the underlying, *pre-rational* moral commitments of humanity *already* are (in Rich's terms, the common human perception of faith, hope, and love). These commitments may be derived and specified theologically, but they need not be. Rich expects that among these commitments there will be a significant amount of agreement, regardless of the ostensible source of their derivation. Therefore the Christian can deploy the method and conclusions of a Rawlsian account of justice, and secure a much wider consensus than they might have done had they promoted their views on theological grounds alone.[171]

[169] BEE, p. 93, n. 75; Rich, *Wirtschaftsethik I*, p. 100, n. 75. See also BEE, pp. 213–14.

[170] BEE, p. 215; Rich, *Wirtschaftsethik I*, p. 218.

[171] Indeed, Rich's work has been rather successful in terms of being heeded beyond the sphere of theological ethics. It has been well received by some economists with an interest in ethics, especially by some who have appreciated his attempt to take economics seriously as a discipline with its own integrity. For example: Karl Homann and others, 'Wirtschaftswissenschaft und

Rich does not think that Christian moral convictions should under any circumstances be *shed* in order to participate in public debate. But he is going further than suggesting that, where the conclusions of one tradition happily coincide with another, a temporary pragmatic alliance may be formed. Rather, Rawls provides him with a *method* appropriate to his belief that Christian convictions should be shaped and expounded dialogically.[172]

To summarize: in some contexts Rich decisively rejects the notion that there is an objective apprehension of morality, and for him this safeguards a continued role for Christian moral convictions in public debate. Yet this does not preclude his appeal to a more general moral awareness. Indeed, in other contexts he asserts that theologically formed moral criteria must be shaped by dialogue with other perceptions of humanity, and even by the canons of rationality to which all have access, in order to maximize moral consensus. Hence, when Rich pursues his theological discussion of eschatology in the next chapter, he identifies it somewhat surprisingly as an 'excursus', and adds, 'Those who shrink from specifically theological considerations may skip the following chapter'.[173] This is significant. Rich is claiming that his overall argument and eventual conclusions may be sustained, even if his theologically disinclined readers 'skip' this chapter. Its interest for the reader, Rich warns, is more autobiographical than substantial: it is 'a critical excursus on the theological positions that have been of importance, both positively and negatively, for the author in the development of his own social-ethical concept'.[174]

Ethik', in *Wirtschaftswissenschaft und Ethik*, ed. Helmut Hesse (Berlin: Duncker & Humblot, 1988), pp. 9–33, esp. pp. 12–13; Rolf-Jürgen Korte, 'Ethische Positionen im Markt sozialer Hilfen', in *Unternehmerische Freiheit, Selbstbindung und politische Mitverantwortung: Perspektiven republikanischer Unternehmensethik*, eds. Peter Ulrich, Albert Löhr, and Josef Wieland (München & Mering: Rainer Hampp, 1999), pp. 139–63, esp. pp. 144ff; Hans Nutzinger, 'Anmerkungen zu Arthur Richs Wirtschaftsethik', *Zeitschrift für Evangelische Ethik* 35.3 (1991), pp. 229–32. See also Strohm, 'Arthur Richs Bedeutung für die Wirtschafts- und Sozialethik', p. 196.

[172] This appears to parallel another aspect of Rawls's thought, namely his account of public reason, at least his more moderate statements of it. We say, 'more moderate' because at times Rawls seems to exclude theological and equivalent considerations outright from the public sphere, as in John Rawls, *A Theory of Justice*, rev. edn. (Cambridge, MA: Harvard University Press, 1999), pp. 397–8. But in later work unknown to Rich, Rawls concedes that theological and other considerations may play a part in public debate, subject to the proviso that they do so only within the 'background culture' of society (everyday public discourse such as conversation, the press, and the academy). In the 'public political' culture (such as a legislature) they must still present their views in publicly justifiable terms. See John Rawls, 'The Idea of Public Reason Revisited', in *The Law of Peoples with 'The Idea of Public Reason Revisited'* (Cambridge, MA: Harvard University Press, 1999), pp. 129–80, esp. pp. 152ff. For a sympathetic critique of Rawls, see Jeffrey Stout, *Democracy and Tradition* (Princeton: Princeton University Press, 2004), chapter 3. For a theological discussion, see Nigel Biggar, '"God" in Public Reason', *Studies in Christian Ethics* 19.1 (2006), pp. 9–19.

[173] BEE, p. 123; Rich, *Wirtschaftsethik I*, p. 128.

[174] BEE, p. 123; Rich, *Wirtschaftsethik I*, p. 128.

HOW NEAR IS THE KINGDOM OF GOD? ESCHATOLOGY AS RICH'S KEY THEOLOGICAL THEME

Rich and Ragaz, Kutter, and Barth

Rich is as good as his word: the chapter on eschatology is structured as a discussion of various theologians or theological approaches in turn, outlining what Rich has learned from each one. He opens with a discussion of what he calls 'the early Barth' ('*Barth in seiner Frühzeit*').[175] Here, Rich lauds the Swiss religious socialist Hermann Kutter (1863–1931), who influenced Barth, for his work in recovering the centrality within Scripture of the message of the breaking in of the Kingdom of God. Rich describes the doctrine as 'the core of the biblical revelation-testimony'.[176]

Rich was initially attracted to the critical attitude towards human affairs that an emphasis on eschatology enabled him to take. Against Hegel's historical idealism and its theological proponents, Kutter and Barth insist that no earthly order can pretend to represent God's Kingdom.[177] Indeed, it is not only human affirmations of social projects which fall short of the Kingdom, but even human criticisms—hence the importance of emphasizing the external absolute of God's rule.[178] Yet, while he sees the great strength of this rigour, Rich fears that such purism will entail political and social paralysis. He concludes that Kutter was too successful in breaking away from romantic idealism in which the Kingdom of God was seen as immanent in human history. He maintained such an emphasis on the radical transcendence of God's rule that it became remote, and unsusceptible of concrete worldly enactment. The way the worldly was called into question was too Platonic, setting reality against a *theoretical* ideal, standing aloof from the world in judgement. Transcendence comes at too high a price: 'the absolute of the Kingdom of God could not enter into a genuine relationship with the relative in the real world, with its conflicting forces and powers'.[179]

[175] By *Frühzeit*, Rich means the period of Barth's radical break with nineteenth-century liberal theology at the beginning of the 1920s in his work on Romans (BEE, p. 130). The drawing of a strong distinction between Barth's early ethics and his supposedly more mature ethics in the *Dogmatics* has been challenged. David Clough argues that the notions of crisis and divine interruption remain essential for rightly interpreting him throughout his life. See his *Ethics in Crisis: Interpreting Barth's Ethics* (Aldershot: Ashgate, 2005).

[176] BEE, p. 130; Rich, *Wirtschaftsethik I*, p. 135.

[177] Cf. Robin W. Lovin's 'Foreword' to Karl Barth's lecture, *The Holy Spirit and the Christian Life: The Theological Basis of Ethics* (Louisville, KY: Westminster/John Knox Press, 1993), pp. ix–xx, esp. pp. x–xiv.

[178] Cf. John Webster, *Barth's Moral Theology: Human Action in Barth's Thought* (London: T & T Clark, 2004), p. 21.

[179] BEE, p. 131; Rich, *Wirtschaftsethik I*, p. 135.

Hence, Kutter held that while God might use a political movement to punish the elite bourgeoisie, this did not invest such a movement with a divine imprimatur. Indeed, he stated that joining the Social Democratic Party was an 'outright betrayal of the Gospel', since it endorsed not merely the social democratic critique of the existing order, but also the (idolatrous) social democratic programme itself.[180] That is, the same faith which drives one to recognize God's censure of the current situation is necessarily the same faith which will condemn improvements as themselves idolatrous and inadequate. Rich's fear is that, if all possibilities are equally damnable, the concept of meaningful action is rendered incoherent. Ethics will be plunged into nihilism.[181]

Rich's hero in resolving this dilemma is Leonhard Ragaz (1860–1945). Ragaz had been 'an optimist in the mould of nineteenth century Idealism'.[182] This was crushed by the Boer War. Ragaz enthusiastically assumed that God himself was at work, enabling the oppressed Boers to regain their freedom. When they were beaten, he was dumbfounded, and driven to reconsider how God's involvement in human history could be perceived.[183] Like Kutter and Barth, he became less comfortable with the notion of history as a medium of divine revelation, and suspicious of identifying the movement of God's Spirit with the course of human history. Yet he refused to replace his idealism with a purely static notion of revelation, in which God's self-disclosure was strictly confined to the earthly life of Christ. He supposed that revelation could also be a present event, although he insisted that this could be discerned only in the light of the definitive past revelation of God in Christ. As Rich puts it in his theological introduction to Ragaz's letters:

> It is by proceeding from the God who has become transparent in the Easter faith . . . that the inscrutable events of history are to be seen as the story of the coming of the Kingdom of God.[184]

One cannot read God's will directly from the passage of history, but in the light of his definitive revelation in Christ one can discern the ways in which aspects of human history might be oriented towards God's Kingdom, and ways in which they might not.[185] History must be evaluated dialectically: some

[180] BEE, p. 131. In Kutter's defence, we might say that this is reminiscent of some of the Hebrew prophets, who regarded the Assyrians and Babylonians as instruments of divine wrath against Israel, but at the same time reserved their most withering invective for the idolatrous self-aggrandizement of these empires.

[181] See BEE, p. 297.

[182] Tonks, *Faith, Hope and Decision-Making*, p. 42.

[183] Tonks, *Faith, Hope and Decision-Making*, p. 42.

[184] Translation from Tonks, *Faith, Hope and Decision-Making*, p. 43; Arthur Rich, 'Theologische Einführung', in *Leonhard Ragaz in seinen Briefen 1: 1887–1914*, eds. Christine Ragaz and others (Zürich: EVZ-Verlag, 1966), pp. ix–xliv, esp. p. xxii.

[185] See Paul Bock, 'Introduction', in Leonhard Ragaz, *Signs of the Kingdom: A Ragaz Reader*, ed. and trans. Paul Bock (Grand Rapids: Eerdmans, 1984), pp. xi–xxii, esp. p. xx.

aspects of particular events, movements, and ideas (such as social democracy) may be affirmed, others refused. The Kingdom is coming *from* God: that is, it is impossible to regard the existing social orders as already God's will, since the Kingdom is yet to come.[186] It is entirely transcendent, radically different from human ways. Hence, history and the Kingdom can never be identified. Yet because it is coming from God, the Kingdom is not an impossible ideal or a theoretical construct. It is a reality, a dynamic and present force in human history. History is not merely under divine judgement. It is also the theatre of God's action, by which it is also proceeding *towards* God. It may be momentary and partial, but there can be genuine motion towards the state of affairs which God wills, although this can only be discerned by faith.

Thus, human efforts for social transformation can be understood as part of God's own activity:

> God goes before us. We have a God who is not just a system, a theory, a past history, but a God who works constantly, a God of the present, of the future.[187]

For Rich this is important, since it enables him to say that the Kingdom is not a mere 'ought', an abstract imperative principle which humanity can never live up to—but an approaching *reality*, in which we can participate. Activity which seeks the Kingdom of God is not idolatrous striving, but a participation in that which God is himself already at work doing:

> 'Eschatological dimension' means . . . not only that the humanity originating from faith, hope, and love is directed towards the Kingdom of God as its ultimate purpose, but even more, that the 'energy of God' (Philippians 2:12–13), which seeks to drive human persons towards this goal, becomes effective in it. With this humanity, understood as the ethical aspect of eschatological salvation in the coming of the Kingdom of God, it is a matter of God's action.[188]

Thus God acts in a way which does not render human action irrelevant but coherent. The living God actually *does* things—which means that the category of history may reappear, albeit cast differently. It need not be construed as a progressive narrative in order to allow for the possibility of genuine improvements. Against what he saw as the one-sidedness of Kutter, Ragaz maintains that both facets of biblical eschatology must be held in a tension *which must not be resolved*. According to Ragaz, this is how the New Testament describes the Kingdom of God:

[186] See Arthur Rich, 'Theologisch-sozial-ethische Einführung', in *Leonhard Ragaz in seinen Briefen 2: 1914–1932*, eds. Christine Ragaz and others (Zürich: Theologischer Verlag, 1982), pp. 9–22, esp. p. 11.

[187] Leonhard Ragaz, 'Thy Kingdom Come', in Ragaz, *Signs of the Kingdom*, pp. 18–23, esp. p. 20.

[188] BEE, p. 125; Rich, *Wirtschaftsethik I*, p. 129.

> The Kingdom must *come*; it cannot be *made*. It is a gift, not something one earns. But this basic view is juxtaposed with a diametrically opposed position. Besides being an affair of God, the Kingdom of God is also presented as being an affair of men. The gift is also a responsibility.... It will not come if there are no people who are waiting for it, praying for it, working for it, fighting, and suffering for its coming.[189]

Any resolution of the tension in favour of one or other of its twin poles would enervate it of its fruitfulness for action.

Yet Ragaz himself was not immune from the temptation to resolve this paradox. Rich considers that Ragaz, with his rather vehement personality, was never able to hold both sides of his dialectic in tension for long, and tended to overstate what can be achieved through human action. Ragaz believed that Reformation theology, in its dread of Pelagianism, had thrown the baby of human action out with the bath water. It may be true in one sense that human action 'does not redeem'.[190] But neither, he notes, does the New Testament consider 'redemption as finished'.[191] The Kingdom can advance here and now, and its presence is by no means coterminous with the church, but may include various developments by which the lot of humanity is improved.[192]

Hence, while not identifying socialism as *the* answer in any permanent way, he saw it as a solution *at this stage* in history to the problem of bourgeois corruption:

> I am convinced that socialism in its basic goals provides the next higher level in historical development. But I do not wish to give the impression that I identify the teachings of Christ with a particular social order.... In theory we certainly need to recognize the possibility that after socialism has made its contribution to the betterment of mankind, a new and better order can arise to serve this end.[193]

Thus, while he refuses the finality of the hope which Marx invested in socialism, Ragaz nevertheless considers it as a stage in human improvement and development. Socialism is better than capitalism, and will be superseded in turn by something better again. Hence Barth and Ragaz fought together against German nationalism and militarism, but Barth soon rejected Ragaz's conflation of particular causes with the Kingdom, such as socialism, democracy,

[189] Leonhard Ragaz, 'The Bible: An Interpretation', in Ragaz, *Signs of the Kingdom*, pp. 118–26, esp. p. 125.

[190] Leonhard Ragaz, *Israel, Judaism and Christianity* (London: Victor Gollancz, 1947), p. 37.

[191] Ragaz, *Israel, Judaism and Christianity*, p. 38.

[192] Leonhard Ragaz, 'The Lord's Prayer', in Ragaz, *Signs of the Kingdom*, pp. 112–13, esp. p. 113. Michael Northcott has argued that this brand of eschatology tends towards the dilution of missiology. See Michael S. Northcott, *The Church and Secularization* (Frankfurt am Main: Peter Lang, 1989), pp. 193–7.

[193] Leonhard Ragaz, 'The Gospel and the Current Social Struggle', in Ragaz, *Signs of the Kingdom*, pp. 3–15, esp. p. 6.

and the League of Nations.[194] Barth saw socialism as a sign or reflection of the Kingdom, but refused to equate them.[195]

Rich's work is therefore an attempt to follow Ragaz's insights more consistently than Ragaz himself. Ragaz tends to collapse the eschatological dialectic into overoptimism; Kutter and Barth, Rich fears, tend to collapse it on the other side into ethical paralysis.[196] Indeed, Rich goes on to argue that Barth is not self-consistent either and, almost despite himself, acknowledges the need to make distinctions in the worldly realm while lacking the conceptual framework to do so in a meaningful way.[197] In support of this, Rich cites a famous passage from Barth's commentary on Romans: 'The revolutionary Titan is far more godless, far more dangerous, than his reactionary counterpart—because he is so much nearer to the truth'.[198] Yet Rich fears that the transcendence in Barth's eschatological perception of reality remains dominant to the extent that 'events in the contemporary world are ultimately inconsequential'.[199] What God has done and is going to do cannot be related to the ordinary course of human events.

Rich sees the promise of this approach, which is to guard against totalitarian political claims, since nothing can pretend to be perfect. Yet its terrible danger is to trivialize the present, as if 'all possible options may be assessed as ultimately of equal validity'.[200] Such a 'moralistic maximalism . . . no longer allow[s] room for the merely better, yet really possible'.[201] Elsewhere, Rich, writing with Siegfried Katterle, phrases this fiercely, partially blaming the dialectical theology of Barth and his disciples for the rise of Nazism, since this theological approach, he argues, exacerbated the withdrawal of Christians from the political realm, leaving it vulnerable and exposed:

[194] Paul Bock, 'Review of *Leonhard Ragaz in seinen Briefen. 2. Band: 1914–1932*', *Journal of the American Academy of Religion* 52.4 (1984), p. 790.

[195] Simon C. R. Ponsonby, 'Natural Theology in the Thought of Karl Barth' (unpublished MLitt thesis, University of Bristol, 1996), p. 2.

[196] Whether Rich's characterization of Barth in this period is accurate cannot, of course, be settled here: our discussion must content itself with Rich's interpretation of Barth. Other interpreters have sought to show that Barth's 'Great Disturbance' by no means necessarily leads to moral paralysis—as indeed it did not in Barth's own life. For example, Nigel Biggar, citing Barth's *Ethics* (1928–9), comments: 'Obedient hastening, then, is more than simply an inner dissatisfaction with the present in the light of the future; for "we are ordered to fight, to build, to work, to organize, to fashion things"'. Obedience is not characterized by paralysis so much as 'provisionality' (Nigel Biggar, *The Hastening that Waits: Karl Barth's Ethics* (Oxford: Oxford University Press, 1993), pp. 84–5).

[197] Indeed, Barth and Ragaz later came to an increasing *rapprochement*—as Barth became (again) more active politically and willing to make positive political suggestions. See Bock, 'Introduction', p. xix.

[198] Karl Barth, *The Epistle to the Romans*, trans. Edwyn C. Hoskyns (Oxford: Oxford University Press, 1933), p. 478.

[199] BEE, p. 137; Rich, *Wirtschaftsethik I*, p. 140.

[200] BEE, p. 137; Rich, *Wirtschaftsethik I*, p. 141.

[201] BEE, p. 129; Rich, *Wirtschaftsethik I*, p. 133.

> In fact, even before that, in the Twenties, the religious motivation and theological rationale of religious socialism were vigorously attacked by the rising dialectical theology. Their total critique of all things in historical existence and all that can be achieved through politics . . . made the struggle of religious socialists to retain the liberal constitutional state . . . and to construct a system of collective security for all nations to save world peace, seem a questionable and presumptuous endeavour, because achieving a more godly state of affairs by human effort was seen as impossible. Thus, sometimes intentionally, sometimes unintentionally, dialectical theology promoted reactionary powers in the time of the Weimar Republic.[202]

Rich observes that Barth himself revised his approach later in his life—a point he will revisit. In the meantime, he is left with the question of how one can therefore construct a historical social ethic at all. He turns to a different approach, 'creation theology' or 'order theology' (*Schöpfungstheologie* and *Ordnungstheologie* respectively), which he thinks avoids some of the problems of Barth's early theology.

Emil Brunner and the 'Orders of Creation'

As a representative of this approach, Rich chooses Emil Brunner. Brunner, under whom Rich studied at Zürich, also had ample exposure to the question of the Kingdom of God in religious socialism since he was taught by Ragaz at Zürich, and was Kutter's Vikar (curate).[203] Like Barth, he was keen to refuse any identification of human political arrangements with the Kingdom of God, but he also perceived that meaningful action is by no means the exclusive preserve of those with access to divine revelation.[204] Brunner did not consider the image of God to be 'formally' obliterated, only 'materially' corrupted.[205] He thus saw special revelation as entirely necessary, and declared: 'We know God's will only through his revelation, in his own Word'.[206] Indeed, the fact that there is a good natural order is one of the very things that must be disclosed in revelation, since it is no longer fully perceptible to defective humanity. Thus

[202] Author's translation of Siegfried Katterle and Arthur Rich, 'Einführung', in *Religiöser Sozialismus und Wirtschaftsordnung*, eds. Siegfried Katterle and Arthur Rich (Gütersloh: Gerd Mohn, 1980), pp. 7–9, esp. p. 7.

[203] BEE, p. 139.

[204] This should not be taken to imply that Barth denies this! But they handle it in very different ways, Barth adopting the 'distinctly aggressive metaphor' of 'annexation' (Biggar, *The Hastening that Waits*, p. 152).

[205] The debate is recorded in Emil Brunner, 'Nature and Grace', and Karl Barth, 'No!: Answer to Emil Brunner', both in *Natural Theology*, ed. John Baillie, trans. Peter Fraenkel (London: Bles, 1946), pp. 15–64 and pp. 67–128 respectively, esp. pp. 22–4 on the *imago Dei*. See the useful analysis in Robin W. Lovin in *Christian Faith and Public Choices: The Social Ethics of Barth, Brunner and Bonhoeffer* (Philadelphia: Fortress, 1984), pp. 62–8.

[206] Emil Brunner, *The Divine Imperative: A Study in Christian Ethics*, trans. Olive Wyon (London: Lutterworth, 1937), p. 114.

the Word does not contradict the natural, only the sinful.[207] It permits—even requires—Christian participation in the 'orders of creation'.

The centrality of this notion to his thought is evident in the title of his magnum opus, *Das Gebot und die Ordnungen*, somewhat obscured by the title of the English translation, *The Divine Imperative*. Indeed, it is the very relation of *das Gebot* (command) and *die Ordnungen* (the created orders of marriage and family life, the economy, government, culture, and the community of faith) which is so crucial: through these orders, the command of God becomes tangible. Because these orders are part of the divine creation, they reveal something of God's will, although this revelation is marred by sin. Thus they are:

> not merely particular spheres of life within which we are to act, but orders in accordance with which we have to act, because in them, even if only in a fragmentary and indirect way, God's Will meets us.[208]

The great gain of this approach is that it makes sense of the way in which goodness may be recognized and participated in, beyond the confines of the community which heeds God's revelation of himself in Christ—clearly a concern we have met earlier in Rich's work. Non-Christians get married, write poetry, govern one another, and so on—and their marriages, poems, and governments are not unequivocally rotten, be they howsoever imperfect. Nor are the poems and marriages of Christians somehow automatically superior, even though they belong to those who have a truer grasp of reality.[209]

So, although their historical forms fluctuate, there is something enduring and divine about the way in which these orders structure human life. For Brunner, this notion was particularly decisive for opposing what he saw as a pervasive and corrosive individualism (evident, for example in the contractarian myth of the pre-social 'primitive state'). Human life is inherently and permanently social, reciprocal, and mutually dependent.[210] Yet as we have noted, Brunner was quick to acknowledge the corruption of the orders by sin, and no instantiation of an order can by any means be claimed as a perfect expression of God's will. But Brunner did not conclude from this that all historical forms were equally damnable:

> Without doubt there are states which are better or worse than others, there are legal codes which are better or worse than others... but their fundamental structure is always the same.[211]

[207] Brunner, *The Divine Imperative*, pp. 61ff, and Ponsonby, 'Natural Theology in the Thought of Karl Barth', pp. 112–13.
[208] Brunner, *The Divine Imperative*, p. 291.
[209] Brunner, *The Divine Imperative*, pp. 210–11.
[210] Brunner, *The Divine Imperative*, p. 212.
[211] Brunner, *The Divine Imperative*, p. 213.

Yet Brunner holds back from asserting that Christians should strive for the improvement of the orders, and clearly this is a point at which he and Rich part company. For example, Brunner is especially suspicious of the Enlightenment impulse towards equality. His appropriation of Martin Buber's personalism led him to believe that it is precisely in the inequality and difference encountered through the orders that humanity discovers its mutual independence: 'Equality always means the removal of fellowship. Fellowship can only exist where people are unequal; fellowship is only possible where we are necessary to each other'.[212] Thus our first duty is to accept the orders as they currently are, in contrast to what Brunner calls 'the insane illusion of the modern man', who is so enamoured of his creative power that he sees the world as formless material to be shaped as he wills:

> Our neighbour and his world are not material which we have to mould first of all. It is presented to us already shaped... in spite of all that human sin may have added to this shape.[213]

Thus the relative good of the existing order should be accepted. This provides a safeguard against the potentially totalitarian impetus of human projects, just as the notion of divine *krisis* did for Barth.

Yet acceptance is only the first task, and not the last: 'the will of God does not merely tell us to adapt ourselves, to accept, but also to resist, to protest, not to be "conformed to this world"'.[214] He was critical of some strands of Lutheranism, which also emphasized the notion of the orders of creation and had degenerated into defeatist surrender to evil masquerading as order. Thus Rich especially admires Brunner for upholding human existence as genuinely responsible, without compromising God's sovereignty.[215] Human action can change things; it can make a difference—at least in theory. At times this approach might even demand a revolutionary response:

> The believer will be found now in the camp of those who maintain and justify the existing order, now in that of those who protest and demand a new order.... We have just said that the first thing necessary is not to alter this vessel but to fill it with new content. But there are vessels which are contrary to this content of love, and it is quite possible that such vessels ought to be smashed.[216]

What Brunner opposed was not the notion of revolution, so much as the anarchist claim that the overthrow of authority was necessary as such.

Nevertheless, Rich ultimately concurs with the criticism frequently levelled at Brunner that his overall conception of the orders inevitably led him into conservatism. In the sphere of economics, Brunner made pertinent and

[212] Brunner, *The Divine Imperative*, p. 213.
[213] Brunner, *The Divine Imperative*, p. 214.
[214] Brunner, *The Divine Imperative*, p. 217.
[215] Rich, 'Denken, das weh tut', p. 79.
[216] Brunner, *The Divine Imperative*, p. 218.

trenchant criticisms of the capitalism of his day, drawing on the work of Marxist economist and sociologist Werner Sombart.[217] Yet notwithstanding these, and his earlier enchantment with religious socialism, Brunner's conviction that acceptance of the orders as they currently are was the primary duty of the Christian drove him to accept capitalism, at least provisionally. One may strain after a better alternative, but until it arrives one must work within the existing conditions:

> Even as a capitalist it is possible to be an anti-capitalist 'at heart.' It is possible to understand the meaning of the words 'vocation,' 'service,' 'love,' and to do one's work in this spirit, as a service to the community within this horrible machinery of the profit system. For—in spite of everything—it is this economic system which supports us all, bad or good; it is this system by means of which God now maintains our lives. As a workman, or a manufacturer or a banker, I may be obliged to do things which run counter to all that can be described as brotherly love; but I need not be infected by the spirit of this economic system. . . . We cannot let the Christian life wait until a better economic order is here; none of us knows whether he will ever know any better order.[218]

So, while Brunner advocates the quest for a better economic order, until one is found it would be profoundly wrong to abolish capitalism: 'The most "humane" economic system is more cruel than an "inhuman" one if it is unable to provide man with that which he needs for his actual existence'.[219] Thus, for example, redistributing wealth might be permissible to mitigate particularly grievous inequalities, but it cannot be made into a constitutive principle of economic order: the capitalist order of ownership is unavoidable, at least for the time being.[220]

So, like Ragaz, Brunner doggedly attempts to hold the two eschatological poles in tension with one another, but he too is inclined to overemphasize one of them, albeit the opposite one to Ragaz. Rich blames this on Brunner's core concept, namely that the existing social structures are fundamentally shaped by the orders of creation.[221] Even in their historical and fallen form, these orders exist by divine volition. The danger is that this invests these fallen forms with an imprimatur of sanctity. Therefore,

[217] Brunner, *The Divine Imperative*, pp. 416ff.

[218] Brunner, *The Divine Imperative*, pp. 423–4. Emphasis mine.

[219] Brunner, *The Divine Imperative*, p. 425.

[220] David A. Krueger, 'Capitalism, Christianity, and Economic Ethics: An Illustrative Survey of Twentieth Century Protestant Social Ethics', in *Christianity and Capitalism: Perspectives on Religion, Liberalism and the Economy*, eds. Bruce Grelle and David A. Krueger (Chicago: Center for the Scientific Study of Religion, 1986), pp. 25–45, esp. pp. 32–3.

[221] BEE, p. 145; Rich, *Wirtschaftsethik I*, p. 148.

> With Brunner, this [conservative] tone is primary and thus dominant. In other words, the static, the preserving, and the existing remain dominantly in the domain of social ethics.[222]

Yet Rich remains warm in his praise for Brunner. In contrast to Rich's interpretation of Barth, Brunner makes a serious attempt to mediate between the unrealizable absolute of God's Kingdom, and the relative of social structures as they actually exist. He seeks to ground ethics theologically, and take existing reality seriously.[223] Yet Rich remains adamant that a way must be found to prevent the highly inadequate relative from hiding behind the claim to be divinely established as a created order.[224]

Eschatology in the Later/'Mature' Barth

Rich chastises the later Barth for a similar fault, although in Barth it is grounded Christologically rather than in creation.[225] Rich argues that Barth's emphasis on the reconciliation and restoration of all things having *already* taken place in Christ has much the same effect:

> In so far as it suggests that this evil actually is in the past, that it has already played itself out, although the world does not yet know it, and that therefore social-ethical thought and action concerning the future possibilities no longer need to take evil seriously . . . the social-political reality . . . is idealistically transfigured.[226]

Thus Barth in this period also endorses the existing state of affairs too much. Brunner, Rich thinks, brings down the Kingdom to the level of the relative. Barth raises the relative to the level of Christ's lordship, in order that the former might be construed as a mediation of the latter.[227] But Rich regards the

222 BEE, p. 145; Rich, *Wirtschaftsethik I*, p. 148.

223 In a personal commemoration of Brunner, Rich attributes his own emphasis on engaging with the world as it actually is, although shaped by sin, to his time as Brunner's student. In contrast to Ragaz's prophetic hostility, Brunner showed the way to fruitful dialogue with practitioners such as economists and businesspeople, so that the ethical demand can be shaped by what is practicably possible. See 'Denken, das weh tut', pp. 80–1.

224 BEE, p. 147.

225 See BEE, pp. 147–54.

226 BEE, p. 154; Rich, *Wirtschaftsethik I*, p. 157. Reinhold Niebuhr made a similar claim, namely that the 'present victory of Christ removes the need to care for the world'. But see Nigel Biggar's rebuttal (*The Hastening that Waits*, p. 157).

227 See the examples Barth gives in 'The Christian Community and the Civil Community' [1946], in *Against the Stream: Shorter Post-War Writings 1946–52*, trans. Stanley Goodman (London: SCM, 1954), pp. 13–50, esp. pp. 35–42. Rich is not the only one to criticize Barth here: cf. Nigel Biggar's summary of the reproaches directed at Barth's political application of the *analogia fidei* in *The Hastening that Waits*, pp. 182–4. In particular, this method, being somewhat arbitrary, could be used to justify almost anything. Biggar concludes that 'the elusiveness that characterizes the logic by which many of the[se examples] are derived from theological premises is fair game for the criticism that has been levelled at it' (Biggar, *The Hastening that Waits*, p. 184).

effect as much the same, namely that they both establish the worldly too directly from the absolute, thus denuding the absolute of its power to critique and thus transform the world.[228]

Liberation Theology

In that case, might liberation theology be germane in helping theology reconstruct a critical power against the status quo? Rich finds this wanting too. He argues that liberation theology on the one hand exaggerates the contrast between the Kingdom of God and the way things are, and on the other posits too much continuity between the Kingdom and revolutionary power. Thus the relative character of the revolution itself is hidden, resulting in a dangerous conformism *to the revolution*:

> The existing orders are already doomed to destruction.... On the other hand, there exists a massive correspondence of the final-will of God to the revolutionary powers in the contemporary order.... And that is the case in a way that conceals their relativity.... In this way there exists here the tendency to a conformism regarding the order-altering powers in the world.[229]

Thus the orders which succeed revolution will inevitably be tyrannous: their self-idealization shields them from the need for further reform, and thus corrupts them. Indeed, Rich regards Barth's insistence that the Kingdom cannot be brought about through human effort as highly salutary here. Hegel, Marx, and their Christian would-be apologists are wrong to presume that significant progress can be made in human history, and revolution must never be conflated with the Kingdom of God. Rich, like Luther, knows that self-assertion and greed can lurk behind revolutionary movements as much as behind conservatism, and any revolution is bound to produce a regime which also falls under divine condemnation.

Rich's Resolution of the Eschatological Dilemma Using Blaise Pascal's Dialectical Method

We have seen that Rich is profoundly arrested by Barth's absolute, eschatologically oriented critique of the existing order. He wishes to harness this for the relentless pursuit of worldly improvement. He is also impressed by Brunner's commitment to dealing with the world as it actually is, attending to the

228 Although see the somewhat grudging defence of Barth as a radical in John C. Bennett, *The Radical Imperative* (Philadelphia: Westminster, 1975), pp. 15–16.

229 BEE, p. 160; Rich, *Wirtschaftsethik I*, pp. 163–4.

possibility of God being at work in the real and existing, and not just in the new and approaching. This opens up history anew as an arena in which genuine improvement and change can take place, be they howsoever piecemeal and inadequate. Yet according to Rich, they both lapse into a conservative paralysis, collapsing Ragaz's dialectic into one of its poles, neither ultimately providing a way for the absolute of God's Kingdom to be brought into a genuine relationship with the relative of existing reality. Ragaz and liberation theology fall into the same predicament, overidentifying the will of God with actual aspects of reality, although they favour new and radical ones rather than entrenched ones. Ultimately, therefore, Rich concludes that there is no satisfactory way to directly relate the Kingdom of God to the existing orders:

> At this point one meets an aporia that is inevitable when one attempts to establish orders that are relative . . . directly from the absolute, and immediately to obtain from that standards for the shaping of the world.[230]

This trap is seemingly inescapable: if one derives the relative from the absolute, one ends up immobile, since the relative will always fall so far short of the ideal, and all the options will seem equally iniquitous. Yet if one does not bring the relative into interaction with the absolute, one will have no way to critique it.

Yet Rich recognizes the valid and necessary points each thinker makes. In contrast to Luther's polemical style and characteristic impatience with those with whom he disagrees, Rich sees the best in each of his interlocutors, showing that even their errors proceed from legitimate intentions. Yet he spots that the strength of each becomes their weakness when they make any given point, although valid in itself, into a fundamental principle. The answer is to take into account the truths for which these thinkers have pressed, without diluting any of them. It is not that they must be *modified* in the light of each other—the sail of belief in human capacity to genuinely alter history for the better cannot be trimmed to fit the wind of the conviction that the Kingdom only comes through the transcendent activity of God, for example. They are to be held concurrently as *mutually opposing* truths.

Rich's method has been formed here by his study of the anthropology of Blaise Pascal, on whom he wrote his *Habilitationsschrift*.[231] Rich was particularly attracted to Pascal's statement of mutually exclusive, opposite truths (*les verités opposées*) in a dialectical mode of expression—indeed, the subtitle of his thesis is *Eine Studie über die Dialektik von Natur und Gnade in den 'Pensées'*. Pascal did not attempt to integrate or synthesize theological claims, as if truth in theology was about achieving sufficient nuance and balance.

[230] BEE, p. 161; Rich, *Wirtschaftsethik I*, p. 164.

[231] Susanne Edel, *Wirtschaftsethik im Dialog: Der Beitrag Arthur Richs zur Verständigung zwischen Theologie und Ökonomik* (Stuttgart: Calwer, 1998), p. 181.

The correct method is to 'stake out the polarities', and let them stand in opposition to one another.[232] Thus, for example, Pascal insists on the total 'incommensurability' between God and humanity.[233] At the same time, he upheld a 'connectedness', and 'analogous relationship' between them. It is not that Pascal is confused as to whether such a relationship exists or not. Both of these things are completely true, but 'on different planes of truth'. Crucially, 'the opposition is not capable of resolution'.[234]

So, Rich does not seek a synthesis, a mélange of truths into one all-encompassing truth. His method, like that of Pascal (and Ragaz when he was behaving himself), is to hold truths together in tension without collapsing either into the other. In particular, he seeks to operate in the arena between Ragaz's two poles, but more rigorously than Ragaz was temperamentally able to do: 'The mediation, therefore, must fail in its complexity if one factor is diminished or completely disregarded in its weight relative to the other'.[235] This tension is insoluble, but properly so. Indeed, it is its insolubility which makes it potent, which licenses a meaningful social ethics without either trivializing worldly distinctions or uncritically endorsing the status quo.

Rich calls this the 'New Way'.[236] By taking both poles seriously without negating either, a mediation can take place between the ultimate of the Kingdom and the penultimate of existence, between the absolute demand of justice and the relative of what is actually possible. This provides Rich with the critical tool he needs to oppose carelessly conservative endorsements of the status quo on the one hand, and overoptimistic assessments of the possibilities of human progress on the other. It provides a perpetual motor for reformist activity, in refusing to accept the way things are, while equally refusing to identify the outcomes of any given reform with the perfection of the Kingdom: 'If Christian existence has to guard against pursuing a utopia . . . it must all the more protect itself from immobility'.[237] At each new moment one is driven to improve reality, yet with each improvement the situation remains thoroughly imperfect—so one is impelled anew to further reform. Although one anticipates with each improvement that the ensuing situation will still fall under divine condemnation, this can nevertheless be embraced, since it represents a *relative* advance over the existing state of affairs. One may not ignore the possibility of improving things just because the improvements do not make things perfect.

232 Tonks, *Faith, Hope and Decision-Making*, p. 89.
233 Tonks, *Faith, Hope and Decision-Making*, p. 75.
234 Tonks, *Faith, Hope and Decision-Making*, p. 79.
235 BEE, p. 160; Rich, *Wirtschaftsethik I*, p. 163.
236 *Neue Wege* was the name of a Religious Socialist journal, of which Ragaz was a central founder in 1906 (Bock, 'Introduction', p. xviii).
237 BEE, p. 128; Rich, *Wirtschaftsethik I*, p. 132.

Rich spells this out as follows with respect to economics. This eschatological outlook means that Christianity can never really endorse any economic order that does or could actually exist:

> No actually existing economic order can claim that it is inspired by the imperative of love in its specific structural principles and their effects. . . . On the contrary, each existing order, again in the words of Paul, belongs to the form of this world, which is passing away.[238]

So, the two sides of the polarity cannot be fruitful if they remain unrelated to one another. The key to making incremental improvements is to allow the two poles to interact, to contradict once another. Thus Rich states 'that the social-political setting of goals in the concrete shaping of society and the world must not be primarily established by the comfort and demand of the ultimate'.[239] At the same time, Christian existence must be 'existence in the penultimate, but in such a way that it lets itself be determined and moved in the penultimate by the call of the ultimate, of the "eschaton"'.[240] Human justice must be shaped by the demand of divine justice, 'even though no human justice can exist before the divine'.[241] It seems that this is to be done by *comparing* the existing state of affairs with the possible improvements that might be made. This naturally leads Rich to emphasize again the importance of practicability and empirical assessment in social structural reform, but he also intends to set out 'criteria' against which these reforms should be evaluated morally.

RICH'S CRITERIA FOR JUSTICE AND HIS SOCIAL-ETHICAL MAXIMS

Introducing Rich's Concepts of Criteria and Maxims

At the conclusion of his chapter on eschatology, Rich takes a moment to outline the basis for his next methodological move. This is jointly based on the 'existential-eschatological approach' of mediating between the absolute and relative, which we have just outlined, and on his earlier resolution (inspired by the work of Gerhard Weisser) of the dilemma regarding the normative significance of particular convictions (especially theological ones) within the realm of the social sciences and in a pluralistic world. Rich's solution is

[238] BEE, pp. 296–7; Rich, *Wirtschaftsethik II*, pp. 41–2.
[239] BEE, pp. 162–3; Rich, *Wirtschaftsethik I*, p. 165.
[240] BEE, p. 128; Rich, *Wirtschaftsethik I*, p. 132.
[241] BEE, p. 129; Rich, *Wirtschaftsethik I*, p. 133.

to propose three 'levels' of social-ethical argument: experience-certitudes, criteria, and maxims.[242]

The experience-certitudes should be entirely theologically conditioned. They cannot and do not need to prove themselves in a rational, universal way, but should be frankly acknowledged. These certitudes in turn give rise to moral criteria which,

> although they are oriented towards the absolute of experience-certitude, should articulate the humanly just in such a way that it can be understood, discussed, and applied even without the fundamental premises.[243]

These criteria are high principles and must guide the quest for justice. But in themselves they are not sufficiently concrete: Rich explicitly disavows Spinoza's doomed endeavour to elucidate ethics on a Euclidean geometric basis all the way from metaphysical axioms to precise and concrete moral stipulations.[244] Rather, concreteness is supplied through 'analyses of social and economic facts'.[245] Such analyses are needed to discover *how* to bring about the best possible state of affairs, to determine 'under what ethical and technical conditions an optimum of human justice can be achieved in the actual circumstances of social life'.[246] Weber's notion of the optimum is therefore the key at this final, determinative level of Rich's method, hence it is imperative to have objective, factual predictions with respect to the material realities of life.

Yet the criteria, although lacking the objectivity Rich will claim for his concept of maxims, still in some sense need to be convincing to those beyond the confines of the church: although not established rationally, 'a certain degree of convincingness is appropriate to them, which can and should become rationally effective in social-ethical argumentation'.[247] This coheres with Rich's contention that theological ethics should be grounded theologically, but still be accessible and persuasive to those who do not share theological assumptions. The criteria must not be calcified into dogma:

> The criteria . . . should by no means prove to be helpful and valid only inwardly, but also . . . with respect to criteria that stand in other ranges of experience. In contrast, dogmas do not need to prove themselves valid. They are simply decreed. Therefore . . . one must go to the trouble of that kind of proof, which is possible only on the basis of persuasive argumentation.[248]

242 BEE, p. 167; Rich, *Wirtschaftsethik I*, p. 170.
243 BEE, p. 167; Rich, *Wirtschaftsethik I*, p. 170.
244 BEE, p. 97; Rich, *Wirtschaftsethik I*, p. 103; cf. Benedict de Spinoza, *Ethics*, ed. and trans. Edwin Curley (London: Penguin, 1996).
245 BEE, p. 97; Rich, *Wirtschaftsethik I*, p. 103.
246 BEE, p. 168; Rich, *Wirtschaftsethik I*, p. 170.
247 BEE, p. 167; Rich, *Wirtschaftsethik I*, p. 170.
248 BEE, p. 96; Rich, *Wirtschaftsethik I*, p. 103.

For Rich, there is no need to choose between theologically grounded conviction and logical argument. They are both necessary: the former to recognize and elucidate the criteria, the latter to argue their case beyond the confines of the theological community. As he expresses this more pithily elsewhere: 'they are also introduced "confessionally" . . . though strong rational grounds can be given for them'.[249]

The interaction of criteria and empirical forecasts yields the third and final level of principle: maxims. They are the ultimate locus of the mediation between theology and general human experience, and between ethical criteria and economic feasibility. They are

> feasible, critically-examinable norms, responsible for mediating the absolute and the relative . . . [and] the normative, humanly just and the situational, economically correct, in such a way that they are able to provide practical guidelines for action, which are both ethically and technically responsible.[250]

This mediatory role gives these maxims a highly relative character in three ways. First, they are always only temporary, being related to the particular facts of the concrete situation.[251] Second, they will not be more reliable than the factual data which they interpret. That is, they are as fallible and contingent as any social-scientific conclusion.[252] For Rich, this is a great gain: being falsifiable, they are acceptable in Popperian terms. Third, although they represent the best chance of gaining consensus in a diverse society, they cannot *command* assent, but must be open to debate:

> Questions about the concrete optimization of human justice can be rationally answered differently in good faith in the same situation, under the same conditions, and by application of the same criteria.[253]

Thus at no stage of the process can an absolute conclusion be claimed. Each level remains subject to revision: the experience-certitudes always need to be refashioned and expressed afresh, which will in turn affect the criteria and maxims, which must also be reformed according to social-scientific findings.

In summary, Rich's method is to move from a particular theological basis, through criteria which can be fairly widely shared, to maxims which seek acceptance among an extensive range of people. Rich establishes his maxims on his criteria, but others may use other criteria and still arrive at similar maxims.

[249] BEE, p. 221; Rich, *Wirtschaftsethik I*, p. 222.
[250] BEE, p. 167; Rich, *Wirtschaftsethik I*, p. 170.
[251] BEE, p. 168.
[252] BEE, p. 97; Rich, *Wirtschaftsethik I*, pp. 103–4.
[253] BEE, p. 168; Rich, *Wirtschaftsethik I*, p. 171.

The Criteria for Justice

As we have seen, Rich's analysis of the core doctrinal theme of eschatology led to a key methodological conclusion, namely that the absolute character of the Kingdom cannot be brought into direct relation to existing reality, but must be *mediated* by comparing a given state of affairs to the states of affairs that might result were possible improvements made. For these relative changes to be affirmed, they must be *oriented* towards the Kingdom using ethical 'criteria of human justice', without seeking directly to deduce them from the Kingdom. Rich identifies seven of these. We cannot explore each in detail, but in this section we will pick out some salient ways in which these are shaped by Rich's methodology so far.

The first two are familiar territory: they express the two poles of the eschatological dichotomy explored in Rich's previous chapter. Rich's criterion of *critical distance* flows from the conviction that no human institution or structure can ever match up to the divine standard of justice. Instead, one must be perpetually aware of the evil encountered in all human structures without exception, so that no economic system can claim to be 'ultimately valid' (*Letztgültigkeit*).[254]

Rich adds an immediate qualification to this: his criterion of *relative reception*. The criterion of critical distance on its own would be nihilistic, inviting despair and paralysis, or radically withdrawing from the world as it actually exists. The criterion of relative reception therefore affirms and receives the relatively good character of the penultimate, and recognizes the possibilities for improving its arrangements.[255] Thus a given order may stand simultaneously under absolute divine judgement on the one hand (providing a constant stimulus to greater reform) while on the other hand receiving a relative human affirmation of its goodness and its scope for improvement. Rich characterizes this as a 'relatively better justice in the world of imperfections'.[256]

It is the insolubility of the tension between these two criteria which Rich regards as so potentially fruitful. Existence shaped by these criteria will be restless—unwilling to conform to the way things currently are, yet willing to accept improvement by small, incremental degrees, acknowledging all the while that the Kingdom of God can never be brought about by human efforts. The key question then becomes *how* these improvements should be evaluated.

He gives a helpful example. The right to property, he argues, cannot stand before the absolute demand of love. Crudely speaking, it would not exist in an ideal world, or in heaven. But in this era it is a relatively acceptable institution,

254 BEE, p. 177; Rich, *Wirtschaftsethik I*, p. 180.
255 BEE, p. 178; Rich, *Wirtschaftsethik I*, p. 182.
256 BEE, p. 297; Rich, *Wirtschaftsethik II*, p. 42.

provided it does not become overly concentrated in the hands of a few.[257] The crucial move here is that instead of comparing the relative to the absolute, one must 'compare the relative to the relative' in order to determine what is 'as just as possible'.[258] That is, the way to bring the absolute into interaction with the relative is paradoxically *to compare one relative option with another*. One must compare alternative *achievable* options in order to assess which of them is the best in the circumstances.

Mediation is also required with regard to the wide sphere of human values commonly discussed with respect to economic life, such as liberty, autonomy, self-interest, and altruism. Rich approvingly quotes the political scientist Alfred Grosser as follows:

> Values are by no means always compatible with one another.... The attempt to realize one of them can often bring us into conflict with the demands of the other. From that we will not conclude, however, that there is a golden middle way to walk along. We will instead sharpen our sense for the tensions between opposing imperatives.[259]

This for Rich is the criterion of *relationality*. By this he means that no one value can fully express moral truth, so none may be treated as absolute in itself. Rather, each value must be related to and accepted in tension with its opposite. Rich gives an example: Luther's famous antithesis that a Christian is both a free lord and a servant of all. Freedom cannot be understood merely as the absence of restraint (in which case the other person becomes a barrier to freedom) 'but always in relation to its complement of servitude' (in which case the other becomes the very realization of freedom).[260] Rich's theological rationale for what might otherwise seem a straight lift from Weber again takes its cue from eschatology: the transcendent order of God's Kingdom stands utterly beyond all human valuations and moral hierarchies. They are all decisively relative—not irrelevant or worthless, but relative. This applies equally to any theologically derived understanding of moral order. Even the absolute imperative of love can never be anchored to a particular set of human values, lest it be corrupted by their relativity: 'a moral order of values will come no closer to this command [to love] than a society, even at its highest imaginable level, will come close to the Kingdom of God'.[261]

Rich seems to have mingled the agonistic political vision of Max Weber with the sublime dialectic of Pascal. For Weber, humanity is a tragic and

257 BEE, p. 180; Rich, *Wirtschaftsethik I*, p. 183. See the very different patristic assessment, as summarized in Charles Avila, *Ownership: Early Christian Teaching* (Maryknoll: Orbis, 1983), esp. pp. 131ff.

258 BEE, p. 180; Rich, *Wirtschaftsethik I*, p. 184.

259 BEE, pp. 186–7; Rich, *Wirtschaftsethik I*, p. 189.

260 BEE, p. 184; Rich, *Wirtschaftsethik I*, p. 187.

261 BEE, p. 182; Rich, *Wirtschaftsethik I*, p. 185.

complex creature, locked in irreconcilable struggle with itself, so the realization of one legitimate value can only come at the expense of the realization of another equally legitimate one. Any comfortable balance between the two is a pernicious illusion. For Pascal, one must be caught up into the dynamic tension between opposing poles: because one can never fully arrive at *the* truth, the best way to express it is to remain *in motion between* truths, even if they seem opposed to one another.

This helps Rich advance his earlier discussion regarding the requirement for theological ethics to adopt moral values from the 'horizon of general human experience'. He now adduces Philippians 4:8 in support of this notion.[262] This by no means implies a mindless replication of whatever values are most in vogue at any given time. They must be received *critically*, which means giving each of them a relative weight by holding them in tension with one another. What must be resisted is the absolutization of any one value, which leads to its corruption:

> Individual responsibility becomes autistic utility-maximization, and the principle of solidarity becomes comfortable laziness; from frugality comes miserliness, and from generosity extravagance.[263]

For example, Rich observes:

> It would be wrong to think that the more equality there is among human persons, the more justice there is.... Egalitarian levelling, however, never corresponds to human justice, but instead proves itself again and again to be a source of injustices. For human persons are essentially not only equal, but also unequal.[264]

This appears to be the very view which Rich criticized in Brunner. In any case, it highlights the *basis* of this relativity of values for Rich: humanity. Each value *expresses an aspect* of humanity:

> The whole in which [values] find their unity is the humanity originating from faith, hope, and love. They themselves can never be this whole. They can, however, refer to it, but only if they understand themselves relationally, and thus do not attempt to become themselves the whole.[265]

The relativity of these values is thus based on the complexity of human nature, theologically defined. Hence, to take an example, Rich's proposal for a just wage is based partly on performance, and partly on need. This ensures the worker shares in the goods they produce, without removing an element of incentive. Both legitimate values must be expressed.

[262] BEE, p. 182. [263] BEE, p. 185; Rich, *Wirtschaftsethik I*, p. 188.
[264] BEE, p. 187; Rich, *Wirtschaftsethik I*, p. 190.
[265] BEE, p. 186; Rich, *Wirtschaftsethik I*, p. 189.

This theological definition is the concern of three more of Rich's criteria: of *creatureliness*, *fellow-humanness*, and *fellow-creatureliness*. These theological concepts (which, as ever, Rich regards as communicable and persuasive to those who do not share their presuppositions) enable Rich to guard against an economy which, for example, asserts human dominance in absolute terms. We cannot escape our creaturely limitations 'by a technocratic feat of strength'.[266] For Rich, this would be inhuman and antihuman, since it would amount to a denial of the way God has made humanity. Conversely, he adds that:

> Promoting an ecological maximalism that blocks the way to a high-performance economy that serves the human person makes no more sense than sacrificing the natural environment to the maximization of economic performance.[267]

The dialectical character of human reality is repeatedly evident here: humans are responsible but finite, social but individual. Humans are fundamentally related to other creatures, which although they are not human are also created by God, but humans are also fundamentally right to shape the world around them. Each aspect is absolutely legitimate and must be acted upon—provided all the time that such action does not transgress the opposite and equally legitimate aspect of human identity. For example, humanity is not God: it is not the Lord of creation. It exists in a relationship of 'ontological difference' to the creator. But it is an agent of the creator, existing also in a relationship of 'personal correspondence' to him.[268] Neither must come at the expense of the other. Responsible creatureliness must be limited by finite creatureliness, and finite creatureliness must not become an excuse for failing to shape history.

In the final criterion, that of *participation*, Rich continues in this more theologically substantial vein. Participation takes its point of departure from the words of John the Baptist—that the one who has two tunics should share with the one who has none. This word can be transposed to the *institutional* sphere.[269] This does not denote simple egalitarianism, which as we have seen would contradict the criterion of relationality. Rather, Rich advocates a just distribution of 'life situations' (*Lebenslagen*), a phrase he borrows from Gerhard Weisser.[270] For Rich this means advocating freedom against the centralized, planned economies of the communist bloc, but it must be a 'freedom that unambiguously stresses the right of every person to participate in the national income and national wealth'.[271] Rich believes that a living wage, full employment, and the welfare state are also required by this criterion, so that

[266] BEE, p. 193; Rich, *Wirtschaftsethik I*, p. 196.
[267] BEE, p. 193; Rich, *Wirtschaftsethik I*, p. 196.
[268] BEE, p. 172; Rich, *Wirtschaftsethik I*, p. 175.
[269] BEE, p. 194; Rich, *Wirtschaftsethik I*, p. 197.
[270] BEE, pp. 203–4, 282; Rich, *Wirtschaftsethik I*, p. 206 and *Wirtschaftsethik II*, p. 28.
[271] BEE, p. 203; Rich, *Wirtschaftsethik I*, p. 206.

even in a market economy, those who cannot contribute directly to production may nevertheless participate in its goods.[272]

Rich's Development of His Concept of Maxims

Having briefly summarized Rich's criteria of human justice, the final stage of his method is the formation of social-ethical maxims. By now it is no surprise to discover that this process is a dialectical one. He suggests that the maxims should be 'determined in a *circular* manner'.[273] One should move from the demands of economic rectitude to those of justice and back again, critically examining the maxim at each stage until one reaches a point at which the maxim meets the demands of each, although Rich admits that there may be times at which one may not be so fortunate as to arrive at such reciprocity.

The process of forming maxims begins with an analysis of the existing state of affairs and its problems.[274] One cannot begin with an entirely blank slate and ask which economic order would be the best per se. One must begin with the existing circumstances, and consider how they may be reformed. Using his example of major inequalities of income and property, the question then posed is: are such inequalities inevitable, or can they be overcome (or at least mitigated)? Here, objective analysis is clearly necessary in order to assess whether alterations will be effective or counter productive:

> If it proves not to be practicable, because it contradicts basic economic data, or if it shows that its actual consequences in a given situation . . . are humanly, socially or ecologically counter-productive, then it should be given up as economically-incorrect and ethically indefensible.[275]

In such cases the maxim should be abandoned or modified.

The maxims are therefore the locus of the integration of 'the supra-rational demand of human justice', and the 'rational demand of economic correctness'.[276] Such integration 'is possible only approximately', hence 'the normativeness of the maxims can be no more than relative'.[277] This does not make the maxims unreliable, but Rich concedes that an accusation likely to be levelled at his method is that 'the relativity of the maxims mean[s] . . . ethical relativism at the practical level, precisely where concrete decisions are to be made and, therefore, where it is most serious'.[278]

272 See variously, BEE, pp. 410–14; Rich, *Wirtschaftsethik II*, pp. 151–5.
273 BEE, p. 226; Rich, *Wirtschaftsethik I*, p. 227. Emphasis original.
274 BEE, p. 224; Rich, *Wirtschaftsethik I*, p. 224.
275 BEE, p. 226; Rich, *Wirtschaftsethik I*, p. 227.
276 BEE, p. 222; Rich, *Wirtschaftsethik I*, p. 223.
277 BEE, p. 222; Rich, *Wirtschaftsethik I*, p. 223.
278 BEE, p. 227; Rich, *Wirtschaftsethik I*, p. 228.

For Rich, though, relativity is not relativism (which he strongly rejects). The relativity of the maxims makes them not unreliable but *flexible*: they should always be open to improvement in the light of his principle of optimization.[279] In short, they are relative *to* something, namely 'to the absolute of the humanity originating in faith, hope, and love'.[280] Their imperfection is indispensable for their relevance, since if maxims pretended to be an 'ethic of the Kingdom', they would remove themselves from the real world:

> At the level of maxims, there is no perfection, no ethic of the Kingdom of God, the Sermon on the Mount.... If one were to aspire to and assert something in this way, only the collapse of each theory of social or economic ethics that grasps for the concrete would become obvious. The maxims contain nothing heavenly. They are norms of fully earthy smell.[281]

So, to be normative they must be relative. Yet because of this 'relative correspondence' to true humanity, they can be a 'first glimpse of the coming Kingdom'.[282] Their very relativity is what keeps them 'critically in motion' towards greater similarity to 'the command of divine justice'.[283]

The question which we will later put to this methodological step is whether Rich's maxims can ever therefore make a forceful moral challenge. We have seen that maxims are, for Rich, highly relative and contingent. They do not have the force of any kind of rule or imperative, since this would diminish the responsibility of those who must make the pertinent decisions: 'Maxims... cannot take the decision away from anyone; they are to be understood as orientation aids for a responsible decision'.[284] This does not negate their normativity, but it means that their normativity is of a relative kind. Because they are relative, even rather subjective, it is difficult to make their selection or rejection morally compulsory.

Rich's conclusions as to *how* the existing economic structures of today should therefore be reformed in the light of these maxims will be the subject of the final section of this chapter. Here we shall see examples of Rich's mediation between the absolute of the Kingdom of God and the ambiguity of the relative. But first, it will be instructive to note Rich's approach to the Bible in all this, a topic that he addresses *within* his discussion of his concept of maxims.

[279] BEE, p. 226; Rich, *Wirtschaftsethik I*, p. 228.
[280] BEE, p. 227; Rich, *Wirtschaftsethik I*, p. 229.
[281] BEE, pp. 227–8; Rich, *Wirtschaftsethik I*, p. 229.
[282] BEE, p. 228; Rich, *Wirtschaftsethik I*, p. 229.
[283] BEE, p. 229; Rich, *Wirtschaftsethik I*, p. 230.
[284] BEE, p. 232; Rich, *Wirtschaftsethik I*, p. 233, n. 16.

Rich and Scripture

Rich's first point is that the Bible contains maxims which are, like the maxims he has just defined, of chiefly *relative* validity, according to the specific situations they address: 'They, although fundamentally of a relative character, nevertheless make a concrete, and for the most part—indeed not always—situational claim to validity'.[285] Some maxims are more generally valid than others (such as the Decalogue), but even these are still situation-specific. Rich points to the fact that the Old Testament contains different versions of the same commands, adapted to new situations. Then in the New Testament Jesus intensifies these commands even further. They remain 'in motion towards a better humanity'.[286]

This metaphor of motion is significant. The Decalogue in Deuteronomy 5 represents for Rich a transition to a qualitatively 'better' humanity than that expressed in Exodus 20. In the older version in Exodus, Sabbath-keeping is a cultic requirement, and wives are treated as part of their husbands' possessions. In Deuteronomy, the Sabbath is grounded not in the cult but the requirements of social justice, and wives are treated as legal entities in their own right.[287] Rich draws the conclusion that the purpose of a given set of maxims is to develop and improve upon previous ones. The relativity of biblical *Maximen* is not merely situation-specific, but progressive. There *are* absolutes for Rich: the demands to love God and neighbour. But all concrete expressions of such love can only be relative. Thus, 'in their normative verbalization they [the Ten Commandments] are not themselves an absolute demand, but rather the relative, and hence variable, expression of an absolute'.[288]

How, then, is one to look to the biblical maxims for ethical guidance, while correctly negotiating their relativity? For Rich this is dependent on his eschatological perspective: whether one deals with them correctly, 'stands or falls with correct mediation between the absolute and relative, between divine and human justice, between love and law'.[289] He provides two worked examples, one from each Testament: the ban on interest (Exodus 22:15), and the injunction not to support those who give up work in expectation of the

[285] BEE, p. 232; Rich, *Wirtschaftsethik I*, p. 234.

[286] BEE, p. 234; Rich, *Wirtschaftsethik I*, p. 235.

[287] BEE, p. 233; Rich, *Wirtschaftsethik I*, pp. 234–5. Assuming Rich is historically correct regarding the chronological priority of the Decalogue in Exodus (and in this he is certainly supported by the majority opinion of critical biblical scholarship), we note in passing that the sharp dichotomy between moral precepts that are grounded in the cult and those that are socially grounded displays a somewhat controversial value judgement to say the least. Still more controvertible is the assumption that the socially grounded are superior and progressive!

[288] BEE, p. 233; Rich, *Wirtschaftsethik I*, p. 235. See the discussion in Walter Brueggemann, *In Man We Trust: The Neglected Side of Biblical Faith* (Richmond, VI: John Knox, 1972), esp. pp. 86–9.

[289] BEE, p. 235; Rich, *Wirtschaftsethik I*, p. 237.

imminent return of Christ and who therefore live off others in the church (2 Thessalonians 3:10).[290] He argues that neither prescription should apply directly today, but that this by no means renders them morally irrelevant. This conclusion is reached on two grounds. First, 'the basic social intention' *behind* the commands themselves can be seen, and must continue to be observed.[291] Thus, for example, the prohibition on interest was intended to prevent the exploitation of the unfortunate by enabling them to secure perpetual access to basic necessities for those who had fallen on hard times.[292]

Second, the *effects* of obeying (or of not adhering to) the command in question must be considered. Thus, Rich points out that the ban on usury in the late Middle Ages made matters worse by driving it underground and enabling lenders to charge extortionate levels of interest.[293] So, interest-bearing loans which are not made to private consumers for the sake of sustaining their bare existence are legitimate on the first ground (since their intention is the mutual acquisition of profit rather than the exploitation of the unfortunate) and necessary, even beneficial, on the second, since the economy of today is dependent upon them and would otherwise collapse.[294]

Rich has thus set out his methodology regarding the use of biblical commands in contemporary social ethics in a programmatic discussion which appears at the end of the first volume of *Wirtschaftsethik*. But apart from the two examples given here, and although he states that biblical maxims *should* be examined to see what they require today, he discusses few other biblical maxims in the second volume. He affirms the need for and legitimacy of engagement with biblical material, and provides a method for doing so. But the second volume is methodologically unable to carry this through, because the normative content for social ethics is not in practice set by this kind of exegetical discourse, but by a social-scientific discussion of concrete facts.[295]

[290] BEE, pp. 234–40; Rich, *Wirtschaftsethik I*, pp. 236–41.

[291] BEE, p. 238; Rich, *Wirtschaftsethik I*, p. 239.

[292] Of course, this claim is controversial. For example, Old Testament scholar Robert Gnuse argues that this prohibition also intended actively to hinder the accumulation of excessive wealth. Robert Gnuse, *You Shall Not Steal: Community and Property in the Biblical Tradition* (Maryknoll: Orbis, 1985), p. 7 and *passim*. Enrique Nardoni makes the same point with regard to Sabbatical legislation, and Timothy Gorringe argues that the Deuteronomists objected not merely to the inhibition of access to the means of life, but the transfer of wealth upwards per se. See Enrique Nardoni, *Rise Up O Judge: A Study of Justice in the Biblical World*, trans. Seán Charles Martin (Peabody, MA: Hendrickson, 2004), pp. 88–9 and Timothy J. Gorringe, *Capital and the Kingdom: Theological Ethics and Economic Order* (London: SPCK, 1994), p. 167.

[293] BEE, p. 237–9; Rich, *Wirtschaftsethik I*, pp. 239–40.

[294] For an alternative study with respect to the biblical prohibition on interest, written by an economist, see Paul Mills, *Interest in Interest: The Old Testament Ban on Interest and its Implications for Today* (Cambridge: Jubilee, 1989), and more briefly, 'The Ban on Interest: Dead Letter or Radical Solution?', *Cambridge Papers* 1.4 (1993).

[295] In the first chapter of *Wirtschaftsethik II*, Rich refers to a handful of biblical texts, encompassing such themes as creation and the character of *agape* love, but there is no sustained discussion of them, nor of other biblical imperatives.

RICH'S CONCLUSIONS

In a study of Rich's methodology, a detailed discussion of his conclusions would be out of place, but as this chapter draws to a close we will note some outcomes of how Rich actually *uses* his method, particularly as they appear in the final chapters of the second volume of *Wirtschaftsethik*. Rich's goal, as we have seen, is not to produce a perfectly just economic order. Such an aim would make things worse, since it would condemn all possible economic forms as unacceptable and therefore abandon the economic sphere as irremediable. The answer is therefore to strive for 'less unjust or, what amounts to the same thing, relatively better' ways of structuring economic systems.[296]

The criterion of participation plays a key role. Justice requires that 'structures are oriented towards the ability to participate of everyone involved'.[297] For example, participation should be reflected in non-confrontational relations between workers and managers, the state and unions, and investors. It should also be reflected in distribution, not only in the sense of output but also with respect to, say, opportunities to work.[298] On this basis, Rich argues that every worker should be paid a living wage sufficient for their needs (and their dependents), rather than being paid as modestly as the market will allow. Thus all have a stake in their own productivity, which is commensurate with their human dignity.

Yet on the basis of the empirically investigable facts, Rich notes a drawback: this 'severely weakens or even eliminates the incentive to perform well'.[299] This in turn diminishes economic efficiency and output, with ultimately negative consequences for poorer social groups. A competitive labour market is needed, as well as a just wage, and unequal incomes should be:

> permitted to the degree that they produce incentives to perform, ensure the efficiency of the economy, and thus form the prerequisite for a better position for precisely the poorest social groups in society.[300]

This reflects Rich's learning from Rawls, of course. Profit is defended on the same basis: it ensures creative entrepreneurial activity, good management of scarce resources, and hard work.[301] What is primarily determinative is not a substantial discussion of the rights and wrongs of the profit motive or self-interest, but an appeal to their positive consequences in the light of the economic facts.

[296] BEE, p. 650; Rich, *Wirtschaftsethik II*, p. 373.
[297] BEE, p. 402; Rich, *Wirtschaftsethik II*, p. 144.
[298] BEE, pp. 403–4.
[299] BEE, p. 411; Rich, *Wirtschaftsethik II*, p. 152.
[300] BEE, p. 411; Rich, *Wirtschaftsethik II*, p. 153.
[301] BEE, pp. 442ff; Rich, *Wirtschaftsethik II*, pp. 183ff.

The criterion of relationality is significant here too. In keeping with Rich's emphasis on not pretending, one can create economic systems *ex nihilo*, but on striving to reform existing ones he delineates two economic systems: the market economy (planned by individuals, coordinated by the market, made efficient by competition) and the centrally planned economy (in which the Party is the sole economic subject, controlling production and coordination, with all the problems this entails).[302] There are only these two possibilities—the *values* behind them are both fundamentally valid, and can coexist relationally, but there is no such thing as a system in which both systems function at the same time: 'They mutually exclude one another. An economic order cannot simultaneously exist on both systematic foundations'.[303]

So, in theory the values of both systems should be held together in dynamic relational tension. In practice only one system can be constitutive at a time. But, one *can* seek to modify one in the light of the other, in order to take account of the relationality of their underlying values, provided one recognizes that one principle or the other will always remain primary.[304] This is desirable for Rich because he wants to reconcile the systems in a way which respects the legitimacy of the different values that each represents: self-interest, liberty, and responsibility on one hand, collective interest, social duty, and solidarity on the other.[305] Just as the underlying values must be held in tension with one another, so must the systems which they generate. So Rich must analyse various proposed combinations of systems, in order to establish which system will be most effective, and whether it actually stands a chance of being realized.[306]

However, given his presupposition that only one or other system can be constitutive, in practice Rich is only willing to consider the market form of the economy. While examples of its abuse are plentiful, it can at least exist in a socially ordered way. It is the most efficient method of coordination, and is the best system for evening out interests and defusing conflicts. Constructed wisely, it need not entail monopolies of self-interest and ecological destruction.[307] In short, the market economy can exist in ways that allow for the values of the centrally planned economy to be expressed.

The same is not true for the collectivist system. Rich believes that the centrally planned economy simply cannot exist in a way that allows sufficient space for individual responsibility, because it tends not to allow any countermeasures. Thus, it 'cannot really be reformed, and thus also cannot be

[302] BEE, pp. 472–3; Rich, *Wirtschaftsethik II*, pp. 212–13.
[303] BEE, p. 503; Rich, *Wirtschaftsethik II*, p. 239.
[304] BEE, p. 505; Rich, *Wirtschaftsethik II*, p. 241.
[305] BEE, p. 486; Rich, *Wirtschaftsethik II*, p. 224.
[306] BEE, pp. 506ff; Rich, *Wirtschaftsethik II*, pp. 242ff.
[307] BEE, p. 514; Rich, *Wirtschaftsethik II*, p. 250.

relativized'.[308] So, for objective reasons, one cannot ever successfully modify a planned economy in the light of the market economy. (Rich argues that China, for example, is not a centrally planned economy with market modifications, but a market economy with a totalitarian political system.[309]) Yet a pure market economy would be unconscionable: the predatory character of a truly laissez-faire market means it would eventually destroy itself, so regulation is economically as well as morally rational.[310] The fully capitalist form of the market is too confrontational, and allows the interests of capital to dominate all others.[311]

Thus, Rich concludes that the fundamental economic system should be a market, in which planning regulates the market without overruling it.[312] He has chosen between the two systems, while acknowledging the relationality of the values behind them. That settles the question of economic *system*. But what kind of plan-modified market economy is best? Rich designates this the question of economic *order*. He is naturally opposed to a laissez-faire approach à la Friedman, given the principles he has laid out: however true one considers Adam Smith's idea of the invisible hand to be, Rich agrees with Keynes that capitalism needs to be managed by the state to avoid boom-and-bust cycles.[313] Government needs a very visible hand, as it were, to ensure the market harmonizes individual and social interests properly.

Therefore the promising area for Rich is in the cluster of forms of the market economy, which are modified in the light of the values which the planned economy sought but was congenitally unable to represent in practice. He discusses different models in turn, moving from the market economy least modified by planning, to the most modified form.[314] In the primarily liberal social market economy of post-1945 Germany, intervention was used lightly and only to safeguard its social purpose. This achieved much, such as subsidized housing, protection against unfair dismissal, and better industrial representation, but there remained unpleasant levels of inequality, unemployment, and environmental damage.[315] Rich also cites the efficiency and prosperity of Thatcherite Britain, which came at the expense of rises in unemployment and

[308] BEE, p. 511; *Wirtschaftsethik II*, p. 247. This does not apply to *socialism*, but to central planning. Similarly, Rich argues that it is inaccurate to equate the market economy with capitalism. It is possible to have a market without self-interested profit maximization being the highest priority (BEE, pp. 526–9).

[309] BEE, p. 522; Rich, *Wirtschaftsethik II*, p. 257.

[310] BEE, p. 600; Rich, *Wirtschaftsethik II*, p. 327.

[311] BEE, p. 617; Rich, *Wirtschaftsethik II*, p. 342.

[312] BEE, p. 615; Rich, *Wirtschaftsethik II*, p. 340.

[313] BEE, p. 533; Rich, *Wirtschaftsethik II*, p. 266.

[314] An almost identical method, although with less concrete conclusions, is adopted by J. Philip Wogaman in *The Great Economic Debate: An Ethical Analysis* (Philadelphia: Westminster, 1977).

[315] BEE, pp. 536–45; Rich, *Wirtschaftsethik II*, pp. 269–77.

inequality. He prefers the democratic market economy of Sweden, which regulates production very lightly, but arranges distribution much more intensively.[316] Wages are not simply remuneration, but reflect each employee's social contribution, hence its flat wage structure. But this makes it harder for weaker companies to survive, which results in unemployment, inflation, and the concentration of capital power in the hands of the few.

Next, the socialist market economy (democratic socialism) involves collective ownership (rather than nationalization) and macro planning, while retaining the efficiency benefits of micro competition.[317] Finally, Rich draws on Ota Šik's proposal for a 'humanly reformed market economy'.[318] Šik proposes to use the market as a system of coordination, to preserve efficient production and investment, but augment it with a plan of democratically decided distribution, including property reform, in order to abolish 'the contradiction between profit and wage interests'.[319] Collaborative ownership could *strengthen* competition, because its correlation of wages and profit gives an incentive to workers and suppresses excessive capital accumulation, which causes monopolies and undermines competition.[320]

Rich also adds that any market economy should be ecologically regulated, both for aesthetic reasons and to protect future resources.[321] This is difficult, as one should not limit economic growth too much, given the genuine shortages in underdeveloped countries, and because unemployment would grow if growth slowed. He suggests using fewer labour-saving machines (which are also energy-intensive), and reducing working hours to distribute jobs. The wage loss would be compensated for by a corresponding increase in the quality of life, and the hours gained could be used for doing more socially useful tasks, which would also bring down the cost of living. This would involve a departure from an overemphasis on maximizing profit or gross national product. These remain legitimate goals, but only among others, such as treating people as responsible subjects and protecting the environment. However, even the distinction between qualitative and quantitative growth should not be pressed into an absolute polarity since, for example, basic needs must still be met, which in an increasingly populous world means quantitative growth.[322]

[316] BEE, pp. 545–53; Rich, *Wirtschaftsethik II*, pp. 277–85.
[317] BEE, pp. 554–65; Rich, *Wirtschaftsethik II*, pp. 285–96.
[318] BEE, pp. 565ff; Rich, *Wirtschaftsethik II*, pp. 296ff.
[319] BEE, p. 570; Rich, *Wirtschaftsethik II*, p. 301.
[320] BEE, p. 578; Rich, *Wirtschaftsethik II*, p. 308.
[321] BEE, pp. 579ff; Rich, *Wirtschaftsethik II*, pp. 308ff.
[322] Economist Bob Goudzwaard disputes this notion in 'Economic Growth: Is More Always Better?', in *Christianity and the Culture of Economics*, eds. Donald A. Hay and Alan Kreider (Cardiff: University of Wales Press, 2001), pp. 153–65.

On this basis, Rich enumerates the following maxims regarding the form of the market economy, modified by the values of the planned economy, which he favours.[323] It must promote competition, which balances the interests of economic subjects and promotes general welfare by inducing efficiency. Regulation is legitimate, but only insofar as is necessary: it might seek to minimize instabilities, keep working conditions humane, and ensure ecological sustainability (perhaps by factoring environmental externalities into tax). Workers should participate in industrial decisions and share profits and losses, to ensure that they benefit from their work and have the incentive to work productively and take entrepreneurial initiative. All this will enhance efficiency—and thus enhance the common good. The social safety net of welfare for those unable to be productive must be added to all this. Welfare is particularly necessary in an industrial economy because of its potentially strong disparity in incomes. It enacts the principle of solidarity between the strong and the weak. Market arrangements must not come at the expense of caring for those unable to perform.

In summary, Rich advocates a competitive market economy which incentivizes hard work through self-interest, governmental intervention in the market in order to ensure fair play and ecological protection, and a strong welfare state. Distribution must take account of needs, while retaining differentiated pay scales and an open labour market. Profit is permitted, to provide an incentive for hard work and efficiency, but harnessed even further using collaborative models of ownership and employee representation, since their incentive to be efficient will be increased when their interests are aligned with those of their company. This will produce responsible rather than confrontational industrial relations, because no one group (unions/workers, politicians, officials, investors, managers) will dominate.

The key, recalling Weber again, is not maximization of profit, but optimization. In short, to borrow Robert Benne's phrase, Rich advocates 'capitalism with fewer tears'.[324] He certainly does not claim that these conditions will produce solely positive consequences. Nobody could be more aware that any arrangement produces mixed results. His argument is that, at this particular moment, these arrangements taken together are likely to produce optimum consequences. One of the questions we will therefore put to Rich in Chapter 3 is whether this conclusion is rather complacent, and leaves him without recourse to critique the existing economic order, or to propose any *substantial* changes to it. Rich acknowledges that there is much scope for reform and improvement, but it seems that effectively the pinnacle of what is just and

[323] BEE, pp. 612ff; Rich, *Wirtschaftsethik II*, pp. 338ff.

[324] Robert Benne, 'Capitalism with Fewer Tears', in *Christianity and Capitalism: Perspectives on Religion, Liberalism and the Economy*, eds. Bruce Grelle and David A. Krueger (Chicago: Center for the Scientific Study of Religion, 1986), pp. 67–78.

feasible is a system which resembles very closely the contemporary European free market in a democratic welfare state. We have essentially already arrived at the optimal possibility in a fallen world.

CONCLUSION

This concludes our commentary on Rich's method in *Wirtschaftsethik*. In this chapter we have briefly outlined some of Rich's biographical details and intellectual development, and we have provided an analysis of selected aspects of Rich's method in *Wirtschaftsethik*, with particular reference to its first volume. The chapter concluded with a summary of the conclusions and prescriptions Rich advances with respect to contemporary economic systems and orders, particularly as they are found in the second volume of *Wirtschaftsethik*. Our next task is to bring our methodological analysis of Rich's economic ethics from this chapter into interaction with our discussion of Luther's method in Chapter 1. It is to this we will turn in Chapter 3.

3

An Analysis of Arthur Rich's Method in the Light of that of Martin Luther

We have explored the methods of Rich and Luther in handling economic ethical questions in our first two chapters, in order to lay the groundwork for this chapter. To restate our aim, we will seek to identify specific ways in which the study of Martin Luther's economic ethics can help contemporary theology to be more self-aware of its own potential shortcomings. This chapter therefore uses what we have found in Luther, in order to discern both strengths and weaknesses of Rich's method. While Rich's approach has much to commend it, we find cause to question some of his fundamental assumptions, and therefore much of his basic methodological approach. This gives our final chapter a potentially frustrating bias for the reader who would naturally suppose that Luther also has much to learn from Rich. No doubt this is also true, and some advantages of Rich's method over Luther's will indeed be noted. But the temptation to structure the chapter as an equal dialogue between the two thinkers has been resisted because its aim is not to achieve a historical comparative study, but to strengthen contemporary economic theological ethics by drawing on a neglected potential resource.

ETHICS AS A SCIENTIFIC, DIALOGICAL DISCIPLINE

We will begin with a very *visually* noticeable difference between the two texts. Luther proceeds fairly directly to the biblical text and expounds it. For Rich, there is a sizeable quantity of preliminary questions to be dealt with, and indeed his first volume is predominantly devoted to these. He explicates and defends his assumptions and maps the phases of his method, so that his project is presented in a systematic, structured way. This might seem inconsequential, but that is the point of studying the method of a theologian who operated in a very different academic milieu (with different but similarly rigorous conventions and structures). It sensitizes us to something we might almost otherwise take for granted, namely Rich's methodical, quasi-scientific structure: narrowing the field of research, identifying presuppositions, and testing and revising hypotheses. This is a gain over Luther, although the latter's philosophical and scholastic training means that he is capable of much more systematic work than he is sometimes given credit for. But the difference between them alerts us to the importance in our own time of considering thoroughly exactly what a project is setting out to achieve and how.[1] Indeed, Rich needs to contend for the very legitimacy of his project in the first place, to secure a space for it in public discourse.

The potential disadvantage of Rich's seemingly scientific approach, however, is that it comes across as a shade defensive. Even the concept of normative ethics must be justified before the substance of an ethical project can be embarked upon. Indeed, we have observed that a corollary of Rich's attempt to yoke normative ethics with social science is that his conclusions (expressed in the form of maxims) can never have the status of unavoidable moral obligations. Like all scientific postulates they are hypotheses, subject to revision in the light of the facts. This means that the human will can never be confronted with a non-negotiable, absolute imperative to which the response can only be either obedience or wilful defiance. Rather, the good is infinitely and perpetually contestable.

By contrast, we find Luther's bellicose self-assurance distasteful today. But there is something compelling about his conviction that he has something worth saying on God's behalf which needs no further justification, but carries its own authority. Yet simultaneously, or perhaps because of this, Luther is far more willing to be ignored—his responsibility is to say what he believes to be true, even if that means being disregarded, whereas Rich's responsibility to optimize outcomes morally obliges him to procure as wide and convincing a hearing as possible. It is therefore proper, even compulsory, for him to mould what he says in order to do so.

A second, very apparent difference is the way in which Luther and Rich engage with other thinkers, particularly those with whom they disagree. Luther is well known for his exaggeration and aggression in his characterization of his opponents (although in fairness we should remember the polemic was by no means all on his side). Rich, of course, is working in a world of academic and political discourse where the standards of civility are very different, at least superficially. Rich's conscientious and scrupulously courteous work enables him to address social scientists and businesspeople who might otherwise be ready to dismiss theological insights. Allowing them to

[1] Of course, this is a hotly contested matter within the philosophy of science. See Paul Feyerabend, *Against Method*, 3rd edn. (London: Verso, 1993) and the response in James F. Harris, *Against Relativism: A Philosophical Defense of Method* (Peru, IL: Open Court Publishing, 1992).

dismiss him as naïve or discourteous would be letting *them* off the hook, and as we have seen Rich is conspicuously more successful in gaining a hearing for a theological perspective within economic circles than most theological contributions have been. Certainly, here is an exemplary model from which the contemporary economic ethicist has much to learn.

At the same time, Luther reminds us that anger is not always out of place in theological discourse, and there is a time for politeness to give way to it. Luther's outrage is not purely circumstantial or temperamental. We tend to assume that his theological method is shaped by what we might call his personality, and there is no doubt some truth in this assumption. But it is equally plausible that his personality was shaped by his theology. Confronted with exploitation and injustice, Luther reminds us that fury may be the proper response, and prompts us to be wary of ways in which academic impartiality may mask indifference or cowardice. Indeed, for Luther impassioned rhetoric was entirely compatible with scholarly rigour.

A major strength of Rich's dialogical method is that it enables him to receive valuable insights from his interlocutors. He is acutely aware of the provisional nature of his conclusions, and stands ready to revise them. He is open to adopting well-founded contributions from beyond his own frame of reference. Whereas Luther's greater clarity tends to lock him into a position, Rich is more fluid and able to improve his by learning from others.

Yet we should also note that while Luther can be notoriously rude about his theological antagonists, he also deliberately learns from them. Indeed, he recognizes that they made him who he was, theologically speaking.[2] And at the Diet of Worms, as every theology student knows, Luther notoriously stated that he was willing to change his mind if anyone could convince him that his views were in contradiction to Scripture or reason.[3] So, like Rich, Luther acknowledges the provisionality of ethical claims. Nobody can ever have the final word because, while God has revealed himself in a trustworthy and final way, our perceptions and grasp of that revelation will be far from perfect.[4]

[2] See David V. N. Bagchi in *Luther's Earliest Opponents: Catholic Controversialists 1518–1525* (Minneapolis: Fortress, 2009), esp. pp. 256–63.

[3] LW v. 32, pp. 111–12. This is borne out by the account of Aleander, the papal nuncio present at Worms. See LW v. 32, p. 124 and Heiko A. Oberman, *Luther: Man between God and the Devil*, trans. Eileen Walliser-Schwarzbart (New Haven: Yale University Press, 1989), pp. 38–40.

[4] What will spring to many minds here is the tag, *ecclesia reformata, quia semper reformanda.* This is sometimes misattributed to Luther and the early Reformers, but was not coined until the mid-seventeenth century, probably by the Dutch Calvinist Johannes Hoornbeeck. It captures something of the spirit of Luther's openness to ever yielding to Scripture afresh, but perverts his intentions if it is taken to locate Reformed identity in the pursuit of perpetual improvement. For Luther, the need for reform was a special case in a dire emergency, not an ongoing badge of honour. See Philip Benedict, *Christ's Churches Purely Reformed: A Social History of Calvinism* (New Haven: Yale University Press, 2002), p. xvi. This work also provides a sober assessment of

A proper humility and willingness to learn from others are thus quite compatible with confidence in theological revelation.

The weakness of Rich's approach, however, is that in holding several competing claims in irreconcilable tension, he ends up trying to straddle several positions at once. Luther learns from his opponents, but by evaluating their views from his own terra firma. Luther's combative and categorical style is unsavoury, and he lacks Rich's meticulous systematic bent. These are major drawbacks, and Rich's approach has a clear advantage here. However, Luther's thought does possess an underlying coherence, which functions as a vantage point from which to critically interact with different standpoints, and this is a gain against Rich, as we shall continue to see.

THE PROBLEM OF ETHICS

The Tragedy and Complexity of Ethics

We turn now to more substantial points. As we have noted, for Rich the ethical question is 'two-dimensional'. The integrity of *ethos* in its absolute sense must be preserved, lest ethics degenerate into an uncritical justification of the status quo. And the integrity of *ethos* in its customary sense must also be defended, lest ethics lapse into a destructive absolutism which fails to heed the real goods yielded by convention. This makes ethics complex and tragic.

Ethics is tragic because one is caught between these two poles, between competing goods. As an example of this tragedy, Rich mentions conscientious objectors who 'were driven to their actions by the most inner urgings'.[5] Yet they could not object with a good conscience, because by refusing to fight they broke the law and thus undermined the social good which the law exists to uphold. Rich quotes the Ukrainian poet Nikolai Gogol: 'Sadness overcomes my soul, because I am not able to see the good in the good'.[6]

This makes it impossible to set out absolute norms in advance of concrete situations. The appropriate norms vary, according to the potential consequences of particular actions. Rich gives the example of a doctor called to assist in a birth with tragic complications: either the mother or the baby will die. The norm ethicist cannot help the doctor, Rich claims, because either way the doctor will fall afoul of the command, 'Do not kill'. Even inaction would be

the Tawney-Weber thesis regarding the relationship of Calvinism to the development of capitalism (pp. 533ff.).

[5] BEE, p. 14; Rich, *Wirtschaftsethik I*, p. 18.

[6] BEE, p. 14; Rich, *Wirtschaftsethik I*, p. 18.

inexcusable, since then two human lives would be lost.[7] So an ethics of absolute norms founders on the exigencies of reality.[8]

Political action in particular is for Rich inescapably 'marked by structural evil and, therefore, cause[s] guilt'.[9] For instance, he regards the use of force as inherently dubious: '[human law] is also never essentially love, for love does not get along with power'.[10] For Luther, of course, law is a form which love may take for the sake of another. In Johannes Heckel's phrase, Luther holds that 'the divine law is the order of divine love'.[11] Yet, like Luther, Rich acknowledges that the use of force is absolutely necessary if order and justice are to be upheld in a fallen world. That is, the employment of a problematic means for an ultimately optimal end is native and appropriate to the political sphere, but nevertheless remains something for which one is culpable. Someone can be guilty even 'when he could only have done what has actually been done'.[12] Because *outcomes* redound upon their originating action, an action can be in a sense right and wrong simultaneously—even if it was the responsible thing to do. Hence ethics is tragic.

And ethics is complex, because the task of ethics is to reshape a complex social reality in order to make it more humane. Because actions produce both good and bad returns, it is difficult to discern which course of action will produce optimal consequences. How is one to weigh them against one another? To such a question there can be no simple answer, hence the ambiguity of action and the need for social-scientific analysis, and Rich rightly does not pretend that such analysis offers watertight security. Thus, the complexity of ethics lies in the complexity of reality: it is not easy to know what should be done. Ethics is inherently a matter of *krisis*: 'This leads to a crisis of morals, not from immorality, but from morality'.[13]

7 BEE, pp. 24–5; Rich, *Wirtschaftsethik I*, p. 29.

8 With respect to 'no-win' moral scenarios such as these, John Milbank notes that 'according to Aristotle such circumstances are usually pre-engineered by a tyrant' and therefore 'one may wonder whether they ever deserve to be baptized with ontological necessity' (John Milbank, 'Enclaves, or Where is the Church', *New Blackfriars* 73 (1992), pp. 341–52, esp. p. 349). 'Ontological necessity' is precisely Rich's characterization of such circumstances, hence his assumption that despite their venality, one must choose between one of the economic systems that already exist. Milbank's alternative is that, while 'one cannot *guarantee* the compatibility of goods, . . . to go on having *faith* in this possibility is part of what it means to read the world as created' (Milbank, 'Enclaves, or Where is the Church', p. 349). As we will see, Rich is suspicious of several aspects of the doctrine of creation.

9 BEE, p. 497; Rich, *Wirtschaftsethik II*, p. 234.

10 BEE, pp. 163–4; Rich, *Wirtschaftsethik I*, p. 166.

11 See Johannes Heckel, *Lex Charitatis: A Juristic Disquisition on Law in the Theology of Martin Luther*, trans. and ed. Gottfried G. Krodel (Grand Rapids: Eerdmans, 2010), p. 47, which provides documentation of Heckel's claim.

12 Quoted and translated by Tonks, *Faith, Hope and Decision-Making*, p. 217.

13 BEE, p. 12; Rich, *Wirtschaftsethik I*, p. 16.

Rich's Response to Tragedy and Complexity: Optimization Rather than Fixed Moral Norms

Rich finds a solution to the problem that this tragedy and complexity create for ethics in Weber's notion of the optimum. For Rich, the optimum represents a mediation between conflicting demands, between the absolute of God's Kingdom and the relative possibilities of human order, between the demand of love and the dictates of economic realism. For example, his criterion of the relationality of human values means that even a 'value' as important as altruism must not be allowed to become absolute, but must be held in tension with legitimate self-interest. To take another example, well-meaning actions may have terrible consequences, while self-interested actions can have ultimately beneficial consequences. Wilfully ignoring these hard facts is irresponsible utopianism, which is just as dangerous as relativistic pragmatism in Rich's view.[14] Even if it cannot stand before divine judgement, self-interest cannot be avoided within human history. It must be reckoned with as a constitutive factor of human behaviour, a necessary value to be held in relational tension with its opposite.

This is why, as we have seen, Rich is reluctant to set out permanent norms of behaviour. No norm can be assumed a priori. So, while Rich strongly affirms the role of convictions in shaping norms, he speaks also of 'the process of finding the normative' (*Findungsprozeß des Normativen*).[15] Humanity's role is not merely to be told about and do the good: it must *discover the normative for itself.* Here, Rich conforms to Kant's rejection of heteronomy.[16] It is not enough for humanity simply to be told what to do, and to do it on the basis of some external incentive, whether punishment or reward. This would fail to be truly moral, since it is grounded in necessity rather than duty. It is intrinsic to morality that it must be something laid out for humanity by itself.

Yet here Rich's adherence to Kant ends, since Rich's rejection of heteronomy leads also in his case to a rejection of moral absolutes. For Rich, 'the process of finding the normative' requires testing the consequences of particular actions. One cannot set out norms in advance, since the consequences of particular actions will vary according to circumstances. Norms must be formulated and tested in the thick of the way things are, and this process is an essential part of what it means to be human. Rich cites the poet, Theodor Storm:

> One asks, 'What will result?'
> The other asks only, 'Is it right?'

[14] BEE, p. 232; Rich, *Wirtschaftsethik I*, p. 233.

[15] BEE, p. 32; Rich, *Wirtschaftsethik I*, p. 36.

[16] See Immanuel Kant, *Groundwork of the Metaphysics of Morals*, trans. and ed. Mary Gregor (Cambridge: Cambridge University Press, 1997 [1785]) p. 41.

> and in this way the free
> Distinguishes himself from the slave.[17]

An ethics which takes it that there are predetermined norms regardless of consequences is a form of slavery. The great strength of this, of course, is Rich's refusal of simplistic solutions. A potential weakness, of course, is that this statement opens the door to a consequentialist ethic. Let us examine this in more depth.

As we saw in the previous chapter, Rich was stung by Marx's charge against Christianity, that the portrayal of humanity as made by a supreme God facilitates capitalist oppression:

> Against this perverted creation faith, which one-sidedly stresses the ontological difference between Creator and creation, and darkens, if it does not completely deny, the existence of the human person as an active, and thus free and responsible subject, Karl Marx justifiably protested.[18]

Rich concludes: 'The reduction of human persons to mere objects of the Creator must lead to their total dehumanization'.[19] Treating humanity as a function of God gives rise to what Rich regards as the legitimate protest of the atheism of Nietzsche, Marx, and Sartre. He argues that human freedom is protected by a biblical picture of the divine–human relation, in which God is not so much an absolute creator as a lover seeking a covenant partner (*deus amans et loquens*, in Pascal's phrase).[20]

Human creatureliness is therefore primarily to be understood in *dialogical*, relational terms.[21] Humanity is special because it is like God on the one hand (although simultaneously unlike him), and like the rest of creation on the other (although simultaneously unlike it).[22] This also enables Rich to assert that there is no inherent difference between human and non-human creation,

[17] BEE, p. 32; Rich, *Wirtschaftsethik I*, p. 36.

[18] BEE, p. 173; Rich, *Wirtschaftsethik I*, p. 176. This protest is justified because, as Harold Tonks summarizes, 'If it is of the nature of man to be dependent for his creation and being upon another . . . then it would in no way be a denial of the essence of man for the proletariat to be the mere function of capital'. Tonks, *Faith, Hope and Decision-Making*, p. 116. Of course, Rich is equally dissatisfied with Marx's solution, since the latter simply substitutes an absolutist account of man in place of an absolute account of God (BEE, pp. 174–5; Rich, *Wirtschaftsethik I*, pp. 177–8).

[19] BEE, p. 172; Rich, *Wirtschaftsethik I*, p. 175.

[20] BEE, p. 173; Rich, *Wirtschaftsethik I*, p. 176.

[21] At the same time, Rich invokes the notion of an ontological difference between creature and Creator, to guard against hubristic appraisals of human capability in which humanity is seen as having the capacity to overcome its estrangement itself (BEE, pp. 171–2; Rich, *Wirtschaftsethik I*, pp. 174–5).

[22] See Arthur Rich, 'Personal Evil and Structural Evil in Human Existence', in Tonks, *Faith, Hope and Decision-Making*, trans. Harold Tonks, pp. 303–17, esp. p. 307. Originally published as 'Personal und strukturell Böses in der menschlichen Existenz', *Theologische Zeitschrift* 24 (1968), pp. 320–37.

so humanity should not treat other creatures in a despotic fashion. What sets humanity apart is not something innate, but that God reveals himself to humanity and calls humanity to respond. This responsiveness is the theological heart of Rich's adoption of the ethics of responsibility, since the personal correspondence between God and humanity bestows on humanity a correspondingly divine responsibility:

> In the human person the creature is responsible to God for the created world.... Responsibility, determined in this manner, in which the human person answers that demand as an active, co-creative agent of the Creator, created in the image of God, is an additional fundamental characteristic of humanity.[23]

The English words 'response' and 'responsibility' reflect the double coding of the term *Verantwortung* for Rich: because it is addressed by God and called to a personal response, humanity is also responsible for itself and for creation. Creatureliness for Rich does not mean existence as a puppet or robot, although he is equally adamant that 'the human person is not... the lord of creation'. But it is 'an agent of the Creator, with the mission of bringing his saving will to effectiveness in the world'.[24] This is human 'maturity' (*Mündigkeit*).[25]

This response of humanity to God cannot be predetermined, which means that history is *open*. Human action and decisions make a definite difference—which of course places a corresponding responsibility upon humanity:

> Theologically, man's being this subject is the reason why, in his dialogical existence, he shares with his maker in creation, in God's history—the goal of which is his Kingdom expressed in the coming to perfection of creation. Thus man is placed in history, and in this history he makes a world, a world within history.[26]

The open question is whether this world will be one of self-assertiveness, or of free response to God's love. This is why Weber's ethics of responsibility, with its focus on optimizing outcomes, is congenial to Rich, since the onus is on human action to construct a just world within history. That is, the human task is to produce a certain set of outcomes. This is why Rich cannot say that some norms may never be transgressed in the quest for justice, because justice is not a feature of particular actions, but a feature of particular outcomes. So, while Rich rejects what he characterizes as the thoroughgoing relativism of Sartre, he is much more positive (although not entirely uncritical) about the approach of a thinker such as Joseph Fletcher, who argues that ethical principles (including biblical norms) should be neither abolished nor ignored but *relativized*.[27] For Rich, like Fletcher, only one thing is absolute, the *Bezugsnorm*, or 'ultimate

[23] BEE, p. 172; Rich, *Wirtschaftsethik I*, p. 175.
[24] BEE, p. 176; Rich, *Wirtschaftsethik I*, p. 179.
[25] BEE, p. 172; Rich, *Wirtschaftsethik I*, p. 175.
[26] Rich, 'Personal Evil and Structural Evil', p. 310.
[27] BEE, p. 29; Rich, *Wirtschaftsethik I*, p. 33.

criterion', of *agape* love. But love defies absolute expression and codification. No other moral claim, whether derived from Scripture or anywhere else, may be treated as absolute. But all norms *are* relative to the absolute of *agape*. Indeed, it is by encountering this absolute that one discovers their relativity in the first place. So this is, paradoxically, a 'normative relativism'.[28]

While Rich affirms the existence of one moral absolute, this is only a very general norm. In practice for Rich, this grounds a consequentialist ethic because, as we have seen, his way of assessing the *agape* value of an action is primarily by analysing its consequences. The contingency of ethics for Rich is therefore not simply that of casuistry, where absolute but generic moral norms yield judgements about specific circumstances which depend on the particularity of those circumstances, and which therefore vary from situation to situation.[29] That is, I take casuistry to be the task of discerning whether an action in a particular case is actually the kind of act proscribed or commanded by the relevant norm. It is therefore an analysis of the case which might include consequences, but would also include other features such as intention, as in the double-effect argument that abortion is legitimate to save the life of the mother. Such an argument includes an acknowledgement that a foreseen but unintended consequence of the act would be the end of the life of the foetus for the sake of the intended consequence of saving the mother's life. So this does take consequences into account. But it is not consequentialist because, while it involves a weighing up of harms against benefits, it takes the intention behind the act to be decisive in assessing the validity of the act, rather than the sum of consequences produced by it. It is casuist, because it is a judgement that this particular case is not a species of a proscribed act, namely the intentional taking of an innocent life. Rich, by contrast, is a consequentialist, because he does not display any interest in analysing the intentions behind actions. He takes the consequences they produce to be decisive in determining their moral value. The contingency of ethics for Rich therefore consists first in the fact that the consequences produced by the same action will vary from situation to situation, and second in the fact that despite the technical prowess of economic science, these consequences are very difficult to predict in advance.[30]

Luther offers an alternative methodological entry point. As we have seen, in the paradigm case of the command for Luther, prior even to the Fall, God commands Adam not to eat from the tree of the knowledge of good and evil. At this stage there is no *inner* need for such a command, because Adam does

[28] BEE, p. 29; Rich, *Wirtschaftsethik I*, p. 33.

[29] For a fuller definition and analysis, see Nigel Biggar, 'A Case for Casuistry in the Church', *Modern Theology* 6.1 (1989), pp. 29–51.

[30] For a general critique of this form of moral argument, see John Finnis, *Fundamentals of Ethics* (Oxford: Clarendon Press, 1983), pp. 80ff.

not yet need to be restrained from wrongdoing. The divine command is not merely a response to sin, nor is it fraught with menace: its original purpose is to give an external form of display to Adam's love-drunk, joyful abandon towards God—a state, of course, which is restored in the Christian. Thus Luther believes in genuinely *good* works, 'which God prepared beforehand' (Ephesians 2:10). Moral action is not inescapably guilty since in human action, God himself can act. The implications of this for social ethics will be explored in a moment.

Meanwhile, we might add that even in this paradigm case, the right course of action cannot be discerned by Adam independently. He must encounter it as an external requirement (although for Luther this does not mean that the command is arbitrary or extrinsic to Adam's nature). This prompts a question regarding Rich's portrayal of moral norms as things to be discovered by human investigation. Rich's description of 'the ethical' suggests he regards it as an independent object of human scrutiny—rather than something which dramatically actively confronts humanity.

The Source of the Problem of Ethics

As we have seen, Luther and Rich see the problem of ethics very differently. For Luther, the problem is not that good deeds are inherently cryptic, but that the human will is corrupt and enslaved. This predicament has three key consequences. First, even when humans recognize what is good, they deliberately refuse to do it. Second, humans wilfully deceive themselves, to excuse their decision not to do good. Thus Luther complains that not only are greed and usury on the increase, but to add insult to injury 'they have had the nerve to seek out certain subterfuges by which they might freely practise their wickedness under the guise of fair dealing'.[31] Third, fallen human perception is not only morally but technically defective. It is simply no longer as competent as God created it to be. So, it is not that Luther denies the existence of an epistemological problem with respect to ethics. But he blames the obscurity on the failure of human perception, rather than on the character of the good itself. The obscurity is only *apparent*.

Since for Luther the problem is the malfunction of human perception and the corruption and bondage of the will, his solution is the revelation of God's commands on the one hand and the treatment of the will on the other. Ethics is not a scientific procedure for unravelling and resolving the fiendishly complex question of what to do, so much as a dramatic confrontation between the duplicitous human will and the divine command. There can be no

[31] LW v. 45, p. 273; WA v. 6, p. 36, ll. 8–10.

negotiation or compromise, since the exposure and subjugation of human selfishness must take place before anything good can actually be done. A better schooling in the gospel is needed, to cultivate alertness to self-deception and avarice. Discernment and vigilance are not to be deployed in order to discern what is good, but to guard against the covert machinations of evil. A motif to be noted here, which will be explored later in greater depth, is that ethics is therefore an aspect of Christian theology, integrally related to conversion and discipleship.

Luther's emphasis on the need for humanity to be encountered by an opposing, crushing standard, which exposes not only one's inability to will what God wills, but also the bankruptcy of self-chosen human morality, immediately generates the question whether Rich's concept of humanity engaging in its own process of discovering the normative can ever free itself from the drive to autonomy and self-assertion which Rich himself acknowledges to be the essence of sin. Luther is not interested in dialogue with others so much as hearing and obeying the command of God—this is the proper creaturely role. The creature is not free to decide what to do, still less competent to select from a number of competing options. Thus the confrontation between the human will and the external command of God is a prerequisite for true moral knowledge.

Yet there is much to be affirmed in Rich's method here. While he rejects the notion of God as *prima causa*, he seeks to preserve the primacy of God by speaking of him instead as *primus loquens* and *primus amans*.[32] This portrays not only God, but also the *humanum* as relational and social from the very outset: the very being of humanity is constituted by hearing and being called to *respond* to the divine speech which calls it into existence. There is no human *as such*, no human who is not a human already created for and called into relationship with God—and, correlatively, relationship with other humans. This enables Rich to avoid the impression of humanity as a mindless robot whose role is to obey God's commands mechanically, without scope for meaningful deliberation.

Rich is right to note that it is irresponsible to regard the sum total of one's moral duty to be mindlessly following rules, without any thought to consequences. But our study of Luther prompts us to ask whether mindlessness is really a necessary corollary of the idea that there are fixed, absolute norms of action. The strength of Rich's consequentialism is its willingness to grapple honestly with particular circumstances, rather than make high and mighty blanket pronouncements about this or that economic circumstance. Its weakness is that it is grounded in such general norms that Rich is actually unable to do so successfully.

[32] BEE, p. 173–4; Rich, 'Personal Evil and Structural Evil', p. 307.

Meanwhile, Luther is certainly capable of operating in the prophetic pronouncement mode. But his discussion of the *Zinskauf* represents an alternative Christian response to the contingency of moral deliberation within particular circumstances, namely casuistry. Having laid out the ground rules for conduct with respect to lending money at interest, he then analyses the *Zinskauf* in detail in order to assess whether this particular contract transgresses them, and in what particular circumstances it might be legitimate or not. On the basis of this, he concludes that the *Zinskauf* is usurious in the majority of cases, but there are exceptions. Luther, as one representative of the casuist stream within Christian ethical thought, has therefore reminded us that consequentialism is not the only possible theological response to contingency and circumstantial particularity. Indeed, we have found Luther's casuistry to be the preferable response, since it enables Luther to enter into the specifics of particular circumstances without losing touch with the morally binding character of ethical norms even within the economic sphere. Indeed, it does not simply enable empirical discussion. It *requires* it, if it is to be successful in its own terms.

Human Responsibility within Social Ethics

A further question also arises here. As we have seen, in Rich's laudable desire to safeguard the reality of human freedom, and to emphasize the gravity of human responsibility, he places an onerous task on the shoulders of humanity: it is called to be nothing less than a co-creator of the Kingdom, an agent of the 'perfection of creation'.[33] His emphasis on the genuine openness of history is for him a cause for great hope since if human history is devoid of improvement, it is devoid therefore also of meaning. What happens in history really *matters*: it is not an arbitrary precursor to what God will bring about anyway. That is, there is hope for the here and now and not merely for the future. Rich is to be praised for seeking to defend Christian economic ethics from a purely other-worldly vision, in which there is no need to confront injustice and evil in this life because in the world to come God will make all things well. But this hope brings a correspondingly great responsibility:

> The human person himself is responsible for the institutional ordering of his society and, therefore, must also accept responsibility collectively for its structural consequences on individual, personal, and environmental behaviour.[34]

Yet our reading of Luther prompts us to question whether, by locating this hope in the scope for free human action within history—and not divine action—Rich ultimately misplaces it.

[33] Rich, 'Personal Evil and Structural Evil', p. 310.
[34] BEE, p. 53; Rich, *Wirtschaftsethik I*, p. 58.

Let us substantiate this claim. Our concern is that Rich has placed too high an emphasis on human responsibility for historical outcomes. Ironically, he is therefore forced into the same error for which he castigated Marx, namely, in the absence of God's direct action in history, the burden of responsibility falls on the shoulders of those most like God, the creatures whom he endowed with creative powers of their own.[35] Rich characterizes Marx's belief that humanity can in some sense master its own ultimate destiny as idolatrous superhumanism, and regards the claim to historical perfectibility as inherently totalitarian.[36] Humans cannot perfect creation or master their *final* destiny.

But Rich's emphasis on the interim openness of history and the responsibility of humanity for shaping it does make it liable for its *temporal* destiny.[37] Doubtless, this is a mitigation of Marx's view, leading to a fairly conservative ethic of reform, as opposed to a radical ethic of revolution. But the inner logic is much the same, so Rich's guiding principle for action is also much the same, namely to produce as good a world as possible in the circumstances through *human* action. The goal might be much more modest than perfection, but the underlying logic is still that of producing outcomes, and the agents of this production are still humans.[38] As John Hughes puts it: 'Marx cannot see that utility and immanence are not incidental to capitalism, but rather . . . instrumental reason *as such* is capitalist'.[39] He therefore tries to

[35] This is why Rich gives the scenario of the doctor considering an abortion to save a mother's life. The consequence of the wretched affair may indeed be that one of the parties dies, but it is not obvious that the doctor is *killing* anyone. Yet Rich regards the unavoidable outcome of the situation as the responsibility of the doctor, a conflation of consequence with intention.

[36] A criticism echoed even by some of Marx's disciples, namely that he makes human labour and action too constitutive of human identity. See, for example, Herbert Marcuse, 'The Foundation of Historical Materialism', in *From Luther to Popper*, trans. Joris de Bres (London: Verso, 1972), pp. 1–48, esp. 12–16.

[37] This point is made in Jean-Louis Chrétien's beautiful essay, 'From God the Artist to Man the Creator', in *Hand to Hand: Listening to the Work of Art*, trans. Stephen E. Lewis (New York: Fordham University Press, 2003), pp. 94–129. A similar point is made by Stanley Hauerwas in 'Work as Co-Creation: A Critique of a Remarkably Bad Idea', in *In Good Company: The Church as Polis* (Notre Dame: University of Notre Dame Press, 1995), pp. 109–24. He notes in relation to the papal encyclical *Laborem Exercens* a tendency to downplay the existing goodness of creation and a corresponding exaggeration of the potential of humanity to improve it through grand plans of varying magnitude. Jean-Louis Chrétien, 'From God the Artist to Man the Creator', in *Hand to Hand*, pp. 94–129. Rob Mackintosh makes the same error in 'Wanted: A Doctrine of Wealth Creation', *Crucible* (1992), pp. 129–36, esp. pp. 132–3.

[38] Cf. Oliver O'Donovan's point with respect to assisted reproduction, drawing on George Grant and Jacques Ellul. He observes that we find it difficult to think of ourselves as simply 'doing' things. Instead, we must ever be busy 'making a better world' or 'building a successful relationship'. This habitually prevents us from accurately interpreting things which are 'not a matter of human construction'—in this case, the economy. Oliver O'Donovan, *Begotten or Made?* (Oxford: Oxford University Press, 1984, 2002), pp. 2–3.

[39] John Hughes, *The End of Work: Theological Critiques of Capitalism* (Oxford: Blackwell, 2007), p. 94.

'think beyond capitalism while retaining its essential spirit'.[40] Much the same thing has happened to Rich: because he remains in thrall to instrumental reason (via Weber and Marx), he is simply unable to think beyond capitalism.

This critical observation is particularly prompted by our discovery of Luther's emphasis on the liberating potential of trusting in God's active presence in the realities and practicalities of daily human existence. It is not merely the case that at some unspecified point in the future, God will do something. The realm for which God is responsible, and in which his activity will bear fruit, is not a distant or abstract one. He is already at work, providing good things for his creatures *in this life* as well as the next. Humanly speaking one may receive money in exchange for one's labour or goods, but theologically speaking Luther insists that one's activity is separated from the provision one receives. So, it is not that the laws of economics (necessarily) predict outcomes wrongly, but that they fundamentally misattribute the source of such outcomes to human action rather than an active and caring God. In the light of this, the prospect that humanity must provide for itself and construct its penultimate reality as best as humanly possible actually seems little more enticing than the Marxist vision of history culminating in a perfect world order. Where Rich sees the hopeful possibilities in human responsibility, our reading of Luther prompts us to regard this prospect as a heavy demand, as a bondage to economistic calculation.

So we have seen that Rich's emphasis on the genuine openness and therefore hopefulness of immediate (not ultimate) history is grounded in his anthropology: humanity, as God's agent, is really capable of improving things here and now. And we have suggested that by locating hope in human rather than divine action, Rich has placed an intolerable burden on the shoulders of humanity. This prompts the question why Rich is reluctant to reckon with God as an ongoing agent within immediate history, and therefore cautious of grounding hope within God's action. The answer to this is found in Rich's eschatological outlook, and this will be the subject of our next section.

ESCHATOLOGY VERSUS CREATION AS A BASIS FOR SOCIAL ETHICS

Eschatology and Social Ethics

Rich shies away from the kind of emphasis which Luther has on God's dynamic and proactive presence in his world because, while he sincerely wants God's Kingdom to make an impact *today*, he is concerned to preserve

[40] Hughes, *The End of Work*, p. 94.

the dramatic otherness of God's work. As we have seen, Rich follows Barth in recognizing in the revolutionary spirit the same self-aggrandizement and greed which revolution itself seeks to displace. Any human order which sets itself up as absolute will degenerate into tyranny, as it arrogates ever more power in its insatiable pursuit of its goals. Rich clearly perceives the danger in supposing that humans can build the perfect world by themselves, and he is surely right to maintain against Marxism and other historicist idealism, that the perfection of creation cannot be realized by human efforts. Rich is equally opposed to theological versions of historicism such as that of Ragaz, which identify divine action with historical human movements. As a bulwark against this, he wants to insist that all human orders stand equally condemned in the light of divine justice. This means that it is hard for him to reckon with God as an active agent within history, lest this be construed as a claim that one particular human order or another has been sanctioned by God.[41]

Rich is rightly afraid of identifying the imperfect circumstances of the world with God's will. This would mistakenly justify and preserve evil. So, to avoid this, he points out the absolute dissimilarity between the fallen world and God's Kingdom. The crucial value of this notion for Rich is that it avoids a conservative endorsement of the status quo, while simultaneously contradicting the historicist view that perfection can be established by human effort.

The dialectic this yields is intended to produce a motor for perpetual reform. But in practice, this becomes an insurmountable obstacle to deeper change because an obvious corollary of Rich's postulation of an absolute, unbridgeable gap between the absolute of God's Kingdom and the relative possibilities of human justice is that they are congenitally unable to interact with one another. If we cannot identify any particular events in history as wrought by God then, by implication, God and God's particular requirements as regards economic ethics become abstracted from immediate reality.

So, despite his very positive expectations of the power of humans to improve history, and the correspondingly high level of responsibility this gives us, for Rich human justice remains an 'ersatz' substitute for divine justice, which is conspicuously 'absent'.[42] Towards the end of his magisterial survey of different economic orders he concludes, 'no basic economic system, even in its ideal form, can prevail in the face of the absolute requirement of the Christian criteria of humanity'.[43] Elsewhere, he quotes Pascal's dictum: 'Nothing will be just if weighed in these scales'.[44] That is, compared to divine

[41] John Hughes makes a similar claim with respect to Barth. Hughes argues that in Barth's vigorous resistance to the *idolatry* of work, in which work becomes seen as salvific, Barth denigrates it too far and finds it difficult to portray it as a holy obligation. See *The End of Work*, pp. 12–13.

[42] BEE, p. 229; Rich, *Wirtschaftsethik I*, p. 230.

[43] BEE, p. 597; Rich, *Wirtschaftsethik II*, p. 325.

[44] BEE, p. 80; Rich, *Wirtschaftsethik I*, p. 87.

justice, human arrangements can never be just. All orders fall equally short in theological terms. But if this is so, then the relative differences between them must defy description in theological terms—hence moral questions must be settled through empirical investigation as to the optimum possible outcomes. Or, to extend Pascal's metaphor, Rich must employ a different set of scales. Therefore, as we have seen, in the event Rich regards it as necessary to choose between one of the actually existing economic systems—quite a concession from the man who opposed Emil Brunner's 'orders theology' on the basis that it resulted in a conservative endorsement of the status quo.[45] And once a system is selected, as we have seen, he only recommends some relatively light tinkering to it, under the rubric of giving it a better 'order'. The potentially perpetually reforming zeal of Rich's eschatological outlook is thus not harnessed. Indeed, it is his eschatological framework, of all things, which sets up his conclusions that the ethical must be circumscribed by the dictates of economic feasibility. What Rich sought as a motor for reform has become for him a snare.

Prima facie, one might expect Luther to be in absolute agreement that human justice is totally inadequate compared to divine justice, and that human effort can never secure the establishment of the Kingdom of God. Yet he navigates all of this quite differently.

As we know, Luther vehemently insists that human righteousness can never procure salvation. Human action is totally invalid if it seeks or pretends to secure a right standing with God. Then, it will be a mask for pride and self-dependence. So, in Rich's terms, divine condemnation does indeed fall absolutely on the order which itself pretends to be absolute. This is a core facet of Luther's censure of the papacy: as far as he was concerned it could have been a perfectly legitimate human institution for the ordering of the church. Imperfect and temporary, to be sure, but useful. The church on earth needs some form of human governance, and there is no particular reason why it should not take such a form—as long as that was all it claimed to be. The disaster was its claim to unlimited and perpetual sovereignty in all matters temporal and spiritual. By staking such a claim, and by pretending this claim was grounded in divine sanction, this entirely licit human arrangement came to embody the spirit of Antichrist.

[45] See Joachim Wiebering, 'Rezension zu «Arthur Richs Wirtschaftsethik II»', p. 61. In various publications, Ulrich Duchrow has particularly sought to show that in any case the choice between capitalism and communism is a false one—not because one can adopt aspects of each within the other, as Rich suggests, but because there *are* other options. See Ulrich Duchrow *Alternatives to Global Capitalism: Drawn from Biblical History, Designed for Political Action*, trans. Elizabeth Hicks and others (Utrecht: International Books; Heidelberg: Kairos Europa, 1995), and Ulrich Duchrow and Franz J Hinkelammert, *Property for People, Not for Profit: Alternatives to the Global Tyranny of Capital*, trans. Elaine Griffiths and others (London: Zed Books and CIIR, 2004).

Absolute condemnation, then, falls on earthly orders and projects which overstep their limitations and pretend to an ultimate significance which they cannot have. Indeed, it is precisely the transposition of legitimate human orders into the realm of human salvation which debases them. So for Luther this *total* invalidity only arises in a particular way, namely when human justice is confounded with divine justice—whereas for Rich this total invalidity is all-pervasive. For Luther, the two forms of justice each relate to a different realm (although this does not mean the two cannot affect one another). In its proper realm, human justice can accomplish much that is genuinely good. It must be acknowledged that its accomplishments will inevitably be partial. But this does not mean it is entirely foul. In particular, the fact that these human orders have been created by God has not been obliterated: by God's grace they are capable of doing genuinely good things. So Luther speaks in terms not of an absolute condemnation of earthly orders but, to use Dietrich Bonhoeffer's language, of 'the absolute condemnation of sin and the relative condemnation of existing human orders'.[46] Crucially, then, Luther is able to differentiate between better and worse human orders, between more or less just ones, because the principle of differentiation is not an ultimate one. For him, the appropriate standard of civil justice is an entirely *earthly* one. So Luther's distinction between the two realms means that he does not consider that divine condemnation falls on every order in an equally sheer way.

In his desire for an insatiable motor for social structural improvement, Rich, on the other hand, emphasizes eschatology because he feels it will boost the critical purchase of social ethics on the status quo, and avoid what he considers to be the social conformism of Brunner and others, with their focus precisely on Luther's orders of creation. He therefore judges earthly justice in the light of eschatological justice, and is overwhelmed by the impossibility of relating the two together. If all human orders are equally bad before God, it is difficult to affirm any improvements to them, since such rearrangements will still fall equally far short of the Kingdom. Intriguingly, Rich criticizes Barth on precisely these grounds, namely that a transcendent eschatological perspective can only lead to indifference.[47] Yet he chooses to retain such a perspective, because as we have seen he believes that only this can provide the necessary

[46] Dietrich Bonhoeffer, *Ethics*, trans. Ilse Tödt and others, eds. Eberhard Bethge and others (Minneapolis: Fortress, 2005), p. 157.

[47] As we have seen, Rich partly blamed the rise of Nazism on what he considered to be the politically 'fateful diffidence' yielded by dialectical theology's emphasis on the sovereignty of God. See Tonks, *Faith, Hope and Decision-Making*, p. 198. John Milbank makes a similar claim with respect to the work of Donald MacKinnon, who draws heavily on Barth, namely that MacKinnon's emphasis on the transcendence of the good unintentionally posits its lack of correspondence with the finite realm. It is thus unknowable. This smuggles tragedy back into ethics. John Milbank, '"Between Purgation and Illumination": A Critique of the Theology of Right', in *Christ, Ethics and Tragedy: Essays in Honour of Donald MacKinnon*, ed. Kenneth Surin (Cambridge: Cambridge University Press, 1989), pp. 161–96, esp. pp. 174–8.

bulwark against totalitarianism *and* a constant goad for reform. However, elsewhere Rich does seem to grasp that there *is* a true worldliness which, because it recognizes its own inadequate, interim character, can do justice without making itself destructively absolute:

> Thus there is also . . . a genuine 'humaneness and worldliness,' which, because it is conscious of the relativity of all its actions, does not bring any absolute tones into its social and political thoughts and actions.[48]

So, Rich has correctly identified the necessary solution. But, because of his rigid opposition between absolute and relative justice, between the Kingdom and history, between divine and human action, he is unable to offer any substantial normative description of what this humble, appropriate worldliness should look like.

Luther is far more able to describe human justice, because he is far more ready to speak of God's activity outside the borders of the Kingdom. His distinction (however it has been distorted by some interpreters) between God's activity in creation (including in fallen creation) and his activity in redemption (in Rich's terms, the Kingdom of God), enables him to speak of God's presence in a fallen world without necessarily mistaking the fallen aspects of such a world for the will of God. His method need not therefore fall afoul of Rich's proper fear of endorsing the corruption of the existing order in God's name. This means that although at times Luther is despondent about the reaction he will garner, his confidence in God's power actually to effect changes here and now enables him to envision and call for radical changes in individual and social behaviour. In short, his belief in God's work in the realm of creation, and not just in salvation, enables him to expect and demand far higher standards of behaviour *within that realm*. On this basis, Luther envisages radical changes of behaviour at an individual level, and substantial reforms at a social and legal level.

Rich's difficulty, then, seems to be caused by seeking to identify human improvements as eschatological at the same time as being vividly aware, and rightly, that such improvements can never be redemptive and salvific (that is, in a sense, they can never be eschatological). He hopes the insolubility of this polarity will be dynamic, but in the end it keeps him static. Luther, on the other hand, is not constrained by Rich's condemnation of all social orders equally rigorously. His oft-quoted dictum that 'you cannot rule the world with the gospel' needs to be read alongside his view that government is a good gift of God by which he upholds order and justice. Rather than representing a conservative discomfiture with change, Luther's slogan equally means that one doesn't *need* to rule the world with the gospel, because the theatre of civil

[48] BEE, p. 136; Rich, *Wirtschaftsethik I*, p. 140.

society is already directed by God to act against sin and the devil. The two forms of government are both aspects of one divine rule, which is dynamically present and active here and now.

The distinction between the two realms also enables Luther to guard against the potential tyrannous encroachments of one realm upon the other. The church cannot rule the world, and civil government may not tell the church what to believe. The law is not competent to know or judge the secrets of the human heart, nor is it capable of changing hearts. 'Faith' that is produced through external compulsion is not really faith at all (since faith is an immediate work of God), so civil government should not seek to compel it. Thus the limits of government are established theologically—not pragmatically.[49]

But this awareness of the impotent and ephemeral aspect of temporal justice with respect to humanity's *inward* condition by no means entailed a minimalism for Luther with regard to *external* demands: one might not be able to change people's hearts, but one can hardly permit people to act in accordance with their hearts. Luther therefore expects human justice to be done. Civil authority has no reason to fail to do as it should, to fulfil its proper God-given task. Keeping divine and human justice distinct means that each can have its own integrity and perform its own role.

For Rich, by contrast, the key question is not one of the *requirements* of external justice, but of its *possibilities*. He claims that 'no human justice can exist before the divine' and, we have noted, that political action always causes guilt because it can never generate a situation that is free of structural evil.[50] This emphasis on the degenerate character of human existence leads to his assumption that only a certain (rather small) level of *external* justice will be possible. Because he considers that everything economic stands condemned, he is rather gloomy about the possibility of substantial as opposed to incremental reform. In his concern to avoid endorsing the existing political and economic orders he struggles to receive them as a divine gift, and, paradoxically, therefore struggles to claim them as arenas in which obedience to God is perfectly proper. Meanwhile, while no one could be more conscious than Luther of the wickedness of the financial arena, he assumes that it

[49] This is acknowledged in Oliver O'Donovan, *Principles in the Public Realm: The Dilemma of Christian Moral Witness* (Oxford: Oxford University Press, 1984), pp. 4–7, which offers an alternative, *theological* model to Rich's for construing the necessity for compromise within legal and juridical contexts without making practicability an overly decisive feature. Plainly, Christians share the public realm with people who do not agree with them. Here, then, what is decisive is securing the maximum possible embodiment of the *truth* in a plural and fallen world, rather than a calculus of the optimum *outcomes* in the circumstances (pp. 12–13). The difference is that one acknowledges one has made an inadequate compromise, rather than claimed it as the best possible outcome in the circumstances (p. 14). An exegetical exploration of the extent to which public law can express Christian moral standards is explored in G. J. Wenham, 'The Gap between Law and Ethics in the Bible', *Journal of Jewish Studies* xlviii (1997), pp. 17–29.

[50] BEE, p. 129; Rich, *Wirtschaftsethik I*, p. 133.

fundamentally belongs to Christ. Activity within it should conform to Christ's teaching and his Kingdom right now, and not to some alien interim ethic.

Furthermore, because for Luther civil justice is evaluated on its own terms, it is only relatively rather than unconditionally bad. That is, it is bad *in specific and concrete ways*, and its wrongdoing can therefore be addressed and corrected as such. Rich, on the other hand, while discussing the significance of eschatology for social ethics per se in great detail, ventures little *description* of what the Kingdom of God is actually like, and how that might affect economics. Indeed he cannot, because he thinks that attempting to derive worldly standards from the absolute of the Kingdom of God would be utopian, and that theology does not add specific moral content to the horizon of general human moral experience. The Kingdom is incessant in its *drive* for improvement, but does not itself offer any *agenda* or means of evaluating it. The Kingdom's significance is formal, not concrete. It remains at the level of a kind of cipher, a total critique of the status quo. So sin also remains relatively undefined. Because he believes all human economic orders fall equally far short of God's Kingdom, he does not give sin any tangible, specific description. It is not something concrete, to be opposed and overcome. Sin is simply the *unbridgeable* gulf between the relative and the absolute:

> In the penultimate of our historical time . . . there exists no identity, no harmony, between [reality and justice], only tension and conflict. . . . This difference . . . in biblical language is called 'sin'.[51]

Christian existence can name the non-identity of reality and justice as sin. But it cannot bridge this gap, because all it knows is that there can never be any identity between them. Sin, in this undifferentiated sense, functions as an immutable obstacle to the performance of justice in human affairs.

Yet without concrete descriptions, one has nothing to measure the status quo against in order to assess it. Still less can one advocate a particular reform on the basis that it is the will of God for this moment in human history. The contribution of Christianity to social ethics is the recognition that it is not possible to improve things much, although one must keep trying. Eschatology is invoked as a critical and motive *power* for economic ethics, but it also functions as an excuse for not testing human arrangements against the specific ways of the Kingdom. Such arrangements must be evaluated in some other way, which is why the notion of the Kingdom explicitly becomes for Rich 'a mediator between politics and scientific rationality'.[52] Rich was attracted to Ragaz's views because there he found the Kingdom characterized as a potent force in human history, but in his own treatment of it the Kingdom is rather distant, and even inert.

[51] BEE, pp. 432–3; Rich, *Wirtschaftsethik II*, p. 173.
[52] BEE, p. 128; Rich, *Wirtschaftsethik I*, p. 132.

Our critique of Rich at this juncture bears much in common with reproaches often aimed at Reinhold Niebuhr, whose work Rich draws upon, and which on several occasions he places in the *Literatur* lists that introduce sections of *Wirtschaftsethik*.[53] Indeed, Rich credits Niebuhr for the very project of framing economic ethics in social-ethical terms.[54] They share some striking similarities: the need to balance and harness competing interests, distaste for so-called utopianism, a desire for a credible Christian public voice to be secured by being realistic, even an anthropology which draws on Blaise Pascal.[55]

Niebuhr fiercely criticized the social gospel, which he argued assigned Jesus a reductionist role primarily as a moral exemplar, who 'reveals the full possibilities of human nature to us'.[56] By contrast, Niebuhr asserts that the *whole* of the 'mythos of the Christ and the Cross' must be taken into account, by which 'not only the possibilities but the limits of human finitude' are illumined.[57] This is also the case in *The Nature and Destiny of Man*, where Niebuhr cites Jesus as 'the norm of human nature' who 'defines the final perfection of man in history'. In dying on the cross he 'reveals divine perfection to be not incompatible with a suffering involvement in historical tragedy'. Yet precisely by doing so Jesus demonstrates that 'the perfection of man is not attainable in history. Sacrificial love transcends history'.[58] This approach has been particularly criticized by writers in the Radical Orthodoxy set.[59] Thus Stephen Long takes issue with Niebuhr's alleged adoption of Paul Tillich's 'spartan' account of the cross, in which the death of Jesus functions as a merely formal and symbolic disclosure of the principle of sin and thus a rebuke to attempts to reform society based on absolute ideals, as opposed to a literal atonement involving the substantial condemnation of actual, material wrongdoing.[60] Sin cannot be eliminated: we must take account of it as best we can.

[53] See Rich, *Wirtschaftsethik I*, pp. 71, 133, 202, 228. These lists are omitted in the English edition.

[54] BEE, p. 65, n. 1.

[55] See, for example, Reinhold Niebuhr, *Christian Realism and Political Problems* (London: Faber, 1954), pp. 13–16. For a sympathetic but critical account, see Mark F. W. Lovatt *Confronting the Will-to-Power: A Reconsideration of the Theology of Reinhold Niebuhr* (Carlisle: Paternoster, 2001), esp. pp. 155–6.

[56] Reinhold Niebuhr, *An Interpretation of Christian Ethics* (New York: Meridian, 1956), p. 111.

[57] Niebuhr, *An Interpretation of Christian Ethics*, p. 112.

[58] Niebuhr, *Nature and Destiny of Man* v. 2, p. 68.

[59] The most obvious item to cite is John Milbank's essay, 'The Poverty of Niebuhrianism', in *The Word Made Strange: Theology, Language, Culture* (Oxford: Blackwell, 1997). Unsurprisingly, several scholars have leapt to Niebuhr's defence, arguing that Milbank misreads and misrepresents Niebuhr. See, e.g., Richard Harries, *Reinhold Niebuhr Reconsidered* (Cambridge: Grove, 2011), esp. pp. 16–23.

[60] D. Stephen Long, *Divine Economy: Theology and the Market* (London: Routledge, 2000), pp. 39–40.

This is what we have discovered in the work of Arthur Rich. For Rich, the cross and resurrection of Christ do not accomplish the historical defeat of particular evils so much as demonstrate God's ongoing faithfulness to his creation, which gives Christians strength to work for justice despite everything.[61] Rich, like Niebuhr, therefore concludes that humanity must take responsibility for its own worldly destiny, but both thinkers are very cautious about the extent to which humanity can really change things.[62]

Creation and Social Ethics

So far we have raised concerns about Rich's theological grounding for social ethics in his doctrine of eschatology. This drove him to draw a rigorous distinction between absolute (divine) and relative (human) justice, which meant that he found it hard to bring the two into interaction with one another.

Rather similarly, Luther's experience in medieval piety was that when salvation was the goal of ethics, at first ethics becomes tyrannous. But then, in order to escape from such tyranny, the inevitable outcome is that ethics is subverted into a more manageable standard. If it is up to humanity to meet a divine standard on its own, as well as placing intolerable pressure on humanity to live up to it, the divine standard tends to be brought into line with human capacity. This is what we have encountered in Rich: on the one hand, ethics is eschatological. That is, ethics bears responsibility for the sake of the condition of humanity as a whole (albeit only temporally)—a burdensome task which Luther's emphasis on the ongoing presence of God in creation has caused us to question. And, in line with what we learned from Luther to expect, the enormity of this requirement leads poignantly to the dilution of its standards: the Kingdom of God is 'a promise, not a feasible, ethical agenda'.[63] Civil justice can only fall short of divine justice.

Rich's problem, then, is methodological: in taking eschatology as his sole theological reference point, there is no *intermediate* place for him to speak of God's presence in creation. The doctrine of the Kingdom was meant to be a radical resource, but Rich's interpretation of the early Barth's eschatological condemnation of human structures, and his overestimation of the importance of human action issues in resignation and conformity.[64] As Oliver O'Donovan explains, the fierce, typically Protestant insistence on the corruption and

[61] BEE, p. 117; Rich, *Wirtschaftsethik I*, p. 123.

[62] See the closely argued analysis in Robert Thomas Cornelison, *The Christian Realism of Reinhold Niebuhr and the Political Theology of Jürgen Moltmann: The Realism of Hope* (San Francisco: Mellen Research University Press, 1992), esp. pp. 92–5, 131–5.

[63] BEE, p. 497; Rich, *Wirtschaftsethik II*, p. 233.

[64] Thus Barth at one point states that humans need redemption not only from sin, but from 'the prior condition of creaturehood'. Karl Barth, *The Holy Spirit and the Christian Life:*

obscurity of creation, although legitimate, is disastrous if it fails to honour the enduring and intrinsic goodness of creation. He summarizes: 'Revelation is the solution to man's blindness, not to nature's emptiness'.[65]

We have argued that, somewhat to our surprise, Luther's creation-based ethic has a much greater, more radical potential. Luther, by his strict demarcation of the two realms of divine governance of creation, allows human justice its own integrity as a good in itself. This means that, in a sense, it has its own absolute demands, which are perfectly appropriate to its own sphere. At the same time, despite his profound awareness of the fallen state of creation, Luther also believes that God is very much at work within this sphere to accomplish his purposes and enabling genuinely good works. Indeed, the fact that God enables such good works in creation and not only in redemption means that it makes sense for Luther to demand them of his hearers here and now. God provides humanity not only with divine justice for eschatological salvation, but also with civil justice and earthly provision. As Kathryn Tanner puts it, 'complacency is ruled out not by a transcendent future but by a transcendent present'.[66] Less is more: the quest to make the created world more like the Kingdom is actually less successful than the quest to make the created world be true to itself.[67]

Should Social Ethics Be Based on Eschatology?

On the basis of such concerns, some theologians have argued that eschatology is a problematic basis for social ethics per se. For example, the criticisms of the work of Jürgen Moltmann by Stephen Williams and Tim Chester bear similarities to our comments about Rich here. Moltmann espouses hope as a core social-ethical concept on the basis that it is a concept of wide appeal beyond the church. In response, Williams and Chester point out that *Christian* hope is just as theologically particular as any other concept, and they doubt that one

The Theological Basis of Ethics, trans. R. Birch Hoyle (Louisville, KY: Westminster/John Knox Press, 1993 [1929]), p. 61.

[65] Oliver O'Donovan, 'The Natural Ethic', in *Essays in Evangelical Social Ethics*, ed. David F. Wright (Exeter: Paternoster, no date), pp. 19–35, esp. p. 26.

[66] Kathryn Tanner, 'Eschatology and Ethics', in *The Oxford Handbook of Theological Ethics*, eds. Gilbert Meilaender and William Werpehowski (Oxford: Oxford University Press, 2005), pp. 41–56, esp. p. 52.

[67] In parallel to this observation, Oswald Bayer argues that the dominant Protestant social-ethical school of thought suffers from a distorted Lutheran emphasis on sin, and the dominant Catholic school on an overly optimistic assessment of natural law. *Both* approaches lead to a reduction in moral standards because they are unable to critique the status quo, albeit for slightly different reasons. See Oswald Bayer, 'Social Ethics as an Ethics of Responsibility', in *Worship and Ethics: Lutherans and Anglicans in Dialogue*, eds. Oswald Bayer and Alan Suggate (Berlin: de Gruyter, 1996), pp. 187–201, esp. pp. 191–2.

needs to believe that admirable aspects of this world will be preserved in the next in order to make the task of improving this present world seem worthwhile. That is, even if human action is not significant eschatologically, it can still have its own authentic significance. And pertinently for our purposes, they suggest that an overemphasis on divine hostility towards the world as it exists profoundly denigrates the notion that creation is inherently good.[68]

While Williams and Chester may make comments that hit their mark, their overall goal of discrediting eschatology as a social-ethical resource as such is unfortunate. Our study of Luther and Rich suggests that the point is not whether social ethics is based on eschatology or not, but how truthful is the eschatological doctrine upon which social ethics is then based. If Moltmann and Rich ultimately fail in their social-ethical projects, we should not assume that this is solely because they drew heavily on the doctrine of eschatology, unless we have first investigated whether the details of that doctrine were adequate or not. Luther's analysis of the narrative of creation and fall in Genesis 1–3, and more recently the work of Henri de Lubac, prompt us to suggest that the problem is the characterization of eschatology as extrinsic to created reality (as opposed to fallen reality), rather than its consummation. De Lubac argued that this leads to suspicion of the natural, which is what we have found in Rich.[69]

As we have seen, Oliver O'Donovan also criticizes what he regards as a Protestant overemphasis on eschatology at the expense of the goodness of creation. But for him, this need not and should not exclude a necessary eschatological dimension to ethics:

> Not even a natural ethic that was entirely obedient to the revealed doctrine of creation could suffice as a complete moral guide.... [In the gospel] we must recognize a demand which falls quite outside the scope of the natural order.[70]

O'Donovan's solution is therefore a 'balance' between nature and history, between creation and eschatology.[71] This is corroborated by recent critical

[68] See Stephen Williams, 'The Partition of Love and Hope: Eschatology and Social Responsibility', *Transformation* 7.3 (July–September 1990), pp. 24–7; Tim Chester, *Mission and the Coming of God: Eschatology, the Trinity and Mission in the Theology of Jürgen Moltmann and Contemporary Evangelicalism* (Milton Keynes: Paternoster, 2006), esp. pp. 124–6, 159. Miroslav Volf offers a rebuttal in 'On Loving with Hope: Eschatology and Social Responsibility', *Transformation* 7.3 (July–September 1990), pp. 28–31, a theme he develops in his 'pneumatological' (rather than simply protological or creation-based) theology of work in *Work in the Spirit: Toward a Theology of Work* (Oxford: Oxford University Press, 1991). See the discussion in Darrell Cosden, *A Theology of Work: Work and the New Creation* (Carlisle: Paternoster, 2004), pp. 41–7.

[69] Cf. Jean-Yves Lacoste, 'Le Désir et l'inexigible: pour lire Henri de Lubac', in *Le Monde et l'Absence d'Œuvre et Autres Études* (Paris: Presses Universitaires de France, 2001), and John Milbank, *The Suspended Middle: Henri de Lubac and the Debate Concerning the Supernatural* (Grand Rapids: Eerdmans, 2005).

[70] O'Donovan, 'The Natural Ethic', p. 28.

[71] O'Donovan, 'The Natural Ethic', p. 27.

study of New Testament eschatology, summarized in the slogan that the Kingdom is 'now and not yet'. The New Testament speaks without hesitation of the *presence* of the Kingdom, without lapsing into the anthropocentric historicism of which Rich is rightly afraid, because in this account the Kingdom's presence is entirely God's work and not a human construction. The ethical corollary of this is that those who enter the Kingdom are empowered by its presence to live within it here and now, even if to others this appears absurd and impractical.[72]

PROBLEMS WITH RICH'S PRACTICE OF SOCIAL ETHICS

Rich's work is unapologetically a piece of social ethics. Yet one unexpected finding of our study is that the practical conclusions Rich draws, despite his good intentions, are rather unadventurous, while Luther, who has stood accused of advocating an individualistic ethic, is in fact rather socially radical. It is worth reflecting on some possible reasons for this disparity.

Earlier, we found much to commend about Rich's decision to look at economic ethics in a primarily social key. For example, he is surely right to arduously oppose privatized, individualized accounts of morality that, provided one adheres to narrowly defined standards of right personal action, absolve one of wider social responsibility. He refuses to excuse the self-satisfied person who considers themselves good because they have never stolen or murdered, but has never acknowledged their complicity in structural injustice from which they profit. They may not have caused the problem intentionally, but they still have a responsibility to address it. Poverty, deprivation, and other social evils are not merely unfortunate happenstance, but the outcome of complex agglomerations of particular human decisions and actions.

Having noted these strengths, let us review Luther's method again in order to consider what critical light it might shed on Rich's work. Luther's method is one of scriptural exegesis in a sermon. Far from being superficial or accidental, this is predicated on his assumption that the main obstacle to right action is

[72] Among the voluminous literature, see, inter alia, George Eldon Ladd, *The Presence of the Future: The Eschatology of Biblical Realism* (London: SPCK, 1974), esp. chapters 4 and 12. He gives a full bibliography in *A Theology of the New Testament*, rev. edn., ed. Donald A. Hagner, (Grand Rapids: Eerdmans, 1993), esp. p. 118. Although Ladd only gives social ethics a page and a half, his interpretation is developed by David G. Peterson in 'Jesus and Social Ethics', in *Explorations 3: Christians in Society*, ed. B. G. Webb, (Homebush West: Lancer, 1988), pp. 73–96, available online at <http://davidgpeterson.com/other-topics/jesus-and-social-ethics/> (accessed 2 May 2011). For a typology of interpretations of New Testament eschatology and their implications for social ethics, see Howard Snyder, 'Models of the Kingdom: Sorting out the Practical Meaning of God's Reign', *Transformation* 10.1 (1993), pp. 1–6.

not that it is hidden and obscure, but that the human heart is stubborn, partial, and self-deceptive. Luther's target, as it were, is the heart and not the head. He regards it as relatively easy to read and expound Scripture, and thus to discover God's will. Yet it is laborious and nigh impossible to overcome human attempts to evade God's commands. Let us borrow Bernd Wannenwetsch's eloquent if cheeky distinction between the 'bureaucratic rather than prophetic use of Scripture': rather than assembling all the possible relevant biblical texts 'so as to make sure they will finally cancel each other out', Luther preaches the full intensity and obligation of the particular biblical text before him so that his hearers and readers will *feel* its full force.[73] Scripture for Luther is not merely a catalogue of divine commands to be heeded (although it does contain categorically binding commands). It is a weapon in the divine arsenal for the conquest of greed and unbelief. Rather than treating Scripture primarily as a fixed deposit of revealed content (although it is also this), it is *God* who is the primary subject in the activity of the exposition of Scripture.[74] The encounter between the divine command and the human agent is not only a matter of analysis and deduction *by* the human, but of the dynamic transformation *of* the human.

This is why Luther is incessantly suspicious towards what he regards as attempts to water down the absolute character of the divine command. This would make it precisely useless in confronting the real problem, namely the evasiveness and obstinacy of the human will. This observation prompts a critical challenge to Rich's method: it seems that Rich does not go far enough back in tracing the origin of social maladies in this way, or in the treatments which he advocates for them. On the one hand, he locates the origin of social structural evils in the egoism, fear, and greed seated in the marrow of human life, *but he does not tackle them on this level.* Indeed, he tends to regard them as intractable facts of reality, which is why, for example, self-interest cannot be excluded from social structures. Instead, social structures must be re-engineered humanely in order to both harness self-interest and prevent it from becoming dominant.[75] In turn, this means that social structures are

[73] Wannenwetsch, '"Intrinsically Evil Acts"; or, Why Abortion and Euthanasia Cannot Be Justified', in *Ecumenical Ventures in Ethics: Protestants Engage Pope John Paul II's Moral Encyclicals*, eds. Reinhard Hütter and Theodor Dieter (Grand Rapids: Eerdmans, 1998), pp. 185–215, esp. p. 187.

[74] Cf. Brian Brock's discussion, drawing on his engagement with Luther and Augustine in *Singing the Ethos of God: On the Place of Christian Ethics in Scripture* (Grand Rapids: Eerdmans, 2007), esp. pp. 253–7. See also John Webster's discussion of the holiness of Scripture in terms of God's *action* in setting it apart (as opposed to some inherent but static quality it possesses) in *Holy Scripture: A Dogmatic Sketch* (Cambridge: Cambridge University Press, 2003), pp. 17, 26–8.

[75] Cf. Jürgen Moltmann's criticisms of Reinhold Niebuhr in his 'Foreword' to Robert Thomas Cornelison, *The Christian Realism of Reinhold Niebuhr and the Political Theology of Jürgen Moltmann: The Realism of Hope* (San Francisco: Mellen Research University Press, 1992), pp. i–v, esp. pp. ii–iii.

inescapably marred by a dimension of tragic inevitability. Thus, while Rich sets out to exploit precisely the provisional and malleable character of human social structures in favour of a more humane and just order, because he only sets out to tackle human corruption on this social level he is unable to envisage a more radical (in the etymological sense of 'of the roots') level of transformation. What begins as a project with grand designs on restructuring society becomes a pact with the existing state of affairs, which can only suggest minor adjustments.

Furthermore, since the social is the primary ethical sphere for Rich, in which the different aspects of ethics are integrated, he cannot countenance withdrawal from it. That would be a retreat from and denial of ethics as such, 'a sterile . . . protest'.[76] In Weber's terms, the ethical purist refuses to take responsibility for the calamitous consequences of his absolutism, and blames them on the obduracy of the world instead of his own unwillingness to accept things as they are:

> If evil consequences flow from an action done out of pure conviction, this type of person holds the world, not the doer, responsible, or the stupidity of others, or the will of God who made them thus'.[77]

No doubt Rich is right to be suspicious of the person who nonchalantly absolves himself of culpability for the consequences of his deeds. Yet the elevation of this suspicion into a principle whereby it is immoral to *refuse* to participate in an unjust social structure is troubling in a Christian ethicist, since it would appear to characterize martyrdom as primarily a posture either of haughty self-congratulation or of resigned indifference to the fate of a world which is too wicked and dreadful to help:

> That already happened with the early Christian enthusiasts, who in their eschatological exuberance saw the present world as already sublated by the future world. . . . Their exodus is either only an apparent one—a romantic flight . . . — or an extremist negation of the existing world.[78]

There is of course good precedent to Rich's caution: Augustine was fully alive to the possibility of a *premature* leap to martyrdom, originating from spiritual *superbia* or a misplaced desire to guarantee one's salvation (which led some to provoke the authorities into 'martyring' them).[79] Augustine is sceptical of this

[76] BEE, p. 33; Rich, *Wirtschaftsethik I*, p. 37.

[77] Weber, 'The Profession and Vocation of Politics', p. 360. Weber is making this point against revolutionaries who, in the name of principle, refused to recognize the good features of the status quo, and were thereby willing to throw them away for a romantic and unrealizable utopia.

[78] BEE, p. 178; Rich, *Wirtschaftsethik I*, p. 182.

[79] Carole Straw, 'Martyrdom', in *Augustine Through the Ages: An Encyclopedia,* ed. Allan D. Fitzgerald (Grand Rapids: Eerdmans, 1999), pp. 538–42, esp. p. 539.

'bravado', and insists that martyrdom must be fundamentally involuntary. Only Christ chooses to suffer and offer himself to death. Indeed, Augustine contends that martyrdom can be a daily, faithful endurance of suffering while performing good deeds in everyday life.[80] We have no quarrel with this. Yet Rich does not merely warn us against withdrawing from the world *too soon*. Rather, he does not seem to think that participation in an economic structure could *ever* constitute direct unfaithfulness to Christ. This seems unduly optimistic.[81]

This is sharply illustrated by Rich's discussion of a virtuous manager of his acquaintance who could not treat his workers justly, not because of any personal unscrupulousness, but because of the corporate structures of which he was a relatively impotent part. Rich regards the manager's participation in such structures as tragic, not immoral.[82] For him, this compels one to press for such structures to be changed. Withdrawal would be immoral, because it would abandon these structures and those trapped within them in favour of 'a sterile protest'. So, not permitted to retreat, the hapless man is obliged to participate in injustice until the structures are changed. Yet we have noted elsewhere that Rich is wary of changing structures too significantly, because the economy is the means of provision for human life. Human welfare depends on these unjust structures.

It therefore seems to be Rich's emphasis on social ethics as the integrating, decisive field of ethics which locks him into the curious conclusion that the only viable course of action is to change social structures (although not too much). In his quest to make the world more Christian, he seems to have lost sight of a Christian way of being *in* the world, and is unable to countenance the manager's resignation as a costly but effective *witness* which divulges an alternative life and thus itself engenders the possibility of social structural reform.[83]

Luther, on the other hand, seems to start with the individual rather than with a grand vision to improve society as a whole, at least in the text we have made our particular focus of study (although, as we have seen, other texts demonstrate that Luther was no stranger to the notion of *collective* moral action or the duty of rulers to govern justly). His primary audience in the *Sermon von dem Wucher* is merchants and potential lenders who want to do

[80] Straw, 'Martyrdom', p. 540.

[81] Ulrich Duchrow argues that in fact the global economy does constitute a 'confessional' case, the only proper response to which is withdrawal, in *Global Economy*.

[82] Rich, 'Personal Evil and Structural Evil', pp. 312–13. See also BEE, pp. 59–60.

[83] This point clearly owes as much to Stanley Hauerwas as it does to Luther. Among his publications, see 'Why the "Sectarian Temptation" is a Misrepresentation: A Response to James Gustafson', in Stanley Hauerwas, *The Hauerwas Reader*, eds. John Berkman and Michael Cartwright (Durham, NC: Duke University Press, 2001), pp. 90–110, esp. pp. 101–6, and 'On Keeping Theological Ethics Theological', in the same volume, pp. 51–74, esp. pp. 69–74.

the right thing. And in writings where Luther does directly address structural questions, he does not propound a general theory of what society ought to be like, but addresses particular people who hold political office as Christians. Individual action is particularly important, although this does not mean that his ethics is private or socially indifferent. Indeed, somewhat to our surprise we have been struck by the way in which Luther *begins* with what Rich would call individual ethics, which permits him to develop a far more radical social ethic than Rich's maxims for guiding social reforms pertinent to their circumstances.

The Need for Consensus in Social Ethics

One particular reason for this is that Rich's method is geared not only to secure as wide an *audience* as possible (against which it is difficult to see any objection), but as wide a *consensus* as possible: 'Christian ethics must attempt to persuade on the basis of reason, which under realistic circumstances can and should mean a practicable optimization of social justice'.[84] The optimization of social justice requires consensus, particularly within a pluralistic and democratic society. This makes it morally incumbent on Christians to advocate their social ethics on rational rather than theological grounds, hence Rich's appeal to John Rawls's theory of justice.

By contrast, the very genre of Luther's work is a sermon (although he may never have actually delivered it orally). This instinctive, almost incidental feature is noteworthy. We have noted the contrast between Rich's methodical, elaborate prolegomena and Luther's confident selection and exposition of a relevant biblical passage. The theological assumptions which underpin this homiletic method liberate him from any need to persuade or convince others of his viewpoint in order to optimize its impact on society at large. He believes he is speaking the Word of God: it is not up to him to secure its reception. Furthermore, because preaching is the voice of God himself, Luther has tremendous confidence in the potency of his words to effect what they proclaim. He expects God himself to act, to secure obedience to his words; hence proclamation is itself a force for social transformation. In short, Luther expects change to take place at a far deeper level than Rich does.

The contrast between Rich and Luther on this point is quite striking. Rich fears that presuming to speak on God's behalf will occasion theological hubris and a parochial inability to learn from others. Yet, perhaps counter-intuitively, we have seen that Luther's belief in God's presence and authority in preaching implies the *unimportance* of the preacher, since it is God's work to make what

[84] BEE, p. 215; Rich, *Wirtschaftsethik I*, p. 218.

is preached effective in his hearers. Luther believes that it is not at all within his power to effect any change within his hearers, and assumes that the preponderance of his hearers will not pay much attention to what he has to say: 'I suppose that my writing will be quite in vain'.[85] This is not a rhetorical flourish. It is grounded theologically in Luther's concept of the perduring stubbornness of the human will.

Although writing at a time of seeming Christian ascendancy, he remains acutely aware of the potentially tyrannical character of government, and its potential to support those he deems to be the enemies of true Christian preaching. He never assumes he is guaranteed a hearing. Rather, his responsibility as a preacher is a modest one: to ensure that those who are disposed to heed Christ's commands are made aware of them. This is how he will gauge the success of his efforts, not on the basis of the external results it produces, so he need not secure widespread agreement for the radical ethic this entails. Indeed, he thinks that few of his hearers will respond—what matters is that they are given the chance. Thus Luther does not feel the need to *persuade* others to adopt his moral beliefs. This almost take-it-or-leave-it attitude enables him to embrace the enormity of Christ's commands, while Rich's yearning for rational consensus prohibits him from stating anything so bluntly.

Social Ethics and Discipleship

Yet one of Rich's strengths remains his reminder that Christian ethics is not the exclusive preserve of a subsection of humanity, huddled together in isolation from the rest of the world. Luther and Rich are in agreement about this. Christ calls *everyone* to repent. So, one *can* commend a Christian ethic to those who are not necessarily Christians. Where they differ is that Luther is more alert to the concurrence of Christ's call to repentance with the other aspect of his summons: to believe the good news. In order to maximize consensus, Rich considers it desirable to commend a Christian ethic on society's own terms, and without connecting such an ethic to a summons to Christian conversion. Morality is intrinsically complex for Rich, because it must make contingent judgements on intricate factual questions to ensure value optimization, whereas for Luther it is not morality but (fallen) humanity that is problematic.

Luther's solution, therefore, is not so much ethics as discipleship. This is precisely what is excluded for Rich, because for him the deployment of reason as a neutral medium of negotiation between Christian and non-Christian, and

[85] LW v. 45, p. 245; WA v. 15, p. 293.

between ethics and science, is decisive. There is no methodological space for an integration of his social ethics with the wider contents of theological reasoning—the very things which, in Luther's terms, actually make a difference. This is a further reason for our characterization of Luther's ethic as more radical than Rich's: Luther's primary audience, as he says, is particular tradespeople who want to do the right thing in their work. He therefore treats such individuals as whole people, and pays attention to ostensibly 'spiritual' matters such as trusting in divine provision, repentance, and worship, which would be quite alien to Rich's understanding of the realm of economic ethics.

For example, Luther's starting place in expounding the 'three degrees' of rightly handling temporal goods is the *basic posture towards them*. He presupposes that if this is not wholesome, neither will be the actions which flow from it. Hence he treats greed as the result in the neighbourly dimension of unbelief in the theological dimension. That is, while he draws a distinction between different spheres or realms, he believes that they directly mirror and affect one another. Greed originates in fear for one's material security—so the solution is to encounter God as trustworthy and to put one's trust in God to provide. This trust liberates one from needing to provide for oneself, and trains one to handle worldly goods rightly. So, a crucial component of *moral* teaching must be to grow the hearer's *faith*. Such resources must be accessed if individual transformation (and therefore social transformation, as we shall see) is to take place. Of course, faith is not an alien concept to Rich. But nurturing it is hardly the role of the economic ethicist. It seems that his inability to address his readers at this deeper level is one of the factors which produce his rather conformist conclusions. Hence Luther's method of starting with the individual yields more radical conclusions than Rich's overtly social ethics of responsibility, because Luther is able to draw on the obligations and resources of discipleship, while Rich must reluctantly accept rather than tackle the hard facts of greed and self-absorption.

Let us see in a little more detail how this works in Luther's thought. He aims for and expects the transformation of human behaviour at a deep level. Importantly, though, he is quite as much a realist as Rich in his awareness of the 'facts' of human selfishness, self-interest, and insecurity, and so part of his response is to seek to curb them through coercive political intervention. Yet neither does he assume that, because they cannot be changed at a deep level by such intervention, these realities may be accepted, still less harnessed to some greater end.[86] Hence he makes no truce with self-interest, let alone selfishness. Greed must be pulverized, not used. It is in this sense that Luther's economic ethics is most radical: his analysis of the causes of injustice is very

[86] The view famously satirized by Bernard Mandeville in *The Fable of the Bees* [1723–8]. See Bernard Mandeville, *The Fable of the Bees and Other Writings*, ed. E. J. Hundert (Indianapolis: Hackett, 1997).

similar to Rich's, but Luther takes the fight to a deeper level, postulating a dramatic confrontation between God's command and the human will, in which God's commandments are not formulaic stipulations, but used by him as efficacious means of *accomplishing* his will.[87] Of course, Rich is right to repudiate the false deduction from this that Christians are therefore a moral elite. Yet Luther has his own way of doing this, namely his view that the crushing, liberating power of the law is operative through civil justice, not just preaching. This approach seems more effective, since it enables Luther to oppose greed and self-interest in society at large rather than resign himself to them.[88]

A further point is relevant here. As we have already noted, Luther's early moral theology suggests that without an emphasis both on the non-negotiable character of God's demands *and* on his comprehensive forgiveness, humans tend to reduce God's will to a more manageable standard, because they are unable to keep God's commands in their own strength. We have already argued that this is what we have discovered in Rich's thought, and here we uncover a further facet of this. The maxims in which Rich ultimately trades are endlessly contestable, because they are a method for accommodating Christian convictions in a secular world and moral convictions in a social-scientific world. He therefore cannot allow for a dramatic confrontation between the divine command and human will. On the other hand, insofar as he advocates moral requirements, he does so in isolation from the theological contents of the Christian faith. The contribution of Christian faith is that it is a particularly sturdy source of much-needed *energy* in the perpetual tussle for reform, a context in which disappointment abounds.[89] Rich therefore bears out the view that propounding a Christian moral standard on non-theological grounds, divorced from the muscle of the wider Christian message, tends towards the subversion of the *content* of such an ethic.

[87] This reflects the point, substantiated in our chapter on Luther, that for him the distinction between law and gospel is not a rigid division of biblical texts into two sections (still less the difference between the Old and New Testaments) but a perception of two aspects to each scriptural text: they are crushing commands *and* liberating, empowering promises. Indeed, in this case, it is *by* crushing rebellion and greed that the commands of Christ *enable* obedience. A classic example of this is the way Luther describes God's pronouncement of *judgement* in Genesis 3 as a passage full of *mercy and comfort*! See LW v. 1, pp. 188ff.

[88] Our suggestion that Christian ethics which is divorced from the call to follow Christ (that is, from evangelism) tends to become ethically distorted is paralleled in some recent missiological thinking, which has argued that evangelism which ignores the moral dimension of following Christ tends to be poor evangelism. Hence missiologist Steve Hollinghurst claims (although not in print) that 'evangelism is the discipleship of not-yet-Christians'. This thinking is outlined in his book *Mission-Shaped Evangelism: The Gospel in Contemporary Culture* (Norwich: Canterbury Press, 2010), esp. p. 242.

[89] See the section entitled 'The Distinctiveness of Christian Social Ethics for Rich', and BEE, pp. 117–19.

Another corollary of the way Luther situates morality in the context of the wider Christian proclamation is the startling urgency this gives his ethics since, for him, this proclamation is deeply concerned with the eternal salvation of the individual. As interpreters of Luther today, we tend to find this rather disquieting, but it is worth probing this disquiet to see what we can learn. Luther's fervent rejection of the notion that salvation flows from one's actions does not prevent his soteriology from shaping his moral thought. One's actions in the human sphere display (and reinforce) one's posture in the theological sphere. Thus in his sermon, Luther is intensely cognizant of the way self-interest puts the very souls of those to whom he preaches in peril.

This may seem to us rather individualistic, even pietistic. The temptation could be to assume that Luther's focus on eternal life leaves him indifferent to worldly affairs. Yet in fact, we have argued that its ramifications for Luther are inescapably social. For him, justification by faith is what liberates one from self-service: good deeds flow from the participation of the believer in Christ's goodness, and are thus always directed to the genuine benefit of one's neighbour. Luther may be interested in the salvation of his individual hearers, but his ethic is not individualist in the sense of being concerned with the moral development of individuals for its own sake. Practices such as fasting are not to 'get closer to God' (in contemporary popular terms), or to cultivate soteriological self-assurance, but to subdue one's self-interest so that one may be more readily disposed to serve one's neighbour. Thus Luther is opposed to a privatized notion of the good; hence his individual ethics are simultaneously entirely social, *because* they are a preacher's summons to his hearers to reject greed and embrace eternal life rather than the generalized address of a moral message which has been disentangled from the rest of the gospel.

Social Ethics and the Role of Government

We have already explored some of the ways in which Luther's ethics begin with the individual, and we have suggested that, counter-intuitively, this leads to what we have called a radical social ethic. A similar thing may be observed with respect to the way Luther addresses himself to the governing authorities.[90]

[90] Readers familiar with Luther's thought may at this point be puzzled by the absence of a discussion of Luther's theology of institutions, or the three 'estates': the church, marriage and the household (which Luther also refers to as 'economy', following the Greek term for household, *oikonomia*), and civil government. The reason for this omission is simply that Luther makes no reference to it in the specific text that we have selected for close study. For a full introduction, see the article, already referred to, by Oswald Bayer, 'Nature and Institution', or his longer introduction in *Martin Luther's Theology: A Contemporary Interpretation*, trans. Thomas H. Trapp (Grand Rapids: Eerdmans, 2008), ch. 6.

In particular, Luther is concerned with what the ruler should do, given his position of responsibility for others. Luther directly addresses such people both in private correspondence and oftentimes through recourse to a kind of open letter. As we have seen, he presupposes both that government is a good gift of God in creation which needs no clerical endorsement, and that those in power should make decisions and govern on a Christian basis. This is not simply because the authorities in question happen to share Luther's Christian faith, since he often seems convinced that the problem is precisely their godless greed and idolatry. Yet his address is couched in entirely theological terms. So we might say that for him, the task of government is a species both of individual ethics and of theological ethics. It is a species of individual ethics because government is composed of the actions and decisions of particular people, who are accountable to God for their deeds. And it is a species of theological ethics because, while the relevant standards for the *Weltperson* may be grounded ontologically in nature, they are known epistemologically through revelation. Hence, for example, usury should be prohibited because it is against natural law, but the way that this is *known* is through biblical law.[91]

The question Luther therefore addresses is not 'what should society be like?', but 'what should particular people in a particular office (such as soldier, merchant, or prince) *do*?' And the standard for determining such individual actions is natural law, expressed in the Golden Rule, the Ten Commandments, and so on. The only difference between a person acting on their own behalf and one acting on behalf of another is that the latter may legitimately use force to pursue justice. Thus the distinction between social and individual ethics, if it is permitted at all, is not a difference in theological and ethical content. As we have shown, Luther's famous stricture against attempting to rule the world with the gospel does not refer to a general double moral standard, but only to the use of force by government. Resigned adaption to the limited possibilities of a fallen world goes thus far—*but it goes no further*. Beyond that, the contents of *what* the government should enforce is defined by natural law, which as we have seen is discerned theologically. So, Luther's seeming individualism does not reduce Christian morality to a private affair, but rather entails the opposite, namely that political action be shaped by faith in Christ.

This feature of Luther's method prompts a suspicion of the methodological distinction drawn by Rich between individual and social ethics. Crucially, Rich envisages that distinctive methods pertain to these different modes of ethics,

[91] An erudite summary of the matter can be found in P. D. L. Avis, 'Moses and the Magistrate: A Study in the rise of Protestant Legalism', *Journal of Ecclesiastical History*, xxvi (1975), pp. 149–72, esp. pp. 152–8, although Avis finds Luther to be less systematic and more arbitrary than we have argued him to be.

which leads to the establishment of two levels of moral standard: the socially unenforceable standard of the Kingdom of God, and the pragmatically feasible extraction of the best possible social consequences given the circumstances of human vice. Luther's rejection of the scholastic distinction between minimal moral standards and the counsels of perfection is pertinent here. For Rich, there is a compulsory ethical standard out of which one may not opt. But this is not *socially* enforceable, so the social minimum is set according to what is attainable and realistic. For Luther, there is one standard of action, which is enforced through political and spiritual means.

Social Ethics as Collective Action

While we have argued that Luther *begins* with the actions of individuals rather than a grand vision of what society should be like, this does not prevent him from calling for social and collective forms of action as well. Luther and Rich are united in their acknowledgement that private charity is not enough. For Luther, charity is a public matter, hence civil government is concerned with charity as well as justice. But this is also a matter for the community as a collective whole, as we see in the common chest arrangement which Luther advocated theologically and supported practically.

Yet here again the configuration of this social ethic is subsumed within the matrix of *good deeds*: how communities, even nations, can *do* the right thing, rather than how they can build a more just society, although the latter may sound like the more radical approach. In particular, for Luther, the basis on which such good works are commended is the same Christian theological one as that which undergirds good deeds performed by individuals, such as the notion that one must not hold on to one's money for one's own sake, but rather adopt a posture of letting go of it and giving it away freely. That is, the texts from the Sermon on the Mount which Luther applies to the actions of individuals also have social implications. Luther's concern for the salvation of individuals is quite compatible with a desire for what we might call a structural solution to hardship, visible in the paradigmatic example of the common chest arrangement.

This concludes our exploration of what we can learn about Rich's commitment to the social structural paradigm for economic ethics from what we have called Luther's seemingly more individual approach to ethics. We have encountered the curious observation that Rich's quest for a radical engagement with social structures seems hampered by the way in which he construes social ethics. He is committed to engaging with the structures of the world as they actually are, and although he traces the provenance of the flawed character of these structures to a deep level in the human being, he gives structural reform priority in a way that inhibits him from grappling with these flaws at their level of origin, and *therefore* from actually reforming the structures of society in any significant way.

His recognition of the incorrigibility of human nature—acquisitive, destructive, and self-involved—is translated into the claim that social structures are inevitably unjust. This overcommitment to engaging with the world on its own terms also prevents Rich from envisaging a legitimate and necessary refusal to participate in structures of injustice, which means that such structures are sustained, and alternatives are not embodied or sought. Despite Rich's best efforts, this leads to a rather conservative economic ethic, while Luther's method puts authenticity first. Perhaps the aim of influencing society as much as possible can act as a distraction from the authenticity which is a prerequisite for actually doing so. Not that we should think mechanistically, as if by not attempting to impact society, one surely will do so. Faithfulness is not a *guarantor* of social transformation, but it is its *sine qua non.*

A further aspect of Rich's desire to engage with the world on its own terms is the respect with which he treats the methods and findings of economic science, and it is to this we will turn in the following section of this chapter.

THE RELATIONSHIP BETWEEN ETHICS AND ECONOMICS

Ethics and Economic Growth

We have just noted that for Luther social ethics is primarily a matter of deeds, while we have shown that Rich construes justice in terms of outcomes. For the latter, justice is not so much something which is *done*, as a state of affairs to which a given society should strive to approximate. This is evident in the way that for Rich, justice is quantifiable: he speaks of continually changing economic structures 'towards more justice' (*auf mehr Gerechtigkeit*).[92] His goal is 'a *more* humane shaping of the conditions in our ever more dubious world'.[93] This is why an assessment of concrete, measurable economic outcomes is essential in order to discern the responsible course of action. Our suggestion was that mensuration of moral success in terms of the *quantity* of justice generated—that is, in terms of outcomes—contributes to Rich's project assuming an overly burdensome sense of responsibility, because justice cannot ever simply be *done*: it must be *achieved* in ever increasing quantities.

[92] BEE, p. 297; Rich, *Wirtschaftsethik II*, p. 42.
[93] Emphasis mine. BEE, p. 186; Rich, *Wirtschaftsethik I*, p. 189.

In particular, human responsibility for optimal outcomes means that the successful creation of material wealth is a necessary aim of the economy for Rich. Advantageous outcomes will not be possible without this: 'If the economy is to be able to do justice to its fundamental purpose of service of life, it must first be effective'.[94] That is, it must meet the needs of the people it serves.[95] For Rich, this is helpful in arguing that the economy is not an end in itself, but is subservient to a more fundamental goal: human life. This means that wealth creation has become an aspect of justice for Rich. Visions of economic life which prohibit economic growth in the name of equality, simplicity, or environmental concern may be recognized as legitimate values, of course, but cannot be allowed to override the unavoidable obligation of economic growth.

Our reading of Luther stimulates a particular critical question here. At times, Luther anticipates that obedience to Jesus's teaching will bring worldly improvements: if people stopped squabbling over petty rights, social life would be more generally agreeable. Yet in the main he assumes that suffering, shame, and death are the signs under which God accomplishes his work of love, glory, and victory. But this is not patent: it can be discerned only by faith, not by sight. So once again Luther prompts us to question Rich. He reminds us that outcomes are often not as they appear. This places a check on the notion that the rightness of an action can be adjudged by the quality of its outcomes. In particular, earthly riches are not generally a token of moral success.

The Role of Economic Science in Economic Ethics

Our reading of Luther has prompted us to question the value base on which Rich proposes to evaluate outcomes and thereby to assess the justice of different economic orders. But what of the overall question of the relation of moral claims to the factual claims made by economic science? This is evidently crucial not only to Rich's project, but to the very field of economic ethical enquiry.

Rich approaches the matter with a spirited defence of the role of moral norms in social science, which we have already discussed.[96] With respect to economics, social science 'can never provide its guiding principle'.[97] This seems an expedient move, but once again our reading of Luther stimulates a

[94] BEE, p. 398; Rich, *Wirtschaftsethik II*, p. 140.

[95] Elsewhere this definition proves to be somewhat elastic. For example, Rich suggests that the historical development of humanity has created new *needs* (BEE, p. 376; Rich, *Wirtschaftsethik II*, p. 120). Therefore, it is *morally* urgent to ensure economic growth continues. An alternative case is argued by Fred Hirsch, *Social Limits to Growth* (London: Routledge, 1977).

[96] BEE, pp. 65–98; Rich, *Wirtschaftsethik I*, pp. 71–104.

[97] BEE, p. 66; Rich, *Wirtschaftsethik I*, p. 73.

critical observation. By making a play for the indispensability of moral norms *in* social science, Rich treats them as a *subset* of social science. Thus social ethics is *dependent* on social-scientific expertise:

> Since the nature of this basic question [of how social institutions should be structured] entails that it can be properly asked only in the context of social reality, social ethics is naturally dependent on the findings and insights of the theoretical and empirical social sciences that have this sphere of reality as their object of study.[98]

Hence, Rich's seemingly assertive plea for the inclusion of norms in social science is actually a rather defensive manoeuvre. The characterization of moral values introduced *into* the realm of facts cannot but make those values appear extrinsic, as if they bear no essential relation to the facts. One could equally well substitute any set of values into the controlling framework of the facts as disclosed by social science.

Not that the facts dictate unilaterally to ethics for Rich: there is a reciprocal influence. As Harold Tonks puts it, 'Faithfulness to facts means faithfulness within a prescribed set of values'.[99] He gives this example: the assumption that the 'purpose of a company is to maximize profits at all costs' will 'elicit appropriate facts'.[100] If, on the other hand, one sees corporate purpose in broader terms, such as providing jobs and serving the local community, different facts will be relevant. One's values will *shape* the direction of one's empirical investigations.[101] Yet one's values do not *determine* the facts, and Rich is concerned that ideological forms of thought should not cloud an appropriately neutral enquiry.

Our exploration of Luther's methodology opens up a fissure in this reasoning. It is tempting for us, in our social-scientific milieu, to regard Luther as ignorant of economic reality, and his intense absorption with Scripture has given some interpreters the impression that he is isolated from his particular circumstances, dwelling instead in a Scriptural idealism. Robin Gill comments that Luther's sermon on usury shows his 'basic ignorance of economic realities'.[102] And in his introduction to *Trade and Usury*, Walther Brandt excuses Luther for this on the grounds that his ignorance is 'in common with the vast majority of his contemporaries' who at that time 'knew very little about economic laws'.[103] Even less sympathetic is Tawney's tart appraisal:

[98] BEE, p. 65; Rich, *Wirtschaftsethik I*, pp. 71–2.

[99] Tonks, *Faith, Hope and Decision-Making*, p. 179.

[100] Tonks, *Faith, Hope and Decision-Making*, p. 179.

[101] Gunnar Myrdal makes a similar point when he observes that the inescapable a priori elements present in economics are bound to determine the very scientific questions which one asks, and it is naïve to suppose otherwise. *The Political Element in the Development of Economic Theory*, trans. Paul Streeten (New Brunswick: Transaction, 1990), p. xli.

[102] Gill, *A Textbook of Christian Ethics*, p. 176.

[103] LW v. 45, p. 233.

> Confronted with the complexities of foreign trade and financial organization, or with the subtleties of economic analysis, [Luther] is like a savage introduced to . . . a steam-engine. He is too frightened and angry even to feel curiosity. Attempts to explain the mechanism merely enrage him; he can only repeat that there is a devil in it, and that good Christians will not meddle with the mystery of iniquity.[104]

Such comments divulge a subscription to the very supposition which Luther sought to expose, namely that finance is an autonomous field. We have suggested that, in reality, Luther is diligently attentive to empirical economic observation. For example, he is well aware that levels of supply and demand determine prices. He observes the realities of wealth and poverty, and takes care to inform himself of mercantile and financial practices. But, to subvert Tawney's analogy, his analysis refuses to *stop* at these mechanical explanations. *Behind* these facts (which to Rich and to us may well assume the guise of brute reality), Luther discerns particular human decisions and acts. In turn, behind these decisions and acts is self-interest. So, rather than explaining circumstances naturalistically, as if things simply *are* this way, Luther explains them *morally*.

Once again, our favoured description of Luther's ethic is therefore 'radical', in the etymological sense of tracing human behaviour deeply, to its *roots*. The facts that economic science describes empirically can also be described morally and theologically, in terms of a primary account of reality which also claims to be factual, because morality is real.[105] An ingredient in this account is a detailed analysis of sin, which generates Luther's profound suspicion of greed and self-deception. Angry he may be, and frightened too. But we should not leap to assume that these emotions originate in ignorance. Rather, they flow from an alternative *understanding* of what is going on.

Our unexpected discovery is therefore that Luther and Rich are aware of the same facts, broadly speaking. But they reach very different conclusions as to what should be done about them. Far from being unyielding phenomena of human existence, Luther regards them as concrete manifestations of injustice committed by particular people against their neighbours. Such facts must be opposed rather than accepted and worked with, while Rich regards moral analysis of reality as complex, even impenetrable, and factual analysis of reality as more manageable. For Luther, it is economics which is impenetrable—not

[104] Tawney, *Religion and the Rise of Capitalism*, p. 98.

[105] Cf. Alasdair MacIntyre's analysis of the distinction between the Aristotelian and what he calls the 'mechanist' concepts of 'fact': 'On the former view human action, because it is to be explained teleologically . . . must be characterized with reference to the hierarchy of goods which provide the ends of human action. . . . On the former view the facts about human action include the facts about what is valuable to human beings . . . ; on the latter view there are no facts about what is valuable'. Alasdair MacIntyre, *After Virtue: A Study in Moral Theory*, 2nd edn. (London: Duckworth, 1985), p. 84.

because it is complex, but because it is deliberately deceptive. The gospel is therefore needed to shed light upon it. Self-interest even lurks behind the deeds which we consider noble and worthy, hence the need for the gospel to expose the motives and intentions behind the facts. Luther therefore provokes us to be wary of the way in which supposedly neutral factual claims about reality can mask or absolve idolatry and greed.

Of course, Rich is not uncritical towards the claims to moral neutrality made by the discipline of economics. But he nevertheless allows it a decisive voice in advising theological ethics as to what is practicable. While he is correct to desire a genuine dialogue with social scientists, and markedly successful in pursuing it, he struggles to ask the necessary but potentially uncomfortable fundamental questions about the adequacy of their discourse in the first place. It seems to us that this overly respectful posture ultimately entails too big a sacrifice.

A good example of this can be found in Rich's method with respect to starting with the existing situation. This reflects his fundamental position that you cannot simply replace the existing order. The notion that one cannot raze everything and start again is a dangerous illusion. So, the question is not which economic order out of all the theoretically possible ones is the best, as if one can start from scratch and build any system one desires. The process of forming maxims takes the existing situation as its starting point. But this means that the process must also take as its starting point the problems of the existing situation too. Such problems, as they appear within social science, are baptized as ethical questions.[106]

Rich gives the example of inequalities in income and property, both within nations and globally, which he describes as 'horrendous'—a view which he assumes rather than justifies. We may agree, but it is striking to note that this is not an empirical claim but a normative one. And incidentally, it is a claim which not a few economists would vehemently dispute, on the basis that wealth differentials stimulate economic growth, creating greater overall prosperity for everyone.[107] This indicates that the supposedly empirical questions which economics throws up may not be as morally neutral as they appear. This is no bad thing in our view, but a frank acknowledgement of the fact would have enabled Rich to embark on a thoroughgoing moral analysis of the

[106] BEE, p. 223–4; Rich, *Wirtschaftsethik I*, pp. 225–6.

[107] For a recent example see the paper by Dalibor Roháč, 'Does Inequality Matter?' (London: Adam Smith Institute, 2011), <http://www.adamsmith.org/files/Does_Inequality_Matter_ASI.pdf> (accessed 11 August 2011). This paper offers a critique of sociologist Richard Wilkinson's arguments for equality in *The Impact of Inequality: How to Make Sick Societies Healthier* (New York: New Press, 2005), and Richard Wilkinson and Kate Pickett, *The Spirit Level: Why Equality is Better for Everyone* (London: Penguin, 2009). For a theological discussion, see Duncan Forrester, *On Human Worth: A Christian Vindication of Equality* (London: SCM, 2001).

questions themselves, as opposed to being restricted to answering the questions which economics poses itself.

An obvious parallel to this is the way in which Luther sets Scripture critically against other sources of human knowledge, particularly tradition and customary morality in his case. This does not mean that he regards such sources of knowledge as utterly destitute, only that Scripture takes primacy. Other sources of knowledge can and should be taken into account. But they should not become the controlling paradigm. So, for example, Luther does not ignore the traditions of the church, nor does he regard tradition as bad in itself. Rather, he is simply aware of its potential to become severely corrupted. Neither was Luther as disparaging towards reason as is sometimes assumed. It is a truism that he was part of the bloom of humanistic arts and sciences, and his assessment of the competence of human reason—as regards earthly matters—is far higher than is sometimes assumed.

In a sermon on Isaiah 60:1–6 from 1522 he wryly observes that 'in Scripture, God does not teach how to build houses, make clothes. . . . For such things, the natural light is enough'. But he immediately adds, 'In divine matters . . . nature is completely blind'.[108] Practical matters which need reason include government and the administration of justice—although that does not imply that reason dictates morality to politics. Within its limits, therefore, reason is supreme, and is what distinguishes humanity from brute animals. As Luther puts it in the theses for the *Disputatio de homine* (1536):

> 4. And it is certainly true that reason is the most important and the highest in rank among all things and, in comparison with other things of this life, the best and something divine. 5. It is the inventor and mentor of all the arts, medicines, laws, and of whatever wisdom, power, virtue, glory men possess in this life.[109]

Later, Luther specifically notes that reason's value and ability are not removed by the Fall (thesis 9).

Luther even thinks that human reason extends to certain features of religion and morality. He grants that reason may be aware that good is to be done and evil avoided (just as St Thomas maintained). The crucial distinction is that reason cannot know *which* things are good and which are evil. In a particularly vivid analogy from a Christmas sermon on John 1:1–14 (1522), he compares reason to a man who knows that there is a road which will take him to Rome, but does not know which.[110] Some scholars (notably Troeltsch) have therefore concluded that Luther was simply incoherent on this point.[111] Others more

[108] WA v. 10.I.I, p. 531, ll. 8–13. See the discussion in Egil Grislis, 'Luther's Understanding of the Wrath of God', *Journal of Religion* 41 (1961), pp. 277–92, esp. p. 285.

[109] LW v. 34, p. 137; WA v. 39.I, p. 175, ll. 9–14.

[110] LW v. 52, pp. 57–8; WA v. 10.I.I, pp. 203–4.

[111] See the discussion in Bernhard Lohse, 'Reason and Revelation in Luther', in *Scottish Journal of Theology* 13.4 (1960), pp. 337–65, esp. pp. 338–9.

recently, such as Oswald Bayer and Bernhard Lohse, have argued that his approach possesses an underlying unity. Bayer concludes that, 'there is no contradiction' between Luther's (in)famous designation of reason as a 'whore', and as 'something divine', *if* one acknowledges Luther's distinction between the soteriological and earthly spheres of operation.[112] It is not reason as such that is the target of his ferocious invective, but its potential conceit in overstepping its limits and pronouncing on matters beyond its capability and scope, where revelation is indispensable.[113] Extra-biblical sources of knowledge are only problematic if they operate beyond their legitimate boundaries or take on independent authority, ceasing to be subordinate to Scripture.

Let us connect this point to our earlier observation of the relative absence of the discussion of Scripture within Rich's social ethics, despite his stated view that biblical maxims should play a role. For Luther, Scripture provides the primary account of reality in which human action can be described and understood, so it is always relevant. But Rich is somewhat hypnotized by the absence of a directly social structural element within New Testament ethics. He attributes this to the early church's expectation of the imminence of the end of the world, which means that 'the question of structural changes in society . . . appear[s] from the outset to be obsolete'.[114] Indeed, he expresses his surprise that such a horizon is not entirely absent from the New Testament. One would expect the question of structural transformation to fade entirely, yet it does not—to the credit of the New Testament writers.

So, under the guise of an ostensible defence of the New Testament's relevance (because this question is not *as* absent as one might expect), Rich has taken for granted that today our eschatological perspective will be different from that of the New Testament writers, whose perspective was induced by an explosion of eschatological fervour which we now believe to be misplaced. Let us note the move that has been made here. Rich's assumption is that one's eschatological entry point for social ethics today *will not be the same as that of the writings of the New Testament.* It perforce ensues that there must be a corresponding ethical difference as well. So it is unsurprising that Scripture plays little substantial role in social reflection for Rich.

[112] Bayer, *Martin Luther's Theology*, pp. 160–1.

[113] Lohse, 'Reason and Revelation in Luther', pp. 348–51. For some good contemporary treatments of this question, see Donald Hay, 'On Being a Christian Economist', in *Christianity and the Culture of Economics*, eds. Donald A. Hay and Alan Kreider (Cardiff: University of Wales Press, 2001), pp. 166–90, and Ronald R. Nelson, 'Faith-Discipline Integration: Compatibilist, Reconstructionalist, and Transformationalist', in *The Reality of Christian Learning: Strategies for Faith-Discipline Integration*, eds. Harold Heie and David L. Wolfe (St Paul and Grand Rapids: Christian University Press/Christian College Consortium and Eerdmans, 1987), pp. 317–39, esp. pp. 319–27.

[114] BEE, p. 194. This oft-repeated claim is exactly the kind of conclusion that George Eldon Ladd criticizes on exegetical grounds. See *The Presence of the Future*, p. 303.

For Luther, theological ethics cannot for a moment assume that we can accurately know the world without constant biblical assistance. Reinhard Hütter explains:

> The first question of Christian ethics should not be 'What ought I now to do?' but 'What does the world really look like?' Situations are not just 'out there' for us to 'bump' into. Rather, the description of a situation is everything; it is the situation itself. In describing a 'situation' the morally decisive choices and moves are already made.[115]

So for Luther, Scripture does not merely tell one what to do. It needs to define the world in which action takes place.[116] This is especially true given his diagnosis of human partiality and the way in which our own descriptions cloak wrongdoing in neutral or honourable terms. As Hütter puts it, we need 'God's constant critical intervention into our construals of "reality." God's commandments thus help us avoid getting trapped by false necessities and givens'.[117] So, it is not that action derives purely from the gospel, without attention to facts. Rather, Luther's evangelical description of reality (which of course includes factual claims), provides factual claims which shape his subsequent analysis of other facts. The problem with Rich's approach is not his emphasis on the findings of social science, but the way he *limits* the notion of 'fact' to mechanistic rather than moral explanations of economic realities and human behaviour.

As we have seen, this means that Rich tends to regard economics as a tool for accomplishing moral goals, rather than a sphere in which action must conform to particular standards.[118] To take some of the examples he gives,

[115] Hütter, 'The Twofold Center of Lutheran Ethics', p. 46.

[116] Economist Geoffrey Brennan unwittingly supports this claim, by observing that accepting God as an active participant in human affairs would require a radical alteration to the methodology of economics. For him, this is an argument *against* such an alteration, since he takes it for granted that God is not active in this way. Of course, this is itself a *factual* claim. See H. Geoffrey Brennan, 'The Impact of Theological Dispositions on Economics: A Commentary', in *Economics and Religion: Are They Distinct?*, eds. H. Geoffrey Brennan and A. M. C. Waterman (Boston: Kluwer, 1994), pp. 163–77, esp. pp. 174–7. Similarly, as Sheila C. Dow puts it, rather understatedly, 'the downgrading of the goal of wealth accumulation in a time frame that extends beyond death also has profound theoretical implications for economics'. And not just theoretical ones, we might add. See 'Economics, Ethics and Knowledge', in *Religion and Economics: Normative Social Theory*, eds. James M. Dean and A. M. C. Waterman (Boston: Kluwer, 1999), pp. 123–30.

[117] Hütter, 'The Twofold Center of Lutheran Ethics', p. 46.

[118] Charles Taylor captures it nicely in his discussion of the fact/value split, which he traces back beyond Hume to the theological debate between nominalism and Thomism: 'reason is no longer defined substantively, in terms of a vision of cosmic order, but formally, in terms of the procedures that thought ought to follow, and especially those involved in fitting means to ends, instrumental reason'. Charles Taylor, 'Justice After Virtue', in *After MacIntyre: Critical Perspectives on the Work of Alasdair MacIntyre*, eds. John Horton and Susan Mendus (Cambridge: Polity, 1994), pp. 16–43, esp. p. 19.

most people agree that it is desirable to cut unemployment, keep the value of money stable, and protect the environment:

> There is probably widespread agreement on the desirability . . . of these particular objectives. . . . The humanity originating from faith, hope, and love has, therefore, nothing special to contribute.[119]

The question is *how* best to achieve these goals. And if this is the question, the process of finding the answer must be a technical matter, best left to the experts without any meddling from ethicists who are well-intentioned but not trained in this particular technical field. So, while Rich is not entirely uncritical towards the discipline of economics, it retains for him a decisive voice which obstructs the radical social engagement he desires. As Oliver O'Donovan puts it:

> As soon as we hand over the understanding of our social existence to the purely descriptive sciences and adopt the position of disinterested observers, we abandon the active hope that society may disclose a loving knowledge of the world to us. In which case we have no practical social philosophy available.[120]

Of course, Rich does argue that social science should not be purely descriptive. But he is the victim of his own assumption that it does nevertheless contain purely descriptive *elements*. The very act of amputating oneself from the world in order to observe it from an Olympian plane means that one must ultimately accept it as a given. Detachment from the world in order to observe it by definition prevents one from altering it. Luther's method demands a no less attentive engagement with his circumstances, but his consciousness of his own location *within* them means he analyses the economic facts as mutable phenomena.

Economics as a Moral not a Positive Science

Before proceeding further, it is worth noting that these concerns are not unusual. Economics has received trenchant criticism from self-critical members of its own fraternity who dispute the notion that it is scientific in the modern sense. Cambridge economics don A. B. Cramp has argued that it is bogus and indeed perilous for economics to adopt the pose of a detached science since, 'in effect, if not in beginning intention, all economics is inescapably normative'.[121] Tomas Sedlacek wryly observes that Milton Friedman's

[119] BEE, p. 609; Rich, *Wirtschaftsethik II*, p. 336.

[120] Oliver O'Donovan, *Common Objects of Love: Moral Reflection and the Shaping of Community* (Grand Rapids: Eerdmans, 2002), p. 39.

[121] A. B. Cramp, 'Mappings of (Economic) Meaning: Here Be Monsters', in *Economics and Religion: Are They Distinct?*, eds. H. Geoffrey Brennan and A. M. C. Waterman (Boston: Kluwer, 1994), pp. 179–91, esp. p. 184. See also his essay, 'In what Sphere is Economics Sovereign?', in

claim that 'economics *should be* a positive science that is value-neutral and describes the world as it is and not how it should be', is itself a normative claim which describes the world as it should be.[122]

This counterclaim tends to be substantiated by tracing the historical genealogy of economics as a discipline, showing the ideological freighting which each stage of its development carried.[123] Pride of place here goes to Swedish economist Gunnar Myrdal, who spent decades disputing what he saw as the naïve idealization of economics as morally disinterested. For him, there is no objective access to economic facts, since one's analysis will always be shaped by one's values.[124] Indeed, he went so far as to argue that the notion of scientific objectivity masks an inherent bias to laissez-faire capitalism.[125] Myrdal favours the view that economics is profoundly different from the natural sciences because it is concerned with human action. It is thus an intrinsically moral discipline.[126]

An interesting example of the genealogical manoeuvre is provided by Robert Nelson, who regards the development of economics as a series of *theological* moves.[127] This claim is independent of the similar case made by representatives of the Radical Orthodoxy theological school, as per John Milbank's thesis in *Theology and Social Theory* that 'the most important governing assumptions of [modern, secular social] theory are bound up with the modification or the rejection of orthodox Christian positions'.[128]

Social Science in Christian Perspective, eds. Paul A. Marshall and Robert E. Vandervennen (Lanham, MD: University Press of America, 1988), pp. 199–217.

122 Sedlacek, *Economics of Good and Evil*, p. 7. Emphasis Sedlacek's.

123 So A. B. Cramp in *Notes Towards a Christian Critique of Secular Economic Theory* (Toronto: Institute for Christian Studies, 1975).

124 Gunnar Myrdal, 'Preface', pp. v–viii, esp. pp. vi–vii, and 'How Scientific are the Social Sciences?', pp. 133–57, esp. pp. 136–41, both in Gunnar Myrdal, *Against the Stream: Critical Essays on Economics* (London & Basingstoke: Macmillan, 1974).

125 Gunnar Myrdal, 'The Place of Values in Social Policy', in *Against the Stream*, pp. 33–51, esp. p. 33. So also Andrew Henley, 'Economic Orthodoxy and the Free Market System: A Christian Critique', *International Journal of Social Economics* 14 (1987) pp. 56–66, esp. pp. 56, 65.

126 See also Gunnar Myrdal, *Objectivity in Social Research* (London: Duckworth, 1969); and *The Political Element in the Development of Economic Theory*.

127 Robert H. Nelson, *Reaching for Heaven on Earth: The Theological Meaning of Economics* (Savage, MD: Rowman & Littlefield, 1991). See also his more recent *Economics as Religion: From Samuelson to Chicago and Beyond* (Pennsylvania: Pennsylvania State University Press, 2001), and more briefly, 'Economics as Religion', in *Economics and Religion: Are They Distinct?*, eds. H. Geoffrey Brennan and A. M. C. Waterman (Boston: Kluwer, 1994), pp. 227–36.

128 Milbank, *Theology and Social Theory*, p. 1. This thesis is developed at length by Stephen Long in *Divine Economy*. This claim has won support even from economists who have criticized the conclusions Long draws in other respects. For example, Paul Oslington supports Long's critique of 'the tendency [within economics] to portray capitalism as a natural system, the way that economics is heir to natural theology, the concentration of religious economics on the doctrine of sin to counter proposals for social reform, and the paradoxical anthropology of freedom that runs through economics'. Oslington, 'Review, *Divine Economy*', p. 137.

Thus Michael Northcott has argued that the concept of scarcity common in economics is a particular historical theological development, replacing an earlier notion of fullness and richness.[129] Yet this notion of scarcity is so obviously *factually* true and necessary to orthodox economics that its denial would be regarded as akin to six-day creationism.[130]

Of course, many or even most economists would be much more supportive of Rich's approach. For example, economist-cum-theologian A. M. C. Waterman challenges Tawney's claim that the church's social teaching 'ceased to count because the church ceased to think', on the basis that it was precisely because the church began to think (that is, to take account of the 'facts') that it ceased to oppose political economy and came to side with it.[131]

In addition to genealogical critiques of economics *qua* science, there have been plenty of philosophical ones too. John Maynard Keynes argued that the *imprimatur* of scientific authority which shrouds economics depends on unrealistic assumptions about the rationality of human behaviour, hence his emphasis on the 'animal spirits' of humanity.[132] Economics derives its theory of human behaviour from a series of beliefs about human individuals, which it extrapolates to a huge scale, assuming that economic agents act consistently on this model.[133] Economist Paul Ormerod questions both whether these underlying beliefs are accurate in the first place, and even if they are, whether they can be reliably extrapolated in the way that they need to be for mainstream economics to operate.[134]

[129] Michael S. Northcott, 'The Parable of the Talents and the Economy of the Gift', *Theology* cvii (2004), pp. 241–9, esp. pp. 245–6.

[130] It is not that the older tradition denied the reality of scarcity, of course, but that it interpreted it differently. For orthodox economics, poverty is a natural phenomenon, and wealth a recent historical novelty. The normative implication of this is that large-scale redistribution of wealth is counterproductive. Instead, the poor need to be taught to *create* wealth too. So Brian Griffiths, *The Creation of Wealth* (London: Hodder & Stoughton, 1984), esp. p. 12 and *Morality and the Market Place* (London: Hodder & Stoughton, 1982), pp. 91–7. The older tradition, taking its cue from the Hebrew prophets, tended to treat poverty as a social phenomenon, blaming it on the refusal of the rich to share out the abundance of God's provision evenly. See Peter Scott, *A Political Theology of Nature* (Cambridge: Cambridge University Press, 2003), pp. 155–6 and 161–5.

[131] A. M. C. Waterman, *Revolution, Economics and Religion: Christian Political Economy 1798–1833* (Cambridge: Cambridge University Press, 1991), pp. 261–2.

[132] John Maynard Keynes, *The General Theory of Employment, Interest and Money* (London: Macmillan, 1936), pp. 161–2. The problematic assumptions made by economics about human desires and emotions are further explored in the work of Wolfgang Palaver. See the relevant sections in *Passions in Economy, Politics, and the Media: In Discussion with Christian Theology*, eds. Wolfgang Palaver and Petra Steinmair-Pösel (Vienna: Lit, 2005), esp. Palaver's own essay, 'Envy or Emulation: A Christian Understanding of Economic Passions', pp. 139–62. In a more recent article he explores some of the consequences of this: 'Challenging Capitalism as Religion: Hans G. Ulrich's Theological and Ethical Reflections on the Economy', *Studies in Christian Ethics* 20 (2007), pp. 215–30, esp. pp. 218–23.

[133] Paul Ormerod, *The Death of Economics* (London: Faber & Faber, 1994), esp. p. 197.

[134] Ormerod, *The Death of Economics*, p. 91.

In short, economics cannot be free of metaphysics.[135] These heterodox economists whom we have surveyed have therefore argued that it needs to pay more attention to getting its metaphysics *right*, or at least a little better—a question it has deliberately tended to avoid due to its origins in the utilitarian quest for socio-political consensus without the possibility of prior metaphysical unanimity.[136]

This bears out our suspicion, born out of our examination of Luther's method, that Rich has far too respectful an engagement with the concept of economic science and its corresponding 'facts'.[137] Luther's analysis of human behaviour does involve empirical observation, but also moral evaluation, which is shaped by his underlying assumptions about human individuals. Where Rich is quite correct is his insistence that love demands an accurate assessment of reality. As Oliver O'Donovan puts it,

> The underlying unity of knowledge and love means that love can take form only as a cognizance of reality. There is an objective measure by which we may differentiate 'better' from 'worse' loves, which is the adequacy of their grasp of reality.[138]

The question is therefore whether the economic account of reality which Rich depends on is really true, and thus whether it really loves.

THE HUMAN PERCEPTION OF THE GOOD

An observation which has come up tangentially in this chapter's analysis, which we will now bring to the foreground, is the contrast between Luther and Rich in their anthropological assumptions concerning the perceptibility of the good to humanity in general, and the implications of this contrast for their methods.

As we have seen, for Rich revelation does not add much to social ethics in the way of concrete *content*. What makes Christian ethics distinctive is not its particular content or stipulations, but its durability. Rich credits humanity with a general awareness of moral reality, which explains why theology does not have a monopoly on morality. For Rich, this is both an ontological claim

[135] See also Alan Storkey, *Foundational Epistemologies in Consumption Theory* (Amsterdam: Vrije Universiteit, 1993), esp. pp. 12ff.

[136] See the historical account in Frederick Rosen, *Classical Utilitarianism from Hume to Mill* (London: Routledge, 2003), esp. part I.

[137] Christian economist Donald Hay bluntly criticizes books written by theologians on economics on the dual grounds that they are 'almost invariably . . . deficient in their understanding of economic analysis, *and far too respectful of it*'. *Economics Today*, p. 8. Emphasis mine.

[138] O'Donovan, *Common Objects of Love*, p. 23.

(namely, moral norms are the same for Christians and non-Christians) and an epistemological one (namely, general human norms may be perceived not only by Christians but also by non-Christians, however partially and imperfectly).

Rich gains numerous advantages from this, from which we can again learn. First, it allows him to uphold the reality of a universally normative moral obligation, without the need to wait to secure unanimous consensus on one metaphysical position, which of course would never happen in any case. Ethics is too important to be put on hold. Second, he is able to make strategic alliances with ethical perspectives which are not theologically derived, but which agree with some of the prescriptions or conclusions of theological ethics. Third, it positions theology as a humble and open discipline: theology can play its part in economic matters, without claiming to be the sole or governing source of legitimate moral knowledge. Fourth, theology is kept from a defensive, siege mentality: theologians can learn collaboratively from others.[139] All this seeks to conserve a credible role for theology in a plural and scientific world, and ensures that those who do not share the metaphysical presuppositions of theology can still engage in discussion with its ethics.

As we saw in the previous chapter, Rich also desires specifically Christian convictions to inform the Christian contribution to social ethics, because a *correlation* is possible between a theological account of justice and the 'horizon of general human experience'.[140] Hence his criteria of justice, while based on 'fundamental experience-certitude' (that is, theological convictions) can also be 'understood, discussed, and applied even without the fundamental premises'.[141] So, Rich's theological criteria set boundaries and rule out certain options, but in themselves they do not and cannot determine 'what a just relationship of rights and duties or just participation in the national income and national wealth means'.[142] This means that Christian social ethics needs to harness a 'compatible' expression of social justice for two reasons. First, to build as wide a social consensus as possible. And second, because theological convictions on their own are not sufficient to facilitate the level of close practical engagement with reality which economic ethics requires. The adoption of a non-theological account of justice (in Rich's case, Rawls's theory of justice, which Rich thinks, 'corresponds in the highest degree to the

[139] For an alternative account of how theological ethics might learn from extra-theological sources, without needing to shape itself around them dialogically, see Michael Banner, 'Some Comments on Two Critics', *Crucible* (January/March, 2002), pp. 20–7, esp. pp. 25–6, and Michael Banner, 'Introductory remarks: Christian Ethical Reasoning', *Transformation* 15.2 (April/June 1998), pp. 15–17, esp. p. 15.

[140] BEE, p. 99; Rich, *Wirtschaftsethik I*, p. 105.

[141] BEE, p. 167; Rich, *Wirtschaftsethik I*, p. 170.

[142] BEE, p. 199; Rich, *Wirtschaftsethik I*, p. 201.

fundamental social-ethical concern expressed in the criteria of relationality and participation') is therefore not simply a possibility, it is a *necessity*.[143]

Our reading of Luther has particularly alerted us to the dangers of diluting the *theological* aspects of moral claims, and once again this seems to shed light on Rich's work. Let us take an example. In the section entitled 'Eschatology Versus Creation as a Basis for Social Ethics', we expressed concern about the lack of material substance to Rich's description of the Kingdom of God. The nearest he comes to a description is his criterion of participation.[144] In one of his few discussions of a biblical passage, Rich takes as his starting point the community of possessions between believers in Acts 4. He is careful to point out that this is just one instantiation of the criterion, which can take many legitimate forms.[145] But its *essence* is that the common experience of salvation led to a sharing of material possessions with the needy. Therefore, 'the humanity originating from faith, hope, and love will never be able to come to terms with conditions in which one has too little and another has too much'.[146] But, he adds, the biblical text should not be interpreted only literally. It is not a mandate exclusively for recurrent almsgiving from the rich to the poor. Therefore, by extrapolation, the criterion also calls for the less materially prosperous to be enabled to participate within the structures of society through, for example, improved industrial democracy.[147] So far, so good.

Yet, for the reasons we have seen, later in the work it is not this mandate at all which Rich takes as decisive for evaluating different economic structural possibilities. Rather, it is the Rawlsian conception of justice which is operative in such cases.[148] Yet there are prima facie reasons why it would seem that a simple equation or correlation of this with John Rawls's 'difference principle' is difficult to vindicate. We may take our cue from Rich's own point, that 'commonly sharing in salvation in Jesus Christ must also lead to common structures that make possible the participation of all in the material goods of the believers'.[149] The community of possessions is here based on a prior common experience, but Rich does not explore how this might pertain in a wider society which does not share such a common experience.

The closest thing to a unifying common experience in Rawls's thought is very different, namely his information deficit or 'veil of ignorance', which in any case is a hypothetical rather than a concrete experience.[150] It therefore appears that the two different foundational common experiences yield

143 BEE, p. 212; Rich, *Wirtschaftsethik I*, p. 215.
144 BEE, pp. 193–8; Rich, *Wirtschaftsethik I*, pp. 196–200.
145 BEE, p. 196; Rich, *Wirtschaftsethik I*, p. 199.
146 BEE, p. 196; Rich, *Wirtschaftsethik I*, pp. 198–9.
147 BEE, p. 196; Rich, *Wirtschaftsethik I*, p. 199.
148 This is made explicit by Rich in BEE, p. 415; Rich, *Wirtschaftsethik II*, p. 157.
149 BEE, p. 195; Rich, *Wirtschaftsethik I*, p. 198.
150 See Rawls, *A Theory of Justice*, pp. 118–23.

correspondingly divergent social implications, namely common *ownership* of goods on the one hand, and equal *distribution* of goods on the other. It is not obvious that these two things can be simply assimilated. It seems that Rich's eagerness to find common ground for appeal to a universal ethical apprehension runs the risk of *altering* the ethical through the very act of translation.

Another example is furnished by Rich's criterion of relationality, which as we have seen holds that all human values have a legitimate place in moral reflection, provided they are held in dynamic tension with their opposites and not permitted to become absolute.[151] Theological ethics can receive all such values as legitimate, provided they are kept in relational tension. Rich cites Philippians 4:8 in theological substantiation of this.[152] He argues that since the concepts of the true, honourable, just, pure, and lovely can be found in Hellenistic and Jewish visions of virtue, 'the humanity to which Paul understands himself to be obligated... does not set any specific values, but rather takes them over from his living circumstances'.[153] This is not to be done uncritically. But theology receives these values critically not by appraising their content, but by grounding them in relation to one another. The specific theological contribution is the prevention of domination by any one value.

From our analysis of Luther, it is difficult to conclude that this is adequate. We have seen that Luther regards the very definition of lending as having been corrupted into a mask for usury. Yet Luther's response was not to reject the term, but to redefine it in the light of Scripture, to 'bring the words to the bath'.[154] For Luther, there is need for a fundamental alteration of *substance* in the light of the gospel. And his relentlessly exegetical method also triggers an exegetical caveat: while it is doubtless true that there are lexical, and perhaps substantial, similarities between New Testament virtues and the Hellenistic ones which Rich believes Paul is referring to, it is stretching this text to breaking to suggest that Paul is advocating their wholesale acceptance, with only the proviso that they be formally relativized in the light of one other. To use terms borrowed from Stanley Hauerwas and Charles Pinches, the formal concept of a virtue might be widely affirmed, and its appellation common to different traditions, but its material content may vary widely.[155]

Indeed, Rich acknowledges this with respect to the virtue of justice:

[151] This criterion is discussed in BEE, pp. 181–9; Rich, *Wirtschaftsethik I*, pp. 184–92.

[152] See BEE, p. 182; Rich, *Wirtschaftsethik I*, p. 185.

[153] BEE, p. 182; Rich, *Wirtschaftsethik I*, p. 185. It is not clear why the translators omitted *christlichen*, which makes Rich's point even more forceful.

[154] Discussed in the section entitled 'The Third Degree: "Do Not Refuse the One Who Would Borrow from You"'.

[155] Stanley Hauerwas with Charles Pinches, 'Courage Exemplified', in Stanley Hauerwas, *The Hauerwas Reader*, eds. John Berkman and Michael Cartwright (Durham, NC: Duke University Press, 2001), pp. 287–306, esp. pp. 290–302. They show the differences between the accounts of the virtue of courage given by Aristotle and Aquinas.

> the merely formal . . . demand for a humanly just economic order . . . is something about which everyone can agree, because it remains in the domain of the undetermined. One is likely to become involved in an argument only if material definiteness is brought to the value. . . . Liberals, Marxists, Christians, etc. can have quite different conceptions of the fundamental demands of human justice.[156]

So, Rich acknowledges that specific definitions of justice are not universal, but argues that the demand for justice as such is in fact 'something about which everyone can agree'. We should note that Rich is somewhat vague about how this universal apprehension of morality works in practice. For example, he substantiates his criterion of fellow-humanness on the basis that '*Somehow* everyone knows that humanity in our society stands or falls with the realization of an optimum of fellow-humanness'.[157] But he does not say *how* everyone knows, and therefore he is not able to propose a way of differentiating between healthy and corrupted perceptions of universal moral reality.

To draw on Alasdair MacIntyre's analysis of Enlightenment moral philosophy, even Rich's more minimal claim that everyone agrees that justice is obligatory, even if they cannot agree on what justice means, exposes a lack of self-awareness as to the culturally conditioned character of morality, and exhibits rather historically naïve assumptions about the universal accessibility of morality.[158] That justice should be the goal of an economy *may* be obvious among certain subsections of Western society (although even this is debatable), but it is not necessarily a universal assumption, historically and globally. Similarly, in relation to the claim that industrial production should continue to expand exponentially, Rich retorts: 'It is obvious to all reasonable persons that it neither should nor can continue like this'.[159] Again, to many people this is not obvious at all.[160]

Why is Rich blind to this? Explanation is at hand in Luther's dim assessment of human character. Despite Luther's passionate stress on the validity of secular vocation, he tends to regard financial dealing as fairly despicable, and

156 BEE, p. 77; Rich, *Wirtschaftsethik I*, p. 83.

157 BEE, p. 190; Rich, *Wirtschaftsethik I*, p. 193. Emphasis mine.

158 MacIntyre has argued this in several places, especially throughout *Three Rival Versions of Moral Enquiry: Encyclopaedia, Genealogy and Tradition* (Notre Dame: University of Notre Dame Press, 1990), esp. pp. 26–30.

159 BEE, p. 74. The German is perhaps not quite so tart: 'Jedem Einsichtigen wird einleuchten, daß es so nicht weitergehen konnte noch weitergehen kann'. Rich, *Wirtschaftsethik I*, pp. 80–1.

160 This theme is explored in Kenneth Boulding's classic essay, 'The Economics of the Coming Spaceship Earth', in *Environmental Quality in a Growing Economy* ed. Henry Jarrett (Baltimore: Johns Hopkins University Press, 1966), pp. 3–14. He observes that 'Economists in particular, for the most part, have failed to come to grips with the ultimate consequences of the transition from the open to the closed earth'. This seems to be the genesis of the aphorism, often attributed to Boulding but not actually in the essay, that 'Anyone who believes exponential growth can go on forever in a finite world is either a madman or an economist'.

business people as generally on the make rather than noble upstanding members of the community. Such a stereotype still goes down well in some quarters today, but on the whole Luther's assumptions strike us as unfair and off-putting. Rich, who spent time personally involved in industry and in close association with many businesspeople, has a dramatically different perception of the world. His desire is to reach out to people within business, rather than to call them out of it. Yet, although Luther's portrait of merchants and bankers may be overdrawn, Luther does alert us to the possibility that people may seem very fine, and may indeed be highly moral in one sense, but they may simultaneously be profoundly *deceived*.

There is no need to adjudicate on Rich's claim as regards a universal moral experience, and Rich is no doubt right to say we should not automatically problematize all moral perceptions beyond Christian theology. He is helpful in offering us a summons to affirm that which is truthful in each so-called human value. Yet our study of Luther suggests that Rich's basic approach must be modified. Luther does not flatly deny a general human awareness of moral reality, but he is acutely sensitive to the ways this awareness can be corrupted and self-deceived—to such an extent that even the seeming pinnacles of moral achievement can mask deep wickedness. The problem, then, is not Rich's claim that non-Christians may accurately perceive the good. Clearly they *may*, and on the basis of such perception Christians can and should seek to *persuade* others of the validity of their moral convictions, and not just adopt a posture of absolute prophetic critique in all circumstances. Rather, the problem is Rich's view that Christian social ethics is *necessarily* not distinctive in this way. That is, he presupposes moral agreement among well-meaning persons.

Yet such agreement cannot be taken for granted. The truth in any given value cannot be accepted on the basis of the purely formal criterion of relationality, but requires a *substantial discussion* (and potentially, a revision) of the value itself. Common terminology and the universality of certain formally similar moral experiences (such as the tension between the demand of the ethical absolute and customary morality) are insufficient grounds on which to conclude that there is a universal *content* to human moral experience. So, non-theological moral claims may not be dismissed merely because they are non-theological, but neither may their veracity be assumed. This must be established by *theological* analysis. Rich's presuppositions mean that he is methodologically unable to perform such an analysis, which means he tends to lack critical purchase on these supposedly universal norms—another reason for the rather conformist conclusions which we documented at the end of Chapter 2.

As we have seen, this proceeds from Rich's conviction that the theological ethicist is obliged to gain a hearing for their views, in order that they might be heeded and implemented. This in turn is a methodological outcome of his principle that one is responsible for ensuring optimal consequences.

Setting him alongside Luther suggests that this is a false economy: by seeking consensus, and therefore greater improvements, by definition Rich tends towards saying things which generally others will be likely to agree with. He is therefore liable to lose the radical edge that is necessary in order to press for precisely such improvements. Seeking to commend a Christian ethic to society *on society's own terms* seems to have compromised that ethic.

Correspondingly, Rich's proposal to generate criteria for justice, which can be understood and applied without necessarily subscribing to their fundamental premises, illuminates the absence of an ongoing detailed theological discussion in *Wirtschaftsethik*. The theological premises are explored in Chapter 6 of volume I (which Rich describes as an 'excursus'), from which the criteria are developed in Chapter 7 (in which there is also a certain amount of theological analysis). After this, theological considerations must take their bow and gracefully quit the scene. Their purpose was to generate criteria which someone could endorse for entirely non-theological reasons. From this point on, there is no further need for them because the application of the criteria is not a theological matter, but a factual enquiry into how these criteria may be optimally realized.

For Luther, by contrast, every stage of the process must be a theological one. This is because the goal is not the optimization of outcomes, but to call people to obey God's commands in Christ's name. These commands require specific actions which can be done right away, somewhat regardless of the social situation. That is, these actions, or good deeds, have inherent significance and value, even if nobody else at all acts the same way, or even notices. And the commands cannot be diluted, which means that they confront the self-deceit and greed of the human will at its deepest level. As we have noted, this means that human behaviour can never be described as a given fact, but is ever subject to theological critique and analysis.

One cannot agree with Luther's conclusions, then, without subscribing to his premises. His conclusions are not only moral or legal prescriptions (although these are not ruled out), but invitations to discipleship expressed in individual and collective action. The strength of Luther's approach is that he can authorize radically different actions, and thus envisage genuinely different outcomes. The disadvantage, especially in contemporary terms, is that such an approach is unlikely to command agreement beyond (or even, one suspects, within) the church, whereas Rich sets out to build consensus.

Yet Rich's approach brings its own snags. He undermines his own goal of making Christian moral claims persuasive and effective in the public sphere, since in order to make these claims persuasive he tends to trim both their particularity (by correlating them with secular norms) and their authority (they cannot stand on their own as divine commands, but must justify themselves as generally reasonable). Rich's desire to avoid ideological arrogance is admirable, and he is right to be cautious of claims to universal validity, given their propensity to become overbearing and to insulate themselves from examination and critique. His quest is for an authentic, self-critical theological voice, which speaks to the outside world *and can be heard by it.* But our reading of Luther prompts us to explore whether Rich's method is the only way to secure this, and indeed whether it is the best way to do so. In contrast, for all his bluster, Luther is a figure par excellence who discovers resources for self-rebuke and self-reconstruction by delving into his own theological heritage (such as Scripture, liturgy, and earlier Christian thinkers). Allegiance to a particular heritage does not preclude his sharp criticism of aspects of it, by drawing on neglected resources internal and integral to it.

CONCLUSION

This concludes our summary of our findings with respect to Rich's perception of a universal horizon of moral awareness. The final chapter of the monograph will summarize both the finding of this chapter and our overall argument, and indicate some potential wider implications of this project.

Conclusion

Our final task is to summarize the findings of our analysis of our interrogation of Rich's method with respect to economic ethics using our prior study of Luther. This will show the ways in which our study of the method of a pre-modern theologian has enabled us to reflect on our own assumptions and methods more critically. Certainly, we found that the methodologies we studied are anything but trivial. They are not neutral vehicles for conveying the real substance of an author's thought, but directly and materially shape that thought. This conclusion will provide a summary of the findings of Chapter 3, following which we shall offer some duly tentative reflections with respect to contemporary Christian social-ethical method in this area.

SUMMARY

We began by noticing the contrast between Rich's careful, academic approach, and Luther's seemingly more ad hoc, expository one. Luther seems to be led primarily by his instincts. He tends to be less overtly self-reflective than Rich, but we have argued that Luther's instincts, as well as his more consciously articulated moves, are often very much to the point, being saturated in Scripture, Christian worship, and the traditions of Christian thought. For example, Luther's understanding of the doctrine of creation profoundly moulds his rejection of usury, but he does not necessarily articulate this directly. The result is that Luther does not so much consciously apply particular biblical texts or doctrinal concepts to a moral question, as allow his very analysis of the question to proceed from his biblically and theologically formed perception of reality.

Rich is much more explicitly self-reflective, devoting his entire first volume to methodological questions. For example, at the end of *Wirtschaftsethik I* he takes the trouble to spell out in some detail a methodology for treating biblical maxims in social ethics. Yet our study of Luther's primarily exegetical *modus operandi* prompted us to note the absence of exegetical material in Rich's substantial ethical discussions in *Wirtschaftsethik II*.

Our own approach, then, enabled us to notice the discrepancy between Rich's explicit methodological proposal and his actual, *concealed* method, and to probe the reasons for the difference. In particular, Rich assumes that performing economic ethics primarily in a social-ethical key renders the Bible largely irrelevant, because of the relative absence of social ethics within its horizon. For him, instead of exegesis, technical discussion of empirical economic facts is required. The primacy accorded to Scripture by Luther, and the way he deploys it critically against other norms, caused us to question this. Rather than assuming the irrelevance of the Bible, because it does not address the questions we are interested in, Luther offers an alternative method, namely to allow Scripture to shape our very social-ethical questions in the first place, and to unmask the avarice and self-deception behind the financial realities that Rich takes for granted. For example, as we have seen, Luther's prior theological vision of reality shapes his definition and interpretation of the facts, such as the nature of lending and the way in which prices and wages are set. Yet this does not make him detached or idealistic. Indeed, his astute description of the various financial tricks of his day render his work illuminating for historians of the period.

This is one example of the way in which our prior reading of Luther gave us a vantage point from which to understand Rich better than he understands himself, as it were. The discrepancy between what someone does and their ability to describe it is the reason we need to compare methodologies from different theological periods. Yet clearly there are also advantages to Rich's more systematic approach: his project seems to benefit from carefully stating where it is going, what it is aiming to accomplish, and how.

In the section entitled 'Ethics as a Scientific, Dialogical Discipline', we admired Rich's patience in systematically explaining and defending his assumptions, just as he also defends the role of moral norms within social science, and theological convictions in a plural society. In contemporary terms this seems proper and necessary if Christian ethics is to have a credible hearing. But our study of Luther, in his very different context, prompted us to ask whether Rich is being *too* defensive. Luther prompted us to ask whether gaining a hearing is the only task of Christian moral theology. For Luther, the task of moral theology includes the confrontation between the non-negotiable divine standard and the human will *incurvatus in se*, because only such a confrontation can liberate humanity from its enslavement to selfishness and greed. Rather than concerning himself with improving the whole of society, Luther is seemingly more modestly concerned. His goal is a pastoral one: the moral guidance and salvation of those in his care, and to alleviate the particular injustices which he sees before him. This is what enables him to tackle sin so radically at an individual level. (We have used the term 'radical' several times with respect to Luther's method, in the etymological sense of pertaining to the roots of something.)

At several junctures, therefore, we have asked, somewhat contrary to our expectations, whether Luther's seemingly more modest concerns are rather more potent for social ethics than Rich's more comprehensive vision. The origin of this vision is Rich's roots in Marx's critique of religion as an ideological force which shores up capitalist oppression by subordinating created humanity to an absolute God. This means that, while Rich is critical of what he regards as Marx's idolatrous utopianism—in which humanity is responsible for its ultimate destiny—Rich lapses into the same logic by positing humanity as responsible for its penultimate, historical destiny. This gives his social ethics great ambition, but this very ambition requires him to come to terms with certain economic realities as given facts, to build as wide a social consensus as possible by justifying his theological convictions at the bar of general human experience and reason, and by adopting suitable conceptions of social justice (in particular that of John Rawls) that can be understood and accepted more widely in society. We have suggested that these factors actually hamper Rich's good intentions: the danger of ruling out utopian attitudes to the facts and any convictions which are not generally palatable to wider society is that by definition one will find it difficult to question the assumptions and verdicts of the existing discourse.

Theologically, Rich's critique of utopianism is grounded in his rigorous eschatological posture. We suggested this also has the opposite effect to the one Rich desires. Instead of acting as a motor for constant improvement, his emphasis on the incommensurability of the Kingdom of God and the present age represses his expectations of what is possible here and now. More problematically, Rich expresses this in Weberian terms, speaking of the complexity and tragedy of the world. It is difficult to know the right thing to do, since one is caught between competing goods, and must take account of the evils attendant on any action. All action thus incurs guilt: there is no such thing as genuinely good action. At the same time, Rich believes that humanity possesses a general desire for and elementary awareness of a transcendent standard of justice, against which all human laws and actions must be judged, and he thinks that this standard should be appealed to in ethical debate—a point that Luther's acute awareness of the human propensity for self-deception has caused us to question.

Luther assumes broadly the opposite. He might agree that the human apprehension of the good remains, but his alertness to its corruption means that it cannot be appealed to as a neutral standard upon which all can agree. So, non-theological sources are in a sense ruled out from his ethical discourse. Where Rich sees ethics as tragic and obscure, Luther regards good deeds as simple, genuinely good, and sufficiently accessible to humanity through God's disclosure of his will in Scripture. Luther's pre-modern construal of the notion of the divine command prompted us to question whether Marx's, and therefore Rich's, caution about this concept was necessarily justified. Luther portrays God's commands not as the arbitrary dictates of an almighty despot, but as a gift to humanity from a caring guardian. God does not issue commands for the sake of securing adherence to his will as such, or to satisfy some extrinsic code of morality, but so that humanity will live according to its created nature. This way, it will flourish and be blessed. Thus the notions of divine monarchy and finite, obedient creatureliness need not be oppressive, but can be liberating and beneficent—although no doubt we would do well to learn from Rich's and Marx's caution that these notions can be abused. Yet, to turn Rich's argument on its head, we have discovered in Luther the possibility that being a mere function of God can even be good for humanity, since humanity is therefore *freed* from having to construct its own destiny.

God's action does not end with the revelation of commands. Luther certainly seems pessimistic at times,[1] but he regards good deeds as genuinely possible here and now, through God's dynamic and proactive agency in worldly affairs. Divine action is not confined to eschatology and redemption: Luther's distinction between the two governments, sometimes mistakenly regarded as establishing a double moral standard, is in fact also a claim that both governments serve God in producing *the same* outward behaviour. Therefore, in contrast to Rich's realism, Luther need not accept certain forms of human action as inevitable. He can demand a totally different form of behaviour from his hearers, while Rich's rigorous eschatological perspective and his desire to speak in terms which everyone in society can understand make it difficult for him to reckon with God as an active participant in contemporary events, and therefore difficult to expect people to act any differently. Our surprising discovery is that less may be more in social ethics: while Luther lacks Rich's grand design to *make* society as just as possible (a state that Rich defines in terms of optimum outcomes), he retains a laser focus on securing obedience to God's commands which will *do* justice in society.

Luther's emphasis on the divine commandment brings us to the question of *authority* in social ethics. His fierce defence of the enormity and inflexibility of the divine command is another consequence of his exegetical method. We have already quoted Paul Althaus's claim that the 'form [of Luther's theology] is basically exegesis'.[2] The reason for this is that its fundamental *location* is the pulpit (whether literally or not). Rather than feeling obliged to provide a coherent and integrated account of an ethical topic, the role of the preacher is, again, more modest: to expound the full force of a particular

[1] In the Genesis commentary Luther bluntly states, 'You will not change the world'. It would be difficult to find a more conspicuous contrast with contemporary popular theology! See LW v. 7, p. 97; WA v. 44, p. 371, l. 37.

[2] Althaus, *The Theology of Martin Luther*, p. 3.

biblical passage. We are somewhat taken aback by how attractive this approach is, compared to that of Rich. Indeed, Luther's intense suspicion towards attempts to 'water down' biblical commands prompts us to question whether Rich is culpable of this. For Rich, the main term which describes biblical injunctions is *Maxim*, a conspicuous semantic contrast to the notion of *Gebot* so apparent in Luther. The latter denotes that which is obligatory and binding, the former suggests more of a guideline or rule of thumb. As we have seen, these maxims are endlessly contestable. This irenic, scholarly approach, while seemingly appropriate to his milieu, holds Rich back from being as radical as he wants to be. Luther is free to tackle injustice with appropriate anger—a feature we have suggested is not merely temperamental or incidental, but *theological*.

This relates to a point that we have appreciated a great deal concerning Rich's work: his dialogical method. Rich learned from Pascal that some statements of theological truth seem to contradict one another—yet they must both be affirmed equally. We remain enthusiastic about the potential of Rich's dialogical method for enabling one to grasp insights from different dialogue partners, while striving to avoid their errors, and without losing sight of the equal but opposite truths hit upon by other thinkers. Thus Rich is able to take on board Marx's critique of the way in which religion can become ideological and support injustice, without abandoning religion as such.

In the work of Ragaz, Rich discovered the dynamic reforming potential of eschatology, which Rich realizes needs to be held in tension with Barth's insight that human reforms cannot measure up to the Kingdom of God. And Barth's insight in turn must be held together with Brunner's view that such reforms are nevertheless valid in their own way. Yet we have questioned the way in which Rich's criterion of relationality transposes the notion of dialogue to Weber's concept of value plurality, so that any human value can be accepted without substantial *theological* discussion. For Rich, this is useful to enable him to speak in language that others will understand, but the danger is his assumption that such values will be materially compatible with theological ones. However, provided we use Luther's insights regarding the human potential for self-deception, and the critical priority of theological revelation against other norms to correct this generalized, insufficiently critical approach, there seems no reason to reject Rich's dialogical method per se. His willingness to learn from different thinkers requires a welcome level of humility, yet such humility need not be incompatible with an appropriate confidence in particular revelation.

This concludes the summary of our findings, which have demonstrated our thesis, namely that attending to the methodological differences between a premodern theological practitioner and a more contemporary one will augment our own self-critical resources with respect to economic ethics.

REFLECTIONS FOR THEOLOGICAL SOCIAL ETHICS TODAY

Having used our study in order to expand the self-critical resources of contemporary social ethics, and summarized our findings, we will now indicate some possible ways in which contemporary theological social ethics might act upon these findings in terms of its method in economic ethics. These indications are tentative, because they do not form part of the thesis which we originally set out to demonstrate, so this research provides only indirect evidence for them. But they may be useful as possible avenues for further reflection, and for nurturing the practice of social ethics today.

We first propose that Christian social ethics should not be padlocked to the dream of public consensus. Of course, consensus is a fine thing, if one does happen to agree with others. But it cannot be taken for granted. In Rich's case at least, making consensus a determinative *objective* of theological ethics tends to render it rather supine. The assumption that agreement is necessary and obligatory runs the risk of subverting the particularity of Christian claims and, despite Rich's ostensibly greater commitment to social change as a goal in itself, this assumption at times stultifies his own intentions, while Luther's method carries a surprising promise for such change because of its endemic refusal to compromise. Another example, closer to home, is provided by Peter Sedgwick, who speaks of the

> great benefits provided by the next stage of global capitalism. The churches need to remain part of the debate on reforming and humanizing that world, and not abandoning it for a rhetoric of Christian identity over against that world. Such a task will appear compromised, but . . . it can also be immensely worthwhile.[3]

The desire to contribute to public discussion is perfectly proper, and it would be premature to assume that Christian identity means opposition to the world. But we may be better served by relinquishing our place at the table, *if* access to that place requires surrendering the theological features of our discourse. This step need not originate in a pietistic desire not to be involved in society. It could be a tactical retreat for the sake of influencing society more radically and therefore more effectively. To put it another way, Rich assumes an overly homogeneous notion of social involvement, when in fact there are many ways to participate in society which do not necessarily require widespread prior consensus. Withdrawing from one particular form of social participation need hardly preclude some other form of involvement.

Similarly, the Reformation rejection of sectarianism and its affirmation of worldly involvement as an authentic and valuable vocation should not be

[3] Peter H. Sedgwick, *The Market Economy and Christian Ethics* (Cambridge: University Press, 1999), pp. 272–3.

misappropriated as a blanket justification for *any* kind of involvement. Rich gave the example of a good manager whose personal convictions were at odds with the unjust social structures in which he participated, and Rich assumed that the manager's withdrawal from such structures would be an idealistic abandonment of the world for the sake of a self-righteous purism. Certainly we are right to be enthusiastic about involvement in the workplace and politics per se. But, if an activity is inherently wrong, the proper course of action is not to participate in it in order to reform it, but to repent and make amends. We need to make up our minds as to the morality of a particular form of action as a *preliminary* to evaluating the validity of Christian involvement in that sphere, rather than assuming such involvement is legitimate or necessary and therefore retrospectively justifying such activity.

Next, we should be wary of assuming that Christian social ethics must make a compromise with the way the world is, in order to improve it. Among Christian writers on economics, there is widespread acknowledgement of the radical incommensurability between a theologically constituted economy and the existing global capitalist order, but the tendency is to sacrifice this radicalism on the altar of improving the way things actually are. Kathryn Tanner forthrightly sketches the characteristics of a genuinely theological economy, and argues that 'theological economy encroaches on and enters within the territory of the economy it opposes'.[4] But she makes the mistake of assuming that if it simply opposes the world as it is, it will be 'sterile', because it would therefore

> leave the world to its own devices, without practical counsel for realistic change.... Its only advice would be the complete overhaul of the present system, the simple replacement of the present system with a wholly different one.[5]

Shying away from this, Tanner observes that matters such as wages, tax, inflation versus employment, protectionism, and so on are 'up for grabs' within the basic structure of capitalism.[6] Since we cannot abolish capitalism, we must work within it, to ameliorate its unfortunate corollaries, to make as good a job of it as possible. We have seen that this tendency, in Rich's case at least, flows from particular assumptions regarding the responsibility of humanity to secure the optimal long-term outcomes in human history.

In contrast to the overly indiscriminate ethic of involvement that we have just criticized, we suggest operating under Luther's assumption that the financial arena fundamentally belongs to Christ and serves him already. Counter-intuitively, we suggest that the problem with accounts of economic ethics which assume that we need to make compromises with the so-called facts is not that they are *excessively* positive about economics, but that they are

[4] Kathryn Tanner, *Economy of Grace* (Minneapolis: Fortress, 2005), p. 89.
[5] Tanner, *Economy of Grace*, pp. 87–8. [6] Tanner, *Economy of Grace*, p. 92.

insufficiently aware of its goodness. They therefore make insufficient moral claims with respect to it. Rather than envisaging the economy as an essentially wicked domain into which Christians must venture in order to improve it, we should assume that the economy already belongs to God and that he is present and active within in it to secure action within it which conforms to his will. It is not grubby or ignoble, but part of God's good creation. Rich's concern with Brunner's orders of creation paradigm was that this would justify the economic status quo, and produce a static and conservative ethic. But unexpectedly, it was Rich with his emphasis on eschatology who became too accommodating, and Luther with his emphasis on creation who demanded that economic activity should conform to Christ's teaching right now.

Just as we should not assume that we must compromise with the supposed economic facts, neither should we assume that we must operate within the matrix of existing economic paradigms. Like Rich, Christian economist Donald Hay compares capitalism and communism from a Christian perspective, and it is hardly surprising when he concludes that a suitably rehabilitated version of capitalism is vastly preferable to the political and fiscal evils of communism.[7] No doubt that is entirely true. But our work on Luther prompts us to question the assumption that these are the only two options. This assumption blinds us to the ways in which our tradition offers other options and practices, such as the just price and wage concept, the prohibition on usury, the Jubilee tradition and the common chest. These do not fit simply into the capitalist bracket any more than the communist one. Instead of fearing the disjunction between a theological economy and the contemporary global economy, we might use it to spur us to more creative thinking and a more imaginative appropriation of our own tradition. This is not to rule out attempts to reform the economic sphere, as we shall see below.

Our next proposal is that we should treat with caution the claims of economics to scientific neutrality. Both Luther and a cross-section of contemporary, unorthodox economists have taught us that these claims overlook the fact that the discipline of economics includes normative as well as empirical claims, and has a tendency to unintentionally camouflage the former as the latter. Luther's emphasis on the validity of human reason *in its proper sphere* suggests we need not quarrel with genuinely empirical economic claims. But we may not assume that all economic claims fall into this category. It is therefore proper and necessary to subject supposed economic facts to *moral* analysis, although an insistence on doing so could jeopardize our place in public discussion even further. A possible avenue for further reflection would be a consideration of how the virtue of prudence might be integrated into an ethic of radical obedience to Christ's commands. This would presumably

[7] Hay, *Economics Today*, p. 311.

involve empirical research, without such research being co-opted into the service of the belief that humanity is responsible for securing optimum overall outcomes.

This relates to our next methodological suggestion, which is that Christian economic ethics should not simply seek to make a contribution on the 'macro' dimension of social structures and systems, but should pay greater attention to the question of discipleship. Work on the interface between theology and economics, with all the mess and imperfection which that entails, may be biting off more than we can chew theologically. In our context, at this lofty social structural plane, the need to compromise seems inexorable to us. Our dilapidation in this area may be because we do not have good foundations on which to construct something more ambitious. Rather than turning to contemporary economic theory, our initial methodological moves should be exegetical and homiletic, deploying biblical and theological material such as the commands of Jesus rather directly in order to shape authentic Christian action. In such a context it is easier to hear the commands of Jesus without treating them as an idealistic bit of hyperbole. Of course, construing social ethics in terms of discipleship would inhibit it from being equally accessible to all members of society. Again, such a move would require us to surrender the dream of consensus. But the promise of such an approach is that it has the potential to nourish radically different forms of action with respect to economics if these are required.

Such an economic ethic will only be viable if it is undergirded by a confidence in God's ongoing presence and activity in the world. As we have seen, it is not enough to tell people what to do. This will not only fail to change their behaviour, it will also tend to subvert the moral standards themselves because, in the face of the sheer magnetic power of human greed, ethics will tend to quail and water itself down to a more manageable standard unless it is undergirded by substantial and potent theological realities.

Luther saw that Pelagianism can manifest itself in two related ways. Confronted with God's seemingly unattainable moral standards, its first and more familiar instantiation pretends that, with effort, human abilities can meet the requisite level of obedience. Luther perceived that the outcome of this was a second, more subtle tendency, namely to dilute the required moral standards to a more practicable level, a seemingly legalistic façade hiding an antinomian reality. He regarded faith as the antidote, that is, a posture of trusting in abundant divine provision which sets us free from our white-knuckle grip on possessions, so we can give away generously. In short, only confidence in God's free gifts of forgiveness and material provision can liberate us to acknowledge the height of God's commandments.

This more modest emphasis on individual discipleship need not prevent us from analysing vested interests, challenging unjust social structures, and establishing structural alternatives. Thus Luther ferociously exposed the way in which the debased forms of pre-Reformation piety reinforced the conditions of the poor by treating poverty and almsgiving as meritorious. Almsgiving meant that help for the poor was immediate, but very temporary, whereas the common chest arrangement sought a structural and durable solution to the *causes* of poverty as well as alleviating particular cases of hardship. Our proposal is that a more modest emphasis on discipleship will enable a more theologically radical approach, which in turn is needed in order to adopt a more radical social-ethical position.

Let us draw these suggestions, and our enquiry, to a close. We have described our proposed approach as simultaneously more modest, and more radical. Indeed, it is the more modest pretensions of such a method which liberate it from the need to dilute its demands in the light of what will be socially acceptable or empirically feasible. We have offered these suggestions regarding method in contemporary Christian economic ethics in a provisional and exploratory fashion, aware that they have been prompted by our findings rather than established directly by them. Clearly there is scope for further reflection—but the next step is perhaps to put these methodological suggestions into practice, in developing the substance of a Christian economic ethic for today. It is to this that we intend to return in future research.

Bibliography

Althaus, Paul, *The Theology of Martin Luther*, trans. Robert C. Schultz (Philadelphia: Fortress, 1966).

Althaus, Paul, *The Ethics of Martin Luther*, trans. Robert C. Schultz (Philadelphia: Fortress, 1972).

Aquinas, St Thomas, *Summa Theologica*, 2nd rev. edn. 22 vols., trans. Fathers of the English Dominican Province (London: Burns, Oates & Washbourne, 1912–36), <http://www.newadvent.org/summa> accessed January 2006–May 2011.

Aron, Raymond, 'Max Weber and Power-politics', in *Max Weber and Sociology Today*, ed. Otto Stammer, trans. Kathleen Morris (Oxford: Blackwell, 1971), pp. 83–100.

Atherton, John, *Christianity and the Market: Christian Social Thought for Our Times* (London: SPCK, 1992).

Augustine, *City of God*, trans. Henry Bettenson (London: Penguin, 2003).

Avila, Charles, *Ownership: Early Christian Teaching* (Maryknoll: Orbis, 1983).

Avis, P. D. L., 'Moses and the Magistrate: A Study in the Rise of Protestant Legalism', *Journal of Ecclesiastical History* xxvi (1975), pp. 149–72.

Bagchi, David V. N., *Luther's Earliest Opponents: Catholic Controversialists 1518–1525* (Minneapolis: Fortress, 2009).

Banner, Michael, 'Introductory remarks: Christian Ethical Reasoning', *Transformation* 15.2 (1998), pp. 15–17.

Banner, Michael, 'Some Comments on Two Critics', *Crucible* (January/March, 2002), pp. 20–7.

Barth, Karl, *The Epistle to the Romans*, trans. Edwyn C. Hoskyns (Oxford: Oxford University Press, 1933).

Barth, Karl, 'No!: Answer to Emil Brunner', in *Natural Theology*, ed. John Baillie, trans. Peter Fraenkel (London: Bles, 1946), pp. 67–128.

Barth, Karl, 'The Christian Community and the Civil Community' [1946], in *Against the Stream: Shorter Post-War Writings 1946–52*, trans. Stanley Goodman (London: SCM, 1954), pp. 13–50.

Barth, Karl, *The Holy Spirit and the Christian Life: The Theological Basis of Ethics*, trans. R. Birch Hoyle (Louisville, KY: Westminster/John Knox Press, 1993 [1929]).

Bastow, Steve, and James Martin, *Third Way Discourse: European Ideologies in the Twentieth Century* (Edinburgh: Edinburgh University Press, 2003).

Bayer, Oswald, 'Luther's Ethics as Pastoral Care', *Lutheran Quarterly* 4.2 (1990), pp. 125–42.

Bayer, Oswald, 'Social Ethics as an Ethics of Responsibility', in *Worship and Ethics: Lutherans and Anglicans in Dialogue*, eds. Oswald Bayer and Alan Suggate (Berlin: de Gruyter, 1996), pp. 187–201.

Bayer, Oswald, 'Nature and Institution: Luther's Doctrine of the Three Orders', *Lutheran Quarterly* 12.2 (1998), pp. 125–59.

Bayer, Oswald, *Living by Faith: Justification and Sanctification*, trans. Geoffrey W. Bromiley (Grand Rapids: Eerdmans, 2003).

Bayer, Oswald, *Martin Luther's Theology: A Contemporary Interpretation*, trans. Thomas H. Trapp (Grand Rapids: Eerdmans, 2008).

Bell, Daniel M., Jr, 'What is Wrong with Capitalism? The Problem with the Problem with Capitalism', *The Other Journal* (May 2005), pp. 1–7. <http://www.theotherjournal.com/2005/04/04/what-is-wrong-with-capitalism-the-problem-with-the-problem-with-capitalism/ accessed 10 May 2007.

Benedict, Philip, *Christ's Churches Purely Reformed: A Social History of Calvinism* (New Haven: Yale University Press, 2002).

Benne, Robert, 'Capitalism with Fewer Tears', in *Christianity and Capitalism: Perspectives on Religion, Liberalism and the Economy*, eds. Bruce Grelle and David A. Krueger (Chicago: Center for the Scientific Study of Religion, 1986), pp. 67–78.

Benne, Robert, 'Lutheran Ethics: Perennial Themes and Contemporary Challenges', in *The Promise of Lutheran Ethics*, eds. Karen L. Bloomquist and John R. Stumme (Minneapolis: Fortress, 1998), pp. 11–30.

Bennett, John C., *The Radical Imperative* (Philadelphia: Westminster, 1975).

Biggar, Nigel, 'A Case for Casuistry in the Church', *Modern Theology* 6.1 (1989), pp. 29–51.

Biggar, Nigel, *The Hastening that Waits: Karl Barth's Ethics* (Oxford: Oxford University Press, 1993).

Biggar, Nigel, '"God" in Public Reason', *Studies in Christian Ethics* 19.1 (2006), pp. 9–19.

Biggar, Nigel, 'Saving the "Secular": The Public Vocation of Moral Theology; An Inaugural Lecture delivered before the University of Oxford on 22 April 2008' <http://www.chch.ox.ac.uk/sites/default/files/njb%20inaugural%20university%20lecture%2008.pdf> accessed 16 February 2011.

Billing, Einar, *Our Calling*, trans. Conrad Bergendoff (Rock Island: Augustana, 1947).

Bock, Paul, 'Introduction', in Leonhard Ragaz, *Signs of the Kingdom: A Ragaz Reader*, ed. and trans. Paul Bock (Grand Rapids: Eerdmans, 1984), pp. xi–xxii.

Bock, Paul, 'Review of *Leonhard Ragaz in seinen Briefen. 2. Band: 1914–1932*', *Journal of the American Academy of Religion* 52.4 (1984), p. 790.

Bonhoeffer, Dietrich, *Ethics*, trans. Ilse Tödt and others, eds. Eberhard Bethge and others (Minneapolis: Fortress, 2005).

Bornkamm, Heinrich, *Luther's World of Thought*, trans. Martin H. Bertram (St Louis: Concordia, 1958).

Bornkamm, Heinrich, *Luther's Doctrine of the Two Kingdoms in the Context of his Theology* (Philadelphia: Fortress, 1966).

Boulding, Kenneth, 'The Economics of the Coming Spaceship Earth', in *Environmental Quality in a Growing Economy*, ed. Henry Jarrett (Baltimore: Johns Hopkins University Press, 1966), pp. 3–14.

Brecht, Martin, *Martin Luther: His Road to Reformation, 1483–1521*, trans. James F. Schaaf (Philadelphia: Fortress, 1985).

Brecht, Martin, *Martin Luther: The Preservation of the Church, 1532–1546*, trans. James F. Schaaf (Philadelphia: Fortress, 1985).

Brecht, Martin, *Martin Luther: Shaping and Defining the Reformation, 1521–1532*, trans. James F. Schaaf (Philadelphia: Fortress, 1985).

Brennan, H. Geoffrey, 'The Impact of Theological Dispositions on Economics: A Commentary', in *Economics and Religion: Are They Distinct?*, eds. H. Geoffrey Brennan and A. M. C. Waterman (Boston: Kluwer, 1994), pp. 163–77.

Brock, Brian, *Singing the Ethos of God: On the Place of Christian Ethics in Scripture* (Grand Rapids: Eerdmans, 2007).
Brown, Malcolm, *After the Market: Economics, Moral Agreement and the Churches' Mission* (Bern: Lang, 2004).
Brown, Malcolm, '"You take Alasdair MacIntyre much too seriously" (Ronald Preston)—But Do Preston or MacIntyre Take the Global Economy Seriously Enough?', *Studies in Christian Ethics* 17 (2004), pp. 173–81.
Brown, Malcolm, and Paul Ballard, 'Plurality and Globalization: The Challenge of Economics to Social Theology', *Political Theology* 4 (May 2001), pp. 102–16.
Brown, Malcolm, and Paul Ballard, *The Church and Economic Life* (Peterborough: Epworth, 2006).
Brueggemann, Walter, *In Man We Trust: The Neglected Side of Biblical Faith* (Richmond, VI: John Knox, 1972).
Brummel, Lee, 'Luther and the Biblical Language of Poverty', *Ecumenical Review* 31.1 (1980), pp. 40–58.
Brunner, Emil, *The Divine Imperative: A Study in Christian Ethics*, trans. Olive Wyon (London: Lutterworth, 1937).
Brunner, Emil, 'Nature and Grace', in *Natural Theology*, ed. John Baillie, trans. Peter Fraenkel (London: Bles, 1946), pp. 15–64.
Bruun, Hans Henrik, *Science, Values and Politics in Max Weber's Methodology*, new edn. (Aldershot: Ashgate, 2007).
Buchan, James, *Adam Smith and the Pursuit of Perfect Liberty* (London: Profile, 2006).
Büchsel, Friedrich, 'Κριτής', in *Theological Dictionary of the New Testament*, eds. G. Kittel and G. Friedrich, trans. Geoffrey W. Bromiley (Grand Rapids: Eerdmans, 1964–76, repr. 2006), v. 3, pp. 942–3.
Cargill Thompson, W. D. J., *Studies in the Reformation: Luther to Hooker*, ed. C. W. Dugmore (London: Athlone Press, 1980).
Cargill Thompson, W. D. J., *The Political Thought of Martin Luther*, ed. Philip Broadhead (Brighton: Harvester, 1984).
Chester, Tim, *Mission and the Coming of God: Eschatology, the Trinity and Mission in the Theology of Jürgen Moltmann and Contemporary Evangelicalism* (Milton Keynes: Paternoster, 2006).
Chrétien, Jean-Louis, 'From God the Artist to Man the Creator', in *Hand to Hand: Listening to the Work of Art*, trans. Stephen E. Lewis (New York: Fordham University Press, 2003), pp. 94–129.
Clough, David, *Ethics in Crisis: Interpreting Barth's Ethics* (Aldershot: Ashgate, 2005).
Clouser, Roy A., *The Myth of Religious Neutrality: An Essay on the Hidden Role of Religious Belief in Theories*, rev. edn. (Notre Dame: University of Notre Dame Press, 2005).
Cornelison, Robert Thomas, *The Christian Realism of Reinhold Niebuhr and the Political Theology of Jürgen Moltmann: The Realism of Hope* (San Francisco: Mellen Research University Press, 1992).
Cosden, Darrell, *A Theology of Work: Work and the New Creation* (Carlisle: Paternoster, 2004).
Cramp, A. B., *Notes Towards a Christian Critique of Secular Economic Theory* (Toronto: Institute for Christian Studies, 1975).

Cramp, A. B., 'In what Sphere is Economics Sovereign?', in *Social Science in Christian Perspective*, eds. Paul A. Marshall and Robert E. Vandervennen (Lanham, MD: University Press of America, 1988), pp. 199–217.

Cramp, A. B., 'Mappings of (Economic) Meaning: Here Be Monsters', in *Economics and Religion: Are They Distinct?*, eds. H. Geoffrey Brennan and A. M. C. Waterman (Boston: Kluwer, 1994), pp. 179–91.

Cranz, F. Edward, *An Essay on the Development of Luther's Thought on Justice, Law, and Society* (Oxford: Oxford University Press, 1964).

Davies, W. D., *The Setting of the Sermon on the Mount* (Cambridge: Cambridge University Press, 1964).

Dean, James M., and A. M. C. Waterman, 'Introduction: Normative Social Theory', in *Religion and Economics: Normative Social Theory*, eds. James M. Dean and A. M. C. Waterman (Boston: Kluwer, 1999), pp. 3–9.

Dickens, A. G., *Reformation and Society in Sixteenth-Century Europe* (London: Thames and Hudson, 1966).

Dieter, Theodor, 'Fundamentals of the Economic Ethics of Arthur Rich', in *Worship and Ethics: Lutherans and Anglicans in Dialogue*, eds. Oswald Bayer and Alan Suggate (Berlin: de Gruyter, 1996), pp. 202–31.

Divine, Thomas F., *Interest: An Historical and Analytical Study in Economics and Modern Ethics* (Milwaukee: Marquette University Press, 1959).

Doherty, Sean, 'Money', in *Living Witness: Explorations in Missional Ethics*, eds. Andy Draycott and Jonathan Rowe (Leicester: Apollos, 2012), pp. 240–57.

Dow, Sheila C., 'Economics, Ethics and Knowledge', in *Religion and Economics: Normative Social Theory*, eds. James M. Dean and A. M. C. Waterman (Boston: Kluwer, 1999), pp. 123–30.

Duchrow, Ulrich, *Global Economy: A Confessional Issue for the Churches?*, trans. David Lewis (Geneva: WCC Publications, 1987).

Duchrow, Ulrich, *Alternatives to Global Capitalism: Drawn from Biblical History, Designed for Political Action*, trans. Elizabeth Hicks and others (Utrecht: International Books; Heidelberg: Kairos Europa, 1995).

Duchrow, Ulrich, and Franz J. Hinkelammert, *Property for People, Not for Profit: Alternatives to the Global Tyranny of Capital*, trans. Elaine Griffiths and others (London: Zed Books and CIIR, 2004).

Ebeling, Gerhard, 'On the Doctrine of the *Triplex Usus Legis* in the Theology of the Reformation', in *Word and Faith*, trans. James W. Leitch (London: SCM, 1963), pp. 62–78.

Ebeling, Gerhard, *Luther: An Introduction to his Thought*, trans. R. A. Wilson (London: Collins, 1970).

Edel, Susanne, *Wirtschaftsethik im Dialog: Der Beitrag Arthur Richs zur Verständigung zwischen Theologie und Ökonomik* (Stuttgart: Calwer, 1998).

Enderle, Georges, 'Buchbesprechung: Arthur Rich, *Wirtschaftsethik: Grundlagen in theologische Perspektive*', in *Zeitschrift für Philosophische Forschung* 40 (1986), pp. 652–4.

Enderle, Georges, 'Introduction to Arthur Rich's *Business and Economic Ethics*', in Arthur Rich, *Business and Economic Ethics: The Ethics of Economic Systems*, ed. Georges Enderle, trans. David W. Lutz and Albert Wimmer (Leuven: Peeters, 2006), pp. xv–xxiii.

Feyerabend, Paul, *Against Method*, 3rd edn. (London: Verso, 1993).

Finnis, John, *Fundamentals of Ethics* (Oxford: Clarendon Press, 1983).
Fischer, Robert H., 'A Reasonable Luther', in *Reformation Studies: Essays in Honor of Roland H. Bainton*, ed. Franklin H. Littell (Richmond, VI: John Knox, 1962), pp. 30–45.
Forell, George W., *Faith Active in Love: An Investigation of the Principles Underlying Luther's Social Ethics* (Minneapolis: Augsburg, 1959).
Forrester, Duncan, *Christian Justice and Public Policy* (Cambridge: University Press, 1997).
Forrester, Duncan, *On Human Worth: A Christian Vindication of Equality* (London: SCM, 2001).
Forrester, Duncan, 'The Scope of Public Theology', *Studies in Christian Ethics* 17.2 (2004), pp. 5–19.
Froehlich, Karlfried, 'Luther on Vocation', in *Harvesting Martin Luther's Reflections on Theology, Ethics and the Church*, ed. Timothy J. Wengert (Grand Rapids: Eerdmans, 2004), pp. 121–33.
Gerrish, B. A., *Grace and Reason: A Study in the Theology of Luther* (Oxford: Clarendon, 1962).
Giddens, Anthony, *The Third Way: The Renewal of Social Democracy* (Cambridge & Oxford: Polity & Blackwell, 1998).
Gill, Robin, *A Textbook of Christian Ethics* (Edinburgh: T & T Clark, 1985).
Gnuse, Robert, *You Shall Not Steal: Community and Property in the Biblical Tradition* (Maryknoll: Orbis, 1985).
Gordon, Barry, *The Economic Problem in Biblical and Patristic Thought* (Leiden: Brill, 1989).
Gorringe, Timothy J., *Capital and the Kingdom: Theological Ethics and Economic Order* (London: SPCK, 1994).
Goudzwaard, Bob, 'Economic Growth: Is More Always Better?', in *Christianity and the Culture of Economics*, eds. Donald A. Hay and Alan Kreider (Cardiff: University of Wales Press, 2001), pp. 153–65.
Graham, Gordon, *The Idea of Christian Charity: A Critique of some Contemporary Conceptions* (Notre Dame: University of Notre Dame Press, 1990).
Gray, John, *False Dawn: The Delusions of Global Capitalism*, new edn. (London: Granta, 2002).
Grenholm, Carl-Henric, *Christian Social Ethics in a Revolutionary Age: An Analysis of the Social Ethics of John C. Bennett, Heinz-Dietrich Wendland and Richard Shaull* (Uppsala: Verbum, 1973).
Grenholm, Carl-Henric, *Protestant Work Ethics: A Study of Work Ethical Theories in Contemporary Protestant Theology* (Uppsala: Acta Universitatis Upsaliensis, 1993).
Griffiths, Brian, *Morality and the Market Place* (London: Hodder & Stoughton, 1982).
Griffiths, Brian, *The Creation of Wealth* (London: Hodder & Stoughton, 1984).
Grislis, Egil, 'Luther's Understanding of the Wrath of God', *Journal of Religion* 41 (1961), pp. 277–92.
Groenewegen, Peter, (ed.) *Economics and Ethics?* (London: Routledge, 1996).
Haakonssen, Knud, 'Introduction: The Coherence of Smith's Thought', in *The Cambridge Companion to Adam Smith*, ed. Knud Haakonssen (Cambridge: Cambridge University Press, 2006), pp. 1–21.

Hann, Roelf L., 'Man and Methodology in Economic Science: About Abstraction and Obedience', in *Social Science in Christian Perspective*, eds. Paul A. Marshall and Robert E. Vandervennen (Lanham, MD: University Press of America, 1988), pp. 219–54.

Harries, Richard, 'Turning into the World before Turning It Upside Down', *Crucible* (2001), pp. 87–105.

Harries, Richard, *Reinhold Niebuhr Reconsidered* (Cambridge: Grove, 2011).

Harris, James F., *Against Relativism: A Philosophical Defense of Method* (Peru, IL: Open Court Publishing, 1992).

Hauerwas, Stanley, 'Work as Co-Creation: A Critique of a Remarkably Bad Idea', in *In Good Company: The Church as Polis* (Notre Dame: University of Notre Dame Press, 1995), pp. 109–24.

Hauerwas, Stanley, 'On Keeping Theological Ethics Theological', in Stanley Hauerwas, *The Hauerwas Reader*, eds. John Berkman and Michael Cartwright (Durham, NC: Duke University Press, 2001), pp. 51–74.

Hauerwas, Stanley, 'Why the "Sectarian Temptation" is a Misrepresentation: A Response to James Gustafson', in Stanley Hauerwas, *The Hauerwas Reader*, eds. John Berkman and Michael Cartwright (Durham, NC: Duke University Press, 2001), pp. 90–110.

Hauerwas, Stanley, with Charles Pinches, 'Courage Exemplified', in Stanley Hauerwas, *The Hauerwas Reader*, eds. John Berkman and Michael Cartwright (Durham, NC: Duke University Press, 2001), pp. 287–306.

Hay, Donald, *Economics Today: A Christian Critique* (Leicester: Apollos 1989).

Hay, Donald, 'On Being a Christian Economist', in *Christianity and the Culture of Economics*, eds. Donald A. Hay and Alan Kreider (Cardiff: University of Wales Press, 2001), pp. 166–90.

Heckel, Johannes, *Lex Charitatis: A Juristic Disquisition on Law in the Theology of Martin Luther*, trans. and ed. Gottfried G. Krodel (Grand Rapids: Eerdmans, 2010).

Hengsbach, Friedhelm, 'Interesse an Wirtschaftsethik', *Jahrbuch für Christliche Sozialwissenschaften* 29 (1988), pp. 127–50.

Henley, Andrew, 'Economic Orthodoxy and the Free Market System: A Christian Critique', *International Journal of Social Economics* 14 (1987), pp. 56–66.

Heyne, Paul, '"If the Trumpet Does Not Sound a Clear Call..."', in *Religion and Economics: Normative Social Theory*, eds. James M. Dean and A. M. C. Waterman (Boston: Kluwer, 1999), pp. 141–51.

Hirsch, Fred, *Social Limits to Growth* (London: Routledge, 1977).

Hobsbawm, Eric J., 'The Fortunes of Marx's and Engels' Writings', in *The History of Marxism Volume One: Marxism in Marx's Day*, ed. Eric J. Hobsbawm (Brighton: John Spiers/Harvester, 1982), pp. 327–44.

Hobsbawm, Eric J., 'Marx, Engels and Pre-Marxian Socialism', in *The History of Marxism Volume One: Marxism in Marx's Day*, ed. Eric J. Hobsbawm (Brighton: John Spiers/Harvester, 1982), pp. 1–28.

Holl, Karl, *Gesammelte Aufsätze zur Kirchengeschichte* (Tübingen: Mohr Siebeck, 1927–8).

Holl, Karl, *The Cultural Significance of the Reformation*, trans. Karl and Barbara Hertz and John H. Lichtblau (New York: Meridian, 1959).

Holl, Karl, *The Reconstruction of Morality*, trans. Fred W. Meuser and Walter R. Wietzke, eds. James Luther Adams and Walter F. Bense (Minneapolis: Augsburg, 1979).

Hollinghurst, Steve, *Mission-Shaped Evangelism: The Gospel in Contemporary Culture* (Norwich: Canterbury Press, 2010).

Homann, Karl, and others, 'Wirtschaftswissenschaft und Ethik', in *Wirtschaftswissenschaft und Ethik*, ed. Helmut Hesse (Berlin: Duncker & Humblot, 1988), pp. 9–33.

Hoppe, Leslie J., *There Shall Be No Poor Among You: Poverty in the Bible* (Nashville: Abingdon, 2004).

Hughes, John, *The End of Work: Theological Critiques of Capitalism* (Oxford: Blackwell, 2007).

Hütter, Reinhard, 'The Twofold Center of Lutheran Ethics: Christian Freedom and God's Commandments', in *The Promise of Lutheran Ethics*, eds. Karen L. Bloomquist and John R. Stumme (Minneapolis: Fortress, 1998), pp. 31–54.

Janz, Denis R., *Luther on Thomas Aquinas: The Angelic Doctor in the Thought of the Reformer* (Stuttgart: Franz Steiner Verlag, 1989).

Jenkins, David, *Market Whys and Human Wherefores: Thinking Again about Markets, Politics and People* (London: Cassell, 2000).

Johnson, Wayne G., *Theological Method in Luther and Tillich: Law-Gospel and Correlation* (Washington, DC: University Press of America, 1981).

Jones, David W., *Reforming the Morality of Usury: A Study of Differences that Separated the Protestant Reformers* (Lanham, MD: University Press of America, 2004).

Kaiser, Helmut, 'Marktwirtschaft, Planwirtschaft, Weltwirtschaft aus sozialethischer Sicht—Die Wirtschaftsethik von Arthur Rich', *Zeitschrift für Evangelische Ethik* 35.3 (1991), pp. 232–6.

Kant, Immanuel, *Groundwork of the Metaphysics of Morals*, trans. and ed. Mary Gregor (Cambridge: Cambridge University Press, 1997 [1785]).

Katterle, Siegfried, and Arthur Rich, 'Einführung', in *Religiöser Sozialismus und Wirtschaftsordnung*, eds. Siegfried Katterle and Arthur Rich (Gütersloh: Gerd Mohn, 1980), pp. 7–9.

Keynes, John Maynard, *The General Theory of Employment, Interest and Money* (London: Macmillan, 1936).

Korte, Rolf-Jürgen, 'Ethische Positionen im Markt sozialer Hilfen', in *Unternehmerische Freiheit, Selbstbindung und politische Mitverantwortung: Perspektiven republikanischer Unternehmensethik*, eds. Peter Ulrich, Albert Löhr, and Josef Wieland (München & Mering: Rainer Hampp, 1999), pp. 139–63.

Krueger, David A., 'Capitalism, Christianity, and Economic Ethics: An Illustrative Survey of Twentieth Century Protestant Social Ethics', in *Christianity and Capitalism: Perspectives on Religion, Liberalism and the Economy*, eds. Bruce Grelle and David A. Krueger (Chicago: Center for the Scientific Study of Religion, 1986), pp. 25–45.

Lacoste, Jean-Yves, 'Le Désir et l'inexigible: pour lire Henri de Lubac', in *Le Monde et l'Absence d'Œuvre et Autres Études* (Paris: Presses Universitaires de France, 2001).

Ladd, George Eldon, *The Presence of the Future: The Eschatology of Biblical Realism* (London: SPCK, 1974).

Ladd, George Eldon, *A Theology of the New Testament*, rev. edn., ed. Donald A. Hagner, (Grand Rapids: Eerdmans, 1993).

Lassman, Peter and Ronald Speirs, 'Introduction', in *Max Weber: Political Writings*, eds. Peter Lassman and Ronald Speirs (Cambridge: Cambridge University Press, 1994), pp. vii–xxv.

Lazareth, William Henry, *Christians in Society: Luther, the Bible, and Social Ethics* (Minneapolis: Fortress, 2001).

Le Goff, Jacques, *Your Money or Your Life: Economy and Religion in the Middle Ages* (New York: Zone Books, 1988).

Lindberg, Carter, 'Theology and Politics: Luther the Radical and Muntzer the Reactionary', *Encounter* 37.4 (1976), pp. 356–71.

Lindberg, Carter, *Beyond Charity: Reformation Initiatives for the Poor* (Minneapolis: Fortress, 1993).

Lindberg, Carter, *The European Reformations* (Oxford: Blackwell, 1996).

Lindberg, Carter, 'Luther's Struggle with Social-Ethical Issues', in *The Cambridge Companion to Martin Luther*, ed. Donald K. McKim (Cambridge: Cambridge University Press, 2003), pp. 165–78.

Lindberg, Carter, 'Luther on Poverty', in *Harvesting Martin Luther's Reflections on Theology, Ethics and the Church*, ed. Timothy J. Wengert (Grand Rapids: Eerdmans, 2004), pp. 134–51.

Lockwood O'Donovan, Joan, 'The Theological Economics of Medieval Usury Theory', *Studies in Christian Ethics* 14.1 (2001), pp. 48–64.

Lockwood O'Donovan, Joan, and O'Donovan, Oliver, *From Irenaeus to Grotius: A Sourcebook in Christian Political Thought 100–1625* (Grand Rapids: Eerdmans, 1999).

Lohse, Bernhard, 'Reason and Revelation in Luther', in *Scottish Journal of Theology* 13.4 (1960), pp. 337–65.

Lohse, Bernhard, *Martin Luther: An Introduction to his Life and Work*, trans. Robert C. Schultz (Edinburgh: T & T Clark, 1987).

Lohse, Bernhard, *Martin Luther's Theology: Its Historical and Systematic Development*, trans. Roy A. Harrisville (Edinburgh: T & T Clark, 1999).

Long, D. Stephen, *Divine Economy: Theology and the Market* (London: Routledge, 2000).

Lovatt, Mark F. W., *Confronting the Will-to-Power: A Reconsideration of the Theology of Reinhold Niebuhr* (Paternoster: Carlisle, 2001).

Lovin, Robin W., *Christian Faith and Public Choices: The Social Ethics of Barth, Brunner and Bonhoeffer* (Philadelphia: Fortress, 1984).

Lovin, Robin W., 'Foreword', in Karl Barth, *The Holy Spirit and the Christian Life: The Theological Basis of Ethics* (Louisville, KY: Westminster/John Knox Press, 1993), pp. ix–xx.

Lubasz, Heinz, 'Adam Smith and the "Free Market"', in *Adam Smith's* Wealth of Nations: *New Interdisciplinary Essays*, eds. Stephen Copley and Kathryn Sutherland (Manchester: University of Manchester Press, 1995), pp. 45–69.

Lütge, Friedrich, 'Agriculture', in *The New Cambridge Modern History: II. The Reformation, 1520–59*, ed. G. R. Elton (Cambridge: Cambridge University Press, 1962), pp. 23–36.
Luther, Martin, *Luthers Werke: Kritische Gesamtausgabe* 65 + vols. (Weimar: H. Böhlau, 1883–), <http://luther.chadwyck.co.uk> accessed August 2005–May 2011.
Luther, Martin, *Luther's Works* 55 vols. (Philadelphia: Fortress and St Louis: Concordia, 1955–1986).
MacIntyre, Alasdair, *After Virtue: A Study in Moral Theory*, 2nd edn. (London: Duckworth, 1985).
MacIntyre, Alasdair, *Three Rival Versions of Moral Enquiry: Encyclopaedia, Genealogy and Tradition* (Notre Dame: University of Notre Dame Press, 1990).
MacIntyre, Alasdair, *Christianity and Marxism* 2nd edn. (London: Duckworth, 1995).
Mackintosh, Rob, 'Wanted: A Doctrine of Wealth Creation', *Crucible* (1992), pp. 129–36.
Mandeville, Bernard, *The Fable of the Bees and Other Writings*, ed. E. J. Hundert (Indianapolis: Hackett, 1997).
Manermaa, Tuomo, *Christ Present in Faith: Luther's View of Justification*, trans. Kirsi Stjerna (Minneapolis: Fortress, 2005).
Marcuse, Herbert, 'The Foundation of Historical Materialism', in *From Luther to Popper*, trans. Joris de Bres (London: Verso, 1972), pp. 1–48.
Marcuse, Herbert, 'A Study on Authority', in *From Luther to Popper*, trans. Joris de Bres (London: Verso, 1972), pp. 49–155.
Marx, Karl, *Capital* v. 1, trans. Ben Fowkes (Harmondsworth: Penguin, 1976 [1867]).
Marx, Karl, *The Communist Manifesto*, trans. Samuel Moore, ed. David McLellan (Oxford: Oxford University Press, 1992 [1848]).
Marx, Karl, and Friedrich Engels, *Early Writings*, trans. and ed. T. B. Bottomore (London: C. A. Watts, 1963 [1833–4]).
Meuser, Fred W., 'Luther as Preacher of the Word of God', in *The Cambridge Companion to Martin Luther*, ed. Donald K. McKim (Cambridge: Cambridge University Press, 2003), pp. 136–48.
Milbank, John, '"Between Purgation and Illumination": A Critique of the Theology of Right', in *Christ, Ethics and Tragedy: Essays in Honour of Donald MacKinnon*, ed. Kenneth Surin (Cambridge: Cambridge University Press, 1989), pp. 161–96.
Milbank, John, *Theology and Social Theory: Beyond Secular Reason* (Oxford: Blackwell, 1990).
Milbank, John, 'Enclaves, or Where is the Church', *New Blackfriars* 73 (1992), pp. 341–52.
Milbank, John, *The Word Made Strange: Theology, Language, Culture* (Oxford: Blackwell, 1997).
Milbank, John, *The Suspended Middle: Henri de Lubac and the Debate Concerning the Supernatural* (Grand Rapids: Eerdmans, 2005).
Mills, Paul, *Interest in Interest: The Old Testament Ban on Interest and its Implications for Today* (Cambridge: Jubilee, 1989).
Mills, Paul, 'The Ban on Interest: Dead Letter or Radical Solution?', *Cambridge Papers* 1.4 (1993).
Moltmann, Jürgen, *On Human Dignity: Political Theology and Ethics*, trans. M. Douglas Meeks (London: SCM, 1984).

Moltmann, Jürgen, 'Foreword' to Robert Thomas Cornelison, *The Christian Realism of Reinhold Niebuhr and the Political Theology of Jürgen Moltmann: The Realism of Hope* (San Francisco: Mellen Research University Press, 1992), pp. i–v.

Mommsen, Wolfgang J., 'The Antinomical Structure of Max Weber's Political Thought', in Wolfgang J. Mommsen, *The Political and Social Theory of Max Weber* (Cambridge: Polity, 1989), pp. 24–43.

Mommsen, Wolfgang J., 'Politics and Scholarship: The Two Icons in Max Weber's Life', in Wolfgang J. Mommsen, *The Political and Social Theory of Max Weber* (Cambridge: Polity, 1989), pp. 3–23.

Mott, Stephen Charles, *Biblical Ethics and Social Change* (Oxford: Oxford University Press, 1982).

Munby, D. L., *Christianity and Economic Problems* (London: Macmillan, 1956).

Myrdal, Gunnar, *Objectivity in Social Research* (London: Duckworth, 1969).

Myrdal, Gunnar, 'How Scientific are the Social Sciences?', in Gunnar Myrdal, *Against the Stream: Critical Essays on Economics* (London & Basingstoke: Macmillan, 1974), pp. 133–57.

Myrdal, Gunnar, 'The Place of Values in Social Policy', in Gunnar Myrdal, *Against the Stream: Critical Essays on Economics* (London & Basingstoke: Macmillan, 1974), pp. 33–51.

Myrdal, Gunnar, 'Preface', in Gunnar Myrdal, *Against the Stream: Critical Essays on Economics* (London & Basingstoke: Macmillan, 1974), pp. v–viii.

Myrdal, Gunnar, *The Political Element in the Development of Economic Theory*, trans. Paul Streeten (New Brunswick: Transaction, 1990).

Nagel, Norman, '*Sacramentum et exemplum* in Luther's Understanding of Christ', in *Luther for an Ecumenical Age: Essays in Commemoration of the 450th Anniversary of the Reformation*, ed. Carl S. Meyer (St Louis: Concordia, 1967), pp. 172–99.

Nardoni, Enrique, *Rise Up O Judge: A Study of Justice in the Biblical World*, trans. Seán Charles Martin (Peabody, MA: Hendrickson, 2004).

Nelson, Benjamin, *The Idea of Usury: From Tribal Brotherhood to Universal Otherhood* (Princeton: Princeton University Press, 1949).

Nelson, M. T., 'Consequentialism', in *New Dictionary of Christian Ethics and Pastoral Theology*, eds. David J. Atkinson and David Field (Leicester: InterVarsity, 1995), pp. 253–4.

Nelson, Robert H., *Reaching for Heaven on Earth: The Theological Meaning of Economics* (Savage, MD: Rowman & Littlefield, 1991).

Nelson, Robert H., 'Economics as Religion', in *Economics and Religion: Are They Distinct?*, eds. H. Geoffrey Brennan and A. M. C. Waterman (Boston: Kluwer, 1994), pp. 227–36.

Nelson, Robert H., *Economics as Religion: From Samuelson to Chicago and Beyond* (Pennsylvania: Pennsylvania State University Press, 2001).

Nelson, Ronald R., 'Faith-Discipline Integration: Compatibilist, Reconstructionalist, and Transformationalist', in *The Reality of Christian Learning: Strategies for Faith–Discipline Integration*, eds. Harold Heie and David L. Wolfe (St Paul and Grand Rapids: Christian University Press/Christian College Consortium & Eerdmans, 1987), pp. 317–39.

Ngien, Dennis, 'Theology of Preaching in Martin Luther', *Themelios* 28.2 (2003), pp. 28–48.

Niebuhr, Reinhold, *The Nature and Destiny of Man: A Christian Interpretation* (New York: Scribners, 1953).
Niebuhr, Reinhold, *Christian Realism and Political Problems* (London: Faber, 1954).
Niebuhr, Reinhold, *An Interpretation of Christian Ethics* (New York: Meridian, 1956).
Noonan, John T., *The Scholastic Analysis of Usury* (Cambridge, MA: Harvard University Press, 1957).
Northcott, Michael S., *The Church and Secularization* (Frankfurt am Main: Peter Lang, 1989).
Northcott, Michael S., 'The Market, the Multitude and Metaphysics: Ronald Preston's Middle Way and the Theological Critique of Economic Reason', *Studies in Christian Ethics* 17.2 (2004), pp. 104–17.
Northcott, Michael S., 'The Parable of the Talents and the Economy of the Gift', *Theology* cvii (2004), pp. 241–9.
Nutzinger, Hans, 'Anmerkungen zu Arthur Richs Wirtschaftsethik', *Zeitschrift für Evangelische Ethik* 35.3 (1991), pp. 229–32.
Nygren, Anders, *Agape & Eros*, trans. Philip S. Watson (London: SPCK, 1982).
O'Donovan, Oliver, *The Problem of Self-Love in St. Augustine* (New Haven: Yale University Press, 1980).
O'Donovan, Oliver, *Begotten or Made?* (Oxford: Oxford University Press, 1984, 2002).
O'Donovan, Oliver, *Principles in the Public Realm: The Dilemma of Christian Moral Witness* (Oxford: Oxford University Press, 1984).
O'Donovan, Oliver, *Resurrection and Moral Order: An Outline for Evangelical Ethics*, 2nd edn. (Leicester: Apollos, 1994).
O'Donovan, Oliver, *The Desire of the Nations* (Cambridge: Cambridge University Press, 1996).
O'Donovan, Oliver, *Common Objects of Love: Moral Reflection and the Shaping of Community* (Grand Rapids: Eerdmans, 2002).
O'Donovan, Oliver, *The Ways of Judgment* (Grand Rapids: Eerdmans, 2005).
O'Donovan, Oliver, 'The Natural Ethic', in *Essays in Evangelical Social Ethics*, ed. David F. Wright (Exeter: Paternoster, no date), pp. 19–35.
Oberman, Heiko A., *Luther: Man between God and the Devil*, trans. Eileen Walliser-Schwarzbart (New Haven: Yale University Press, 1989).
Ormerod, Paul, *The Death of Economics* (London: Faber & Faber, 1994).
Osborne, Peter, *Marx* (London: Grant, 2005).
Osborne, Thomas M., Jr, *Love of Self and Love of God in Thirteenth-Century Ethics* (Notre Dame: University of Notre Dame Press, 2005).
Oslington, Paul, 'A Theological Economics', *International Journal of Social Economics* 27.1 (2000), pp. 32–44.
Oslington, Paul, 'Review, *Divine Economy: Theology and the Market* by D. Stephen Long', *Journal of Markets and Morality* 4.1 (Spring 2001), pp. 136–41.
Otteson, James R., 'The Recurring "Adam Smith Problem"', *History of Philosophy Quarterly* 17.1 (2000), pp. 51–74.
Ozment, Steven E., *The Age of Reform, 1250–1550: An Intellectual and Religious History of Late Medieval and Reformation Europe* (New Haven: Yale University Press, 1980).

Palaver, Wolfgang, 'Envy or Emulation: A Christian Understanding of Economic Passions', in *Passions in Economy, Politics, and the Media: In Discussion with Christian Theology*, eds. Wolfgang Palaver and Petra Steinmair-Pösel (Vienna: Lit, 2005), pp. 139–62.

Palaver, Wolfgang, 'Challenging Capitalism as Religion: Hans G. Ulrich's Theological and Ethical Reflections on the Economy', *Studies in Christian Ethics* 20 (2007), pp. 215–30.

Parsons, Talcott, 'Value-freedom and Objectivity', in *Max Weber and Sociology Today*, ed. Otto Stammer, trans. Kathleen Morris (Oxford: Blackwell, 1971), pp. 27–50.

Peterson, David G., 'Jesus and Social Ethics', in *Explorations 3: Christians in Society*, ed. B. G. Webb (Homebush West: Lancer, 1988), pp. 73–96 <http://davidgpeterson.com/other-topics/jesus-and-social-ethics/> accessed 2 May 2011.

Peura, Simo, 'Christ as Favor and Gift: The Challenge of Luther's Understanding of Justification', in *Union with Christ: The New Finnish Interpretation of Luther*, eds. Carl E. Braaten and Robert W. Jenson (Grand Rapids: Eerdmans, 1998), pp. 42–69.

Peura, Simo, 'What God Gives Man Receives: Luther on Salvation', in *Union with Christ: The New Finnish Interpretation of Luther*, eds. Carl E. Braaten and Robert W. Jenson (Grand Rapids: Eerdmans, 1998), pp. 76–95.

Ponsonby, Simon C. R., 'Natural Theology in the Thought of Karl Barth' (unpublished MLitt thesis, University of Bristol, 1996).

Pope, Stephen J., 'Aquinas on Almsgiving, Justice and Charity: An Interpretation and Reassessment', *Heythrop Journal* 32.2 (1991), pp. 167–91.

Prien, Hans-Jürgen, *Luthers Wirtschaftsethik* (Göttingen: Vandenhoeck & Ruprecht, 1992).

Prien, Hans-Jürgen, 'Wirtschaftsethik der Reformationszeit bei Martin Luther', <http://offenes-forum-wiesbaden.dike.de/wirtschaftsethik/Luther_wirtschaftsethik.htm> accessed 15 April 2006.

Ragaz, Leonhard, *Israel, Judaism and Christianity* (London: Victor Gollancz, 1947).

Ragaz, Leonhard, 'The Bible: An Interpretation', in Leonhard Ragaz, *Signs of the Kingdom: A Ragaz Reader*, ed. and trans. Paul Bock (Grand Rapids: Eerdmans, 1984), pp. 118–26.

Ragaz, Leonhard, 'The Gospel and the Current Social Struggle', in Leonhard Ragaz, *Signs of the Kingdom: A Ragaz Reader*, ed. and trans. Paul Bock (Grand Rapids: Eerdmans, 1984), pp. 3–15.

Ragaz, Leonhard, 'The Lord's Prayer', in Leonhard Ragaz, *Signs of the Kingdom: A Ragaz Reader*, ed. and trans. Paul Bock (Grand Rapids: Eerdmans, 1984), pp. 112–13.

Ragaz, Leonhard, 'Thy Kingdom Come', in Leonhard Ragaz, *Signs of the Kingdom: A Ragaz Reader*, ed. and trans. Paul Bock (Grand Rapids: Eerdmans, 1984), pp. 18–23.

Raunio, Antii, 'Natural Law and Faith: The Forgotten Foundations of Ethics in Luther's Theology', in *Union with Christ: The New Finnish Interpretation of Luther*, eds. Carl E. Braaten and Robert W. Jenson (Grand Rapids: Eerdmans, 1998), pp. 96–124.

Rawls, John, *Political Liberalism* (New York: Columbia University Press, 1993).

Rawls, John, 'The Idea of Public Reason Revisited', in *The Law of Peoples with 'The Idea of Public Reason Revisited'* (Cambridge, MA: Harvard University Press, 1999), pp. 129–80.

Rawls, John, *A Theory of Justice*, rev. edn. (Cambridge, MA: Harvard University Press, 1999).

Rich, Arthur, *Die Anfänge der Theologie Huldrych Zwinglis* (Zürich: Zwingli Verlag, 1949).

Rich, Arthur, *Pascals Bild vom Menschen: Eine Studie über die Dialektik von Natur und Gnade in den 'Pensées'* (Zürich: Zwingli Verlag, 1953).

Rich, Arthur, 'Theologische Einführung', in *Leonhard Ragaz in seinen Briefen 1: 1887–1914*, eds. Christine Ragaz and others (Zürich: EVZ-Verlag, 1966), pp. ix–xliv.

Rich, Arthur, 'Personal Evil and Structural Evil in Human Existence', in Harold Tonks, *Faith, Hope and Decision-Making*, trans. Harold Tonks, pp. 303–17. Originally published as, 'Personal und strukturell Böses in der menschlichen Existenz', in *Theologische Zeitschrift* 24.5 (1968), pp. 320–37.

Rich, Arthur, 'Biographische Notizen', in *Aufrisse: Vorarbeiten zum sozialethischen Denken*, ed. Hans ten Doornkaat Koolman (Zürich: Zwingli Verlag, 1970).

Rich, Arthur, 'Das «Humanum» als Leitbegriff der Sozialethik', in *Humane Gesellschaft: Beiträge zu Ihrer Sozialen Gestaltung; Zum 70. Geburtstag von Heinz-Dietrich Wendland*, eds. Trutz Rendtorff and Arthur Rich (Zürich: Furche/Zwingli, 1970), pp. 13–45.

Rich, Arthur, *Mitbestimmung in der Industrie: Probleme—Modelle—Kritische Beurteilung; Eine sozialethische Orientierung* (Zürich: Flamberg, 1973).

Rich, Arthur, *Radikalität und Rechtsstaatlichkeit: Drei Beiträge zur politischen Ethik* (Zürich: Theologischer Verlag, 1978).

Rich, Arthur, 'Sozialethische Kriterien und Maximem humaner Gesellschaftsgestaltung', in *Religiöser Sozialismus und Wirtschaftsordnung*, eds. Siegfried Katterle and Arthur Rich (Gütersloh: Gerd Mohn, 1980), pp. 10–30.

Rich, Arthur, 'Theologisch-sozial-ethische Einführung', in *Leonhard Ragaz in seinen Briefen 2: 1914–1932*, eds. Christine Ragaz and others (Zürich: Theologischer Verlag, 1982), pp. 9–22.

Rich, Arthur, *Wirtschaftsethik I: Grundlagen in theologischer Perspektive* (Gütersloh: Gerd Mohn, 1984).

Rich, Arthur, 'Denken, das weh tut', in *Emil Brunner in der Erinnerung seiner Schüler*, eds. Werner Kramer and Hugo Sonderegger (Zürich: Theologischer Verlag, 1989), pp. 78–82.

Rich, Arthur, *Wirtschaftsethik II: Marktwirtschaft, Planwirtschaft, Weltwirtschaft aus sozialethischer Sicht* (Gütersloh: Gerd Mohn, 1990).

Rich, Arthur, *Business and Economic Ethics: The Ethics of Economic Systems*, ed. Georges Enderle, trans. David W. Lutz and Albert Wimmer (Leuven: Peeters, 2006).

Rieth, Ricardo, *'Habsucht' bei Martin Luther* (Weimar: Hermann Böhlaus Nachfolger, 1996).

Rieth, Ricardo, 'Luther on Greed', in *Harvesting Martin Luther's Reflections on Theology, Ethics and the Church*, ed. Timothy J. Wengert (Grand Rapids: Eerdmans, 2004), pp. 152–68.

Robbins, Anna M., *Methods in the Madness: Diversity in Twentieth-Century Christian Social Ethics* (Carlisle: Paternoster, 2004).

Rogers, Kelly, (ed.) *Self-Interest: An Anthology of Philosophical Perspectives* (London: Routledge, 1997).

Roháč, Dalibor, 'Does Inequality Matter?' (London: Adam Smith Institute, 2011), <http://www.adamsmith.org/files/Does_Inequality_Matter_ASI.pdf> accessed 11 August 2011.

Rosen, Frederick, *Classical Utilitarianism from Hume to Mill* (London: Routledge, 2003).

Roth, Hans Erich, 'Arthur Richs Wirtschaftsethik II—Eine fundierte Orientierungshilfe für die Wirtschaft', *Zeitschrift für Evangelische Ethik* 35.3 (1991), pp. 236–8.

Ruh, Hans, 'Einführung zu Arthur Richs Wirtschaftsethik', *Zeitschrift für Evangelische Ethik* 35.3 (1991), p. 229.

Rupp, E. G., 'Luther and the German Reformation to 1529', in *The New Cambridge Modern History: II. The Reformation, 1520–59*, ed. G. R. Elton (Cambridge: Cambridge University Press, 1962), pp. 70–95.

Schluchter, Wolfgang, 'The Paradox of Rationalization: On the Relation of Ethics and World', trans. Guenther Roth in *Max Weber's Vision of History*, eds. Guenther Roth and Wolfgang Schluchter (Berkeley: California University Press, 1979), pp. 11–64.

Schluchter, Wolfgang, 'Value-Neutrality and the Ethic of Responsibility', trans. Guenther Roth in *Max Weber's Vision of History*, eds. Guenther Roth and Wolfgang Schluchter (Berkeley: California University Press, 1979), pp. 65–116.

Schwanke, Johannes, 'Luther on Creation', in *Harvesting Martin Luther's Reflections on Theology, Ethics and the Church*, ed. Timothy J. Wengert (Grand Rapids: Eerdmans, 2004), pp. 78–98.

Scott, Peter, *A Political Theology of Nature* (Cambridge: Cambridge University Press, 2003).

Sedgwick, Peter H., *The Market Economy and Christian Ethics* (Cambridge: Cambridge University Press, 1999).

Sedlacek, Tomas, *Economics of Good and Evil: The Quest for Economic Meaning from Gilgamesh to Wall Street*, trans. Douglas Arellanes (Oxford: Oxford University Press, 2011).

Sen, Amartya, *On Ethics and Economics* (Oxford: Blackwell, 1987).

Skevington Wood, A., *Captive to the Word: Martin Luther, Doctor of Sacred Scripture* (Exeter: Paternoster, 1969).

Smith, Adam, *The Wealth of Nations* (New York: Bantam, 2003 [1776]).

Smith, Adam, *The Theory of Moral Sentiments* (Mineola, NY: Dover, 2006 [1790]).

Snyder, Howard, 'Models of the Kingdom: Sorting out the Practical Meaning of God's Reign', *Transformation* 10.1 (1993), pp. 1–6.

Sockness, Brent W., 'Luther's Two Kingdoms Revisited: A Response to Reinhold Niebuhr's Criticism of Luther', *Journal of Religious Ethics* 20.1 (1992), pp. 93–110.

Song, Robert, *Christianity & Liberal Society* (Oxford: Oxford University Press, 2006).

de Spinoza, Benedict, *Ethics*, ed. and trans. Edwin Curley (London: Penguin, 1996).

Stackhouse, Max L., with others (eds.), *On Moral Business: Classical and Contemporary Resources for Ethics in Economic Life* (Grand Rapids: Eerdmans, 1995).

Storkey, Alan, *Foundational Epistemologies in Consumption Theory* (Amsterdam: Vrije Universiteit, 1993).

Stout, Jeffrey, *Democracy and Tradition* (Princeton: Princeton University Press, 2004).

Straw, Carole, 'Martyrdom', in *Augustine Through the Ages: An Encyclopedia*, ed. Allan D. Fitzgerald (Grand Rapids: Eerdmans, 1999), pp. 538–42.

Strohl, Jane E., 'Luther's Spiritual Journey', in *The Cambridge Companion to Martin Luther*, ed. Donald K. McKim (Cambridge: Cambridge University Press, 2003), pp. 149–64.

Strohm, Theodor, 'Arthur Richs Bedeutung für die Wirtschafts- und Sozialethik: Aus Anlaß des 80 Geburtstags von Arthur Rich', *Zeitschrift für Evangelische Ethik* 34 (1990), pp. 192–7.

Suggate, Alan, *William Temple and Christian Social Ethics Today* (Edinburgh: T & T Clark, 1987).

Suggate, Alan, 'Whither Anglican Social Ethics?', *Crucible* (2001), pp. 106–22.

Tanner, Kathryn, *Economy of Grace* (Minneapolis: Fortress, 2005).

Tanner, Kathryn, 'Eschatology and Ethics', in *The Oxford Handbook of Theological Ethics*, eds. Gilbert Meilaender and William Werpehowski (Oxford: Oxford University Press, 2005), pp. 41–56.

Tappert, Theodore G. (trans. and ed.), *The Book of Concord: The Confessions of the Evangelical Lutheran Church* (Philadelphia: Fortress, 1959).

Tawney, R. H., *Religion and the Rise of Capitalism: A Historical Study* (Harmondsworth: Penguin, 1938).

Taylor, Charles, 'Justice After Virtue', in *After MacIntyre: Critical Perspectives on the Work of Alasdair MacIntyre*, eds. John Horton and Susan Mendus (Cambridge: Polity, 1994), pp. 16–43.

Taylor, Simon, 'How to Speak of God and Mammon: Some Methodological Remarks on Theological Approaches to Economics', *Crucible* (2004), pp. 15–28.

ten Doornkaat Koolman, Hans (ed.), Arthur Rich, *Aufrisse: Vorarbeiten zum sozialethischen Denken* (Zürich: Zwingli Verlag, 1970).

Tertullian, *Second Book to his Wife* [c. 200], trans. S. Thelwall, in *Ante-Nicene Fathers*, eds. Alexander Roberts, James Donaldson, and A. Cleveland Coxe (Peabody: Hendrickson, 1994), v. 4.

Thompson, Mark D., *A Sure Ground on which to Stand: The Relation of Authority and Interpretative Method in Luther's Approach to Scripture* (Carlisle: Paternoster, 2004).

Tiemstra, John P., 'Every Square Inch: Kuyperian Social Theory and Economics', in *Religion and Economics: Normative Social Theory*, eds. James M. Dean and A. M. C. Waterman (Boston: Kluwer, 1999), pp. 85–98.

Tomlin, Graham, *The Power of the Cross: Theology and the Death of Christ in Paul, Luther and Pascal* (Carlisle: Paternoster, 1999).

Tonks, Harold, *Faith, Hope and Decision-Making: The Kingdom of God and Social Policy-Making; The Work of Arthur Rich of Zürich* (Frankfurt am Main: Peter Lang, 1984).

Tribe, Keith, 'Natural Liberty and *Laissez Faire*: How Adam Smith Became a Free Trade Ideologue', in *Adam Smith's* Wealth of Nations*: New Interdisciplinary Essays*, eds. Stephen Copley and Kathryn Sutherland (Manchester: University of Manchester Press, 1995), pp. 23–44.

Troeltsch, Ernst, *The Social Teaching of the Christian Churches*, 2 vols., trans. Olive Wyon (Chicago: University of Chicago Press, 1976).

Uhlhorn, Gerhard, *Christian Charity in the Ancient Church* (New York: Scribners, 1883).

Ulrich, Hans G., 'On Finding Our Place: Christian Ethics in God's reality', *European Journal of Theology* xviii (2009), pp. 137–44.

Vajta, Vilmos, *Luther on Worship: An Interpretation* (Philadelphia: Muhlenberg, 1958).

Vandrunen, David, *Natural Law and the Two Kingdoms: A Study in the Development of Reformed Social Thought* (Grand Rapids: Eerdmans, 2010).

Vickers, Douglas, *Economics and Ethics: An Introduction to Theory, Institutions, and Policy* (Westport, CT: Praeger, 1997).

Volf, Miroslav, 'On Loving with Hope: Eschatology and Social Responsibility', *Transformation* 7.3 (July–September 1990), pp. 28–31.

Volf, Miroslav, *Work in the Spirit: Toward a Theology of Work* (Oxford: Oxford University Press, 1991).

Wannenwetsch, Bernd, '"Intrinsically Evil Acts"; or, Why Abortion and Euthanasia Cannot Be Justified', in *Ecumenical Ventures in Ethics: Protestants Engage Pope John Paul II's Moral Encyclicals*, eds. Reinhard Hütter and Theodor Dieter (Grand Rapids: Eerdmans, 1998), pp. 185–215.

Wannenwetsch, Bernd, 'Caritas fide formata: "Herz und Affekte" als Schlüssel zu "Glaube und Liebe"', *Kerygma und Dogma* 46.3 (2000), pp. 205–24.

Wannenwetsch, Bernd, 'You Shall Not Kill—What Does It Take? Why We Need the Other Commandments if We Are to Abstain from Killing', in *I Am the Lord Your God*, eds. Christopher R. Seitz and Carl E. Braaten (Grand Rapids: Eerdmans, 2005), pp. 148–74.

Wannenwetsch, Bernd, 'Conversing with the Saints as they Converse with Scripture: In Conversation with Brian Brock's *Singing the Ethos of God*', *European Journal of Theology* xviii (2009), pp. 125–35.

Waterman, A. M. C., *Revolution, Economics and Religion: Christian Political Economy 1798–1833* (Cambridge: Cambridge University Press, 1991).

Waterman, A. M. C., *Political Economy and Christian Theology Since the Enlightenment: Essays in Intellectual History* (Basingstoke: Palgrave Macmillan, 2004).

Watson, Philip S., *Let God be God!: An Interpretation of the Theology of Martin Luther* (Philadelphia: Fortress, 1970).

Weber, Max, 'The Meaning of "Ethical Neutrality" in Sociology and Economics', in *The Methodology of the Social Sciences*, trans. and eds. Edward A. Shils and Henry A. Finch (Glencoe: Free Press, 1949), pp. 1–47.

Weber, Max, 'The Nation State and Economic Policy', in *Political Writings*, trans. and eds. Peter Lassman and Ronald Speirs (Cambridge: Cambridge University Press, 1994), pp. 1–28.

Weber, Max, 'The Profession and Vocation of Politics', in *Political Writings*, trans. and eds. Peter Lassman and Ronald Speirs (Cambridge: Cambridge University Press, 1994), pp. 309–69.

Webster, John, *Holy Scripture: A Dogmatic Sketch* (Cambridge: Cambridge University Press, 2003).

Webster, John, *Barth's Moral Theology: Human Action in Barth's Thought* (London: T & T Clark, 2004).

Wendland, Heinz-Dietrich, 'The Theology of the Responsible Society', in *Christian Social Ethics in a Changing World: An Ecumenical Theological Enquiry*, ed. John C. Bennett (New York: Association Press, 1966), pp. 135–52.

Wendland, Heinz-Dietrich, *Einführung in die Sozialethik* (Berlin: de Gruyter, 1971).

Wenham, G. J., 'The Gap between Law and Ethics in the Bible', *Journal of Jewish Studies* xlviii (1997), pp. 17–29.

West, Cornel, 'Neo-Aristotelianism, Liberalism and Socialism: A Christian Perspective', in *Christianity and Capitalism: Perspectives on Religion, Liberalism and the Economy*, eds. Bruce Grelle and David A. Krueger (Chicago: Center for the Scientific Study of Religion, 1986), pp. 79–89.

Wiebering, Joachim, 'Rezension zu «Arthur Richs Wirtschaftsethik II»', *Theologische Literaturzeitung* 117 (1992), pp. 60–2.

Wiemeyer, Joachim, 'Neuere Literatur zur Wirtschaftsethik', *Jahrbuch für Christliche Sozialwissenschaften* 29 (1988), pp. 213–26.

Wilkinson, Richard G., *The Impact of Inequality: How to Make Sick Societies Healthier* (New York: New Press, 2005).

Wilkinson, Richard G., and Kate Pickett, *The Spirit Level: Why Equality is Better for Everyone* (London: Penguin, 2009).

Williams, Stephen, 'The Partition of Love and Hope: Eschatology and Social Responsibility', *Transformation* 7.3 (July–September 1990), pp. 24–7.

Wingren, Gustaf, *The Christian's Calling: Luther on Vocation*, trans. Carl C. Rasmussen (Edinburgh: Oliver and Boyd, 1958).

Witte, John, *Law and Protestantism: The Legal Teachings of the Lutheran Reformation* (Cambridge: Cambridge University Press, 2002).

Wogaman, J. Philip, *The Great Economic Debate: An Ethical Analysis* (Philadelphia: Westminster, 1977).

Wogaman, J. Philip, *Economic Ethics: A Christian Inquiry* (Philadelphia: Fortress, 1986).

Wright, William J., *Martin Luther's Understanding of God's Two Kingdoms: A Response to the Challenge of Skepticism* (Grand Rapids: Baker, 2010).

Wuthnow, Robert, *Communities of Discourse: Ideology and Social Structure in the Reformation, the Enlightenment, and European Socialism* (Cambridge, MA: Harvard University Press, 1989).

Yeago, David S., 'Martin Luther on Grace, Law and Moral Life: Prolegomena to an Ecumenical Discussion of Veritatis Splendor', *The Thomist* 62.2 (1998), pp. 163–91.

Index